CHASING THE CATS

CHASING THE CATS

A Kentucky Basketball Journey

Jamie H. Vaught

Acclaim Press
MORLEY, MISSOURI

Acclaim Press
— Your Next Great Book —

P.O. Box 238
Morley, MO 63767
(573) 472-9800
www.acclaimpress.com

Editor: Randy Baumgardner
Book & Cover Design: Frene Melton

ISBN: 978-1-948901-56-7 | 1-948901-56-0
Library of Congress Control Number: 2020930287

First Printing 2020
Printed in the United States of America
10 9 8 7 6 5 4 3 2 1

This publication was produced using available information.
The publisher regrets it cannot assume responsibility for errors or omissions.

Contents

Acknowledgments

This book about University of Kentucky men's basketball program – fifth one in a series – would not have been possible without many cooperative folks, including the ones I interviewed. Without them, this volume wouldn't have taken place. Like my previous UK basketball books, including the first one which was published in 1991, *Crazy About the Cats: From Rupp to Pitino,* this new book is primarily another enjoyable look at the Kentucky Wildcats' hoops program through the eyes of student managers, broadcasters, players, and coaches. A couple of national personalities not from UK were also thrown in for good measure.

By the way, it wasn't easy to find the time for this book project, which for the most part began in 2017, as I'm also a professor at Southeast Kentucky Community and Technical College in Middlesboro, where former UK football standout Dr. Vic Adams is the president. Yes, it's really difficult to believe that I covered Adams at UK during my early days as a sports journalist, including *The Cats' Pause.* And now he is my boss. I'm very thankful the college has been supportive of my writing efforts since I arrived on the Middlesboro campus in 1991. In addition to my family, supporting two teenagers who also participate in high school sports, I also write columns for various outlets and edit my own media website.

During the latter stages of the manuscript, I was beginning to wonder when *Chasing the Cats: A Kentucky Basketball Journey* would be finished. If I didn't stop adding chapters or writing about the other former players who have been a part of UK's rich hoops tradition, the book certainly would have become a huge encyclopedia. In my other four volumes, nearly 60 individuals were profiled, including Dan Issel, Herky Rupp, Wallace "Wah Wah" Jones, Rick Pitino, Joe B. Hall, Tubby Smith, C.M. Newton, Dwane Casey, Louie Dampier, and Sam Bowie, and the list just goes on and on. So, as you can imagine, there are many others I'd have liked to feature in this volume. As we all agree, UK basketball history is loaded with tons of entertaining stories. If you're interested, you can find my out-of-print books online via Amazon, eBay, etc.

Most of the material for this book has not been published previously, as I personally interviewed all of the subjects face-to-face and via email. However, there are some passages throughout the book that have been published in my other books and syndicated columns appearing in media outlets in Kentucky such as *KyForward.com, Middlesboro Daily News,* and *KySportsStyle.com Magazine,* among others. All of the outlets have been great to work with and I really appreciate them, including Judy Clabes of *KyForward.com* and Anthony Cloud of *Middlesboro Daily News.* Even though my columns are syndicated, the outlets graciously have given permission to use my column material. Old media guides from the universities, especially UK, and even Jon Scott's Big Blue History website were helpful for background information, box scores and statistics. The Atlanta Hawks' media guide was helpful as well. Some portions of transcripts of players' and coaches' interviews and press conferences provided via the universities and ASAP Sports were utilized as well. I also used quotes from various newspapers or outlets, and credit is given within the book where appropriate.

UK Athletics has outstanding media relations folks in its Communication and Public Relations department led by Tony Neely, one of the best in the country. Eric Lindsey and Deb Moore were very helpful in arranging interviews, including one with John Calipari, and providing photos.

I'm also very grateful to Eastern Kentucky University's Steve Fohl who arranged interviews with Dan McHale and Steve Lochmueller. Jenny Elder of Georgetown College was helpful as well. I also would like to recognize former Mason County High School coach Chris O'Hearn for helping me to get in touch with Darius Miller and his father. Thanks to Tripp Ramsey and Barbara Isham for helping me to reach Cliff Hagan.

In addition, I'd like to acknowledge several folks who helped with the book in various ways. Special thanks go to two editors who are also authors – Joe Cox, a talented writer who has written several noteworthy sports books, and Carlton Hughes, an outstanding college professor – for proofreading and editing the manuscript. Kudos to Jim O'Brien, the founding editor of *Street and Smith's Basketball Yearbook* who is now a well-known author from Pittsburgh, for allowing me to use some of his materials. Also thanks to Marie Jackson, a wonderful lady who is the widow of UK team physician Dr. V.A. Jackson, for letting me use some of their book materials about Adolph Rupp. Her grandson, Steve Vick, helped me reach Mrs. Jackson after we lost touch for nearly 20 years. Gratitude to photographer Dr. Michael Huang for submitting several pictures of the Rupp family. Thanks to general manager Darrell Bird of *The Cats' Pause* for giving permission to use some passages. Thanks to Kimberly Rice, daughter of my friend Russell Rice (a former UK publicist who passed away), for giving me permission to feature a chapter about him and use some of the materials from his football and basketball books. Thanks to Doug Sikes of Acclaim Press for allowing me to use statistics, scores and other background information from *Kentucky High School Basketball Encyclopedia 1916-2013* by Jeff Bridgeman. Lastly but most importantly, I want to express gratitude to the Lord for guidance and support every step of the way in my entire life. If I have left out anyone else, I'm sorry. Enjoy the book!

–Jamie H. Vaught
October 2019

Prologue

Of course, if I didn't like sports, there is no way I could've written this book or my other four volumes about University of Kentucky men's basketball.

Thankfully, I grew up in a sports-oriented family in Kentucky. My dad, Hartford Vaught, played basketball at the old Science Hill High School, and he later often attended state high school basketball tournaments in Louisville. Unfortunately, nine years before I was born, he got himself in big legal trouble at the 1947 state tourney, which was won by Maysville High. He was among nearly 30 men, including three high school basketball coaches, who were arrested for gambling. They were front-page news in the Sunday edition of Louisville's *The Courier-Journal*. According to that article, my 29-year-old dad paid the heaviest fine, $25, which would be around $300 in today's dollars. He never told me this story, and I had to look it up after hearing stuff from my mother, Betty, and my older sister, Nancy, who became a high school cheerleader. If I remember correctly, he also spent one night in jail during that gambling incident before coming home during the pre-Interstate days. My mom didn't attend that tournament, staying home and taking care of my then-seven-year-old sister.

In addition, after doing some research for this book, I accidentally saw a couple of my dad's comments (including one on UK star Cliff Hagan) which were published in Earl Ruby's sports columns in *The Courier-Journal*. Ruby, who was the sports editor at the time, often ran portions of letters sent by his faithful readers.

Then I came along in the late 1950s and eventually became a fan of the Pittsburgh Pirates and their star outfielder Roberto Clemente in the mid-1960s. I'm not exactly sure why I picked the Pirates as my favorite major league baseball team. Not even the local favorites in southeast Kentucky – the Cincinnati Reds and the Atlanta Braves – interested me. Anyhow, my parents took me to Cincinnati pretty often, so I could watch my beloved Pirates battle the Reds at 30,000-seat Crosley Field. And I got to meet my childhood hero.

Believe or not, I was one lucky kid who got to know Clemente personally after our chance meeting at a very nice downtown hotel where the team stayed in Cincinnati. At first, I'm sure he felt kind of sorry for me because he probably saw my "old-style" hearing aid and I couldn't hear very well, but that is okay. We stayed in touch and I have many warm memories of our friendship, including a breakfast with the superstar in Atlanta (just the two of us). He once asked my mom why I didn't drink milk, worrying about my health.

Clemente also didn't smoke or drink. For me, he was a very good role model. He gave us free tickets in Cincy, and the seats were usually behind home plate. He invited my dad and me to his hotel room, giving me an autographed photo. Also, he once delivered his autographed personal bat to me during a game via a security guard. After receiving his Louisville Slugger bat, I glanced toward the Pirates dugout and Clemente waved at me. He wanted to make sure that I had his bat. A couple of old Clemente biographies, which were published during the 1970s, mentioned this "bat" episode. And I sure didn't know what to think when I first saw my name in one of the Clemente biographies that I had checked out from a local library, with the book discussing that "bat" incident very briefly.

Then I had another love during the winter months, the Kentucky Wildcats. In 1966, my brother-in-law, a former high school basketball coach who was about 20 years older than me, and his friend took me to Lexington to watch the Kentucky-Tulane matchup at Memorial Coliseum in the last game of the regular season. That was the year of the famed Rupp's Runts. I was excited and we had good seats – about 15 rows from the floor. It was the first UK basketball game that I had ever seen in person. I was 10 years old, attending Science Hill Elementary, perhaps the smallest public school in the state of Kentucky.

Coach Adolph Rupp's club was having a sensational year, losing only one game (to Ray Mears' Tennessee club), despite having a small lineup which featured a 6-foot-5 sophomore center by the name of Thad Jaracz. During the pre-Internet days, the top-ranked Wildcats were the talk of the nation that day. *Sports Illustrated*, in its March 7, 1966 issue, featured Rupp and the Wildcats in a cover story written by legendary sportswriter Frank Deford.

While a preliminary game involving the UK freshman team, coached by Harry Lancaster, and Jerry's YMCA squad (which had several former Wildcat standouts) was taking place on the hardwood floor, my brother-in-law poked my elbow. He pointed toward the UK varsity players who were sitting in the stands and watching the Kentucky freshmen play. I immediately recognized future Hall of Famer Louie Dampier after seeing him on television, as well as in pictures in the Louisville and Lexington daily newspapers. I was thinking, "Wow!"

"You want their autographs?" questioned my brother-in-law.

I nodded in agreement. I got up and nervously walked over to the players. They were polite and I was happy to obtain autographs from Dampier, Pat Riley, Tommy Porter and Tom Kron as they signed on a 25-cent game program titled "The Wildcat Tipoff."

That Monday evening was my first early memory involving the Wildcats. What a thrilling moment for a future sportswriter! And I still have that game program today.

As it turned out, the Rupp's Runts, as they were popularly called, defeated Tulane 103-74 before an overflow crowd of 12,000. We saw three Wildcats – Dampier, Kron and Riley – score at least 20 points. Needless to say, we obviously came home happy.

Kentucky then moved on to the 22-team National Collegiate Athletic Association (NCAA) tournament, defeating Dayton and Michigan (which had All-American Cazzie Russell who later became the No. 1 overall pick of the 1966 National Basketball Association Draft), for a Final Four spot, joining Duke, Utah and Texas Western (now Texas-El Paso).

After beating Duke 83-79 in the national semifinals, the Wildcats faced a scrappy Texas Western squad in the national championship showdown. In the previous week, Coach Don Haskins' Miners had upset heavily-favored Kansas in two overtimes in the regional finals.

So, my parents and I tensely watched the national title game on a black-and-white television set in our home in Science Hill, a very small rural town in Pulaski County with a population of around 500. I certainly remember my feelings that evening. I was really uneasy as the all-white Wildcats struggled to pull away from Texas Western, which featured a starting lineup of five African-Americans. The teams battled back and forth before the Miners won in a stunning upset, winning 72-65. UK finished the year with a 27-2 mark.

As you can imagine, it was a horrible Saturday night for a 10-year-old hearing-impaired kid, and I sure remember crying hard. I was really heartbroken, like thousands and thousands of Wildcat fans in the Big Blue Nation.

That was a Wildcat memory I'd like to forget.

As for my poor hearing, my family and doctors didn't know what was the cause of it. Likely, it was because I was prematurely born. I came into this world two months early, weighing four pounds. "Jamie was such a tiny baby that he kept us all scared to death," wrote my mother, who was a librarian and a teacher, in a baby album. I have been told that, prior to my birth, the doctor had even suggested to mother that she should consider the possibility of having an abortion because her life could be in danger. Thankfully, Mother prayed about it and said no. And I survived despite very early struggles, staying in a hospital (likely in an incubator) for two months before coming home.

For the next couple of years, my parents and my sister, who was 16 years older than me, didn't know their new family member had hearing problems. They noticed that I was a grouchy baby and didn't respond to them very well. They knew something was wrong. It was later determined that I was severely hard of hearing and that I'd need lots of help with my speech development.

So, my mother and maternal grandmother started to work with me on a daily basis. We also began our weekly two-hour trips to UK campus for speech therapy under the direction of audiologist C.I. Whipple and then professor Beverly Stanley (who many years later won a Great Teacher Award at UK in 1992). The trips continued until I was a sophomore at Somerset High School. In the latter years of my speech therapy, a very helpful Ms. Stanley, along with her senior students, worked with me two hours at a time, usually on a Monday afternoon, and we often talked about UK basketball. And I can't lie about this – I sure didn't mind having pretty female students helping me with my school assignments and speech patterns.

But there were times when I really didn't want to go to speech therapy for different reasons. I had to miss school after lunch when we journeyed to Lexington. To make my trip more enjoyable, my parents would try to get tickets for the UK basketball game being played that same evening when my all-time favorite Wildcat Dan Issel was playing along with Mike Pratt and Mike Casey. Fortunately, we were successful most of the time in getting tickets at Memorial Coliseum approximately three hours before the tipoff and the seats were good. As Wildcat fans will note, the three Issel-Pratt teams were really good, compiling a rather impressive overall record of 71-12, a winning percentage of nearly 86, along with three Southeastern Conference titles. That was another early great memory.

Very gratefully, I still have some hearing, but not much. I may hear some sounds such as a siren or a very loud voice from the radio or television without a hearing aid. It's bad enough that I can't use a regular smartphone to speak with a friend. However, with the help of a good hearing aid, lip-reading, determination, and intelligence, I somehow managed to excel in the classroom as a highly motivated student and as an aspiring sportswriter during the early days when we had no TV captioning and Internet. Also, during the radio broadcasts of UK games that weren't televised (live or delayed basis), my dad often would relay the scores and provide comments since I couldn't use or hear the radio. In case you're wondering about the taped interviews that I have done, don't worry. I have used professional transcription services to transcribe the interviews for me. In the past, I also have had to ask my mother (who since has passed away) or even my daughter Janna to transcribe. And I haven't forgotten the good Lord who has helped me in mysterious and spiritual ways.

Because of my love for sports, which also included the Kentucky Colonels of the now-defunct American Basketball Association, I continued to have many more great remembrances in following UK hoops as a fan and then as a writer. Over the next four decades or so, I chased the Wildcats like crazy, including trips to the 2012 and 2015 NCAA Final Four, as a credentialed sports columnist.

As I just revealed some of my earliest Wildcat memories, I think you'll enjoy this volume which contains remarkable stories about the UK men's basketball program for the past 70 years through interviews with folks who are or have been connected with the storied program. If you are a Wildcat fan, you'll relish reading about the Big Blue memories in *Chasing the Cats: A Kentucky Basketball Journey*. Go Big Blue!

CHASING THE CATS

A Kentucky Basketball Journey

Chapter One
Chip Rupp and His Grandfather

When UK held its so-called hoops family reunion back in August 2017, featuring two contests – Legends Game and UK Alumni Charity Game – Chip Rupp had lots of fun that special evening at a massive facility named after his legendary grandfather, Adolph Rupp.

A former Vanderbilt and West Virginia player, Adolph Rupp's grandson was actually coaching the Blue team against ex-UK mentor Joe B. Hall of the White team in the Legends game, featuring older Wildcats like Kevin Grevey, Kyle Macy, Kenny Walker, Jack Givens, and Rex Chapman, among others.

It was definitely a memorable moment for Chip Rupp, who still lives in Lexington.

"Having the opportunity to coach the Legends team was the thrill of a lifetime," he said.

"Growing up, I couldn't understand the magnitude of my grandfather's contribution to the game of basketball and his accomplishments at the University of Kentucky. To me, he was just my grandfather, and everybody seemed to know who he was.

"As time has passed, I have come to understand, and fully appreciate, his remarkable accomplishments and his contributions to the UK as well as the state of Kentucky as a whole. I had always envisioned myself one day being the head basketball coach at UK. Unfortunately, that hasn't been my career path.

"So, to hear my name announced as the coach of the Blue team was an unbelievable experience. The whole experience was amazing, and it gave me a great opportunity to reflect on his life and his legend. Beginning with the pre-game [activities], having the chance to mingle with the former players and hear their stories, to walking out of the tunnel and taking my place on the bench and being announced as the coach for the Blue team, it made for an amazing experience."

Chip's dad, Herky Rupp, was also active in athletics. The only child of Adolph and Esther Rupp, Herky played at UK for three years when he was a reserve forward during the late 1950s and early 1960s. He also was head coach at three Kentucky high schools, including two years at Shelby County High, where he took a couple of teams to the state tournament, reaching the quarterfinals both times at Louisville's Freedom Hall. Among his various jobs, he later taught at MMI (Millersburg Military Institute near Paris, Ky.) for several years and raised cattle on his family farm. Herky passed away at the age of 75 during the summer of 2016.

When 6-foot-7 Chip Rupp starred at Henry Clay High School, where he was a two-year starter and played on the school's 1983 state championship team as a sophomore, he had several schools pursuing him, including Kentucky, Louisiana State University (LSU), and Vanderbilt. In December of 1984, UK coach Joe B. Hall offered a scholarship to Rupp, who eventually decided to play elsewhere.

"[Hall] offered me at a Christmas tournament my senior year," recalled Rupp, who averaged 14 points and 13 rebounds that season. "He made me aware that he would be retiring at the end of the season and that he wouldn't be the coach but said that he thought I was deserving of the scholarship offer and would like for me to play for the Wildcats.

"At that time, Coach Hall was bringing in top-ranked recruiting classes with several McDonald's All-Americans, and I truly felt like it was a token gesture and that I wouldn't have an opportunity to play. I wanted to play in the SEC at a place where I had a better opportunity to compete for playing time. Additionally, UK still hadn't decided on a successor for Coach Hall at the spring signing period, so I decided that I would go to Vanderbilt and play for Coach [C.M.] Newton [who was a former Wildcat player for Adolph Rupp].

"As for regrets, I can't say that I have regrets. I do wonder from time to time what it would have been like to play at UK, but I don't regret the decision that I made."

It didn't hurt that Chip Rupp's high school coach was Al Prewitt, who played standout basketball for Newton when the latter was the head coach at Transylvania University.

Anyhow, as a Wildcat opponent, he got to play at Rupp Arena as a freshman in 1987. Rupp grabbed two rebounds in seven minutes as Vanderbilt dropped to coach Eddie Sutton's club, which had freshman sensation Rex Chapman. And he nearly dunked on Chapman.

"I remember that game vividly," recalled Rupp in 2017. "Growing up as a UK fan, I have been going to games at Rupp Arena since the day that it opened [in 1976]. My family's seats have always been on the first row at midcourt, and from attending games routinely, I got to know most of the people that sat around us as well as many of the people that work at the scorers' table.

"As you can tell from the stat line in that game, I was a reserve on the Vanderbilt team my freshman season. I knew coming into the game that I would see some action, but I didn't know how much or when it would come. When Coach C.M. Newton turned to me and told me to check into the game, the next couple of minutes seemed like a dream. When I walked to the scorers' table to check in, I kneeled down and took a quick glance back, and I vividly recall seeing the faces of so many people that I had sat with at games over the years cheering for the Cats, and now I would be checking into the game as one of those players that we cheered so hard against.

"I was a little nervous about how I would be received by the crowd when they announced my entrance into the game, but the crowd gave me a nice applause, which I thought was a really classy gesture. It was a strange experience after being announced and actually entering the game. From regularly attending UK games and playing pickup basketball games with the UK players over the years, I knew some of the UK players better than I knew some of my [Vandy] teammates. To say the least, a scouting report wasn't necessary because I had played with these guys so often that I knew their games and I also knew enough about them to know just how good they really were.

"The game was competitive throughout [and won by UK 65-54]. At the time when I checked in, the game was very close. I recall, after a timeout, we came back onto the court with the ball out of bounds under our basket, and Kentucky was in a man-to-man full court press. Rex Chapman was guarding me on the inbounds, and I was able to shake free for a long pass over his head. We were running stride for stride down the court, and by all accounts, I had a path to the basket for a layup. Knowing Rex and knowing about his great leaping ability, I thought better of potentially getting posturized in Rupp Arena, so I pulled the ball out and waited for my teammates to join me at the offensive end of the court.

"From time to time, I still think about that possession and what it would have been like to throw down a dunk in Rupp Arena, but looking back on it now, I think I made a good choice."

Even though he enjoyed his Vanderbilt days, he moved on to West Virginia, which was coached by ex-Kentucky aide Gale Catlett. "I realized that I didn't

Chip Rupp and his family at Rupp Arena. (Photo by Dr. Michael Huang)

want to spend another season on the bench at Vanderbilt," explained Rupp. "[But] I really enjoyed playing for Coach Newton. Many of the things that I tell the kids that I coach in AAU [Amateur Athletic Union] basketball are things that Coach Newton taught me years ago."

And during the 1989-90 campaign, Rupp finished his collegiate career with 26 games, averaging 9.7 minutes, at West Virginia, including two as a starter. Not long after graduating from WVU in May 1990, he served as a coach and counselor at Rick Pitino's basketball camp at Kentucky and Gale Catlett's camp at West Virginia during the summer.

Asked about his favorite memory of his grandfather, Chip had this to say:

"I have a lot of great memories of my grandfather. I was 11 years old when my grandfather passed away [in December 1977 at the age of 76]. Probably the one memory that sticks out above all the others was in the spring of 1977. I didn't know that he had terminal cancer, but he knew that he wasn't doing well and that his time was short.

"I think that most of his coaching peers realized that the 1977 season would be his last. That year, the men's Final Four was held in Atlanta, and he took me with him. That was such a great experience, getting to spend time with him, just the two of us. Although he didn't feel well and had to rest a lot, he did his best to make the rounds and show me a good time. We went and attended the practices, and I had a chance to meet and have pictures taken with [coaches] John Wooden, Lee Rose, Al McGuire, Dean Smith, as well as so many others.

"During the Final Four weekend every year, the National Association of Basketball Coaches hold their national convention. They asked my grandfather to give the address at the convention, and I recall sitting in the back of a large crowded room while he gave his speech. I really can't remember much about the speech, but what I do recall was the huge applause that he received after the speech and all of the coaches waiting around afterwards to shake his hand and wish him well. Although I was only 11 years old, I could sense the respect that these men had for him and his accomplishments."

For the record, Marquette, coached by colorful Al McGuire, captured the 1977 NCAA title, beating Dean Smith's North Carolina squad. Interestingly, it was McGuire's last game as coach, and the national television audience saw him crying on the bench at the end. As you may recall, Kentucky native Lee Rose and his North Carolina-Charlotte club also appeared in the Final Four, along with controversial coach Jerry Tarkanian and his Nevada-Las Vegas team.

Chip Rupp also shared another memory about his grandfather, who retired as college basketball's all-time winningest coach with a record of 876-190, including four national championships and 27 SEC titles from 1930-72. The four-time national coach of the year also served as assistant in the 1948 Summer Olympics when his "Fabulous Five" team, along with the Phillips 66 Oilers squad, won the gold medal for U.S. in London.

"Many people thought my grandfather was this mean, grouchy, old man, but actually he had a soft, loving side when it came to my sister [Farren] and I," Chip commented. "When my parents would go out for the evening, we would go to my grandfather's house. We would spend hours playing cards. He was very patient with my sister and I, and he gave us his undivided attention while we played hand after hand of 'Go Fish' or 'War.' "

There are many Adolph Rupp stories, and the author has one that was told by college football legend and Louisville native Howard Schnellenberger in 2014. In one of my columns appearing in KyForward.com, I wrote that a young Schnellenberger did something that was forbidden on the UK campus around 1960 while working as an assistant football coach for the Wildcats under Blanton Collier.

Since he was late for a team meeting, Schnellenberger hurried to find a parking space, and after a second go-around, he saw an empty spot and parked his car near Memorial Coliseum (where UK basketball team practiced and played their home games during that time). And that parking space was fairly close to Stoll Field, which was the home of UK football from 1916 to 1972 and was located across the street (Avenue of Champions) from Memorial Coliseum.

But as it turned out, the assistant coach wasn't so lucky after all. His car had taken a prime parking spot that belonged to someone else who was very famous. And that someone else was Adolph Rupp.

Uh-oh. Schnellenberger was in trouble. "It wasn't long after the meeting when I was summoned to the basketball coaches' office to explain why I had trespassed and parked in Adolph Rupp's parking spot," recalled Schnellenberger. "Coach Rupp sat me down in his office and told me that it was a poor decision to park in his spot, that everyone on campus knew it was his spot.

"He said, 'You should have known that, you should have known,' and that this wasn't something to put on my resume if I was ever to move up in the coaching world. Everyone laughed at me. 'Who would have been so stupid to park in Adolph Rupp's parking spot!'"

But there is a good ending from this Rupp-Schnellenberger episode. "We became closer as a few years went by, and in fact, I was one of the few non-basketball people that he would allow to watch any of his UK practices," added Schnellenberger, who also played football at UK where he was a first-team All-American in 1955. As you may remember, in 1959 Schnellenberger was a member of a very impressive coaching staff at UK which was loaded with future National Football League head coaches like Don Shula, John North and Bill Arnsparger in addition to Collier. Chuck Knox, a Collier assistant in 1961 and '62, also became the head coach of three NFL teams over three decades.

Anyhow, that was before Schnellenberger became a household name with his head coaching success at several stops – including rebuilding then-lowly teams Miami and Louisville, and starting a new program from scratch at Florida Atlantic. He retired from coaching after the 2011 campaign.

During his early days, Chip Rupp had a favorite team that wasn't even Kentucky.

Former Tennessee coach Ray Mears told the author in an interview during the early 1990s that Rupp's grandson liked the Vols, pointing out the youngster had decorated his room with the Big Orange stuff. Obviously, Coach Rupp and his family weren't too thrilled about it.

Mears said Coach Rupp "couldn't figure out why his grandson would root for Tennessee. You know Rupp hated Tennessee."

Chip, who has met Mears several times, said the UT coach's story is true. "As a child, I was a huge Tennessee fan," he added. "My family couldn't understand it, but I just loved the bright orange uniforms and thought the team, 'The Ernie and Bernie Show,' was really fun to watch.

"Much to my parents' and my grandmother's dismay, I would cheer whenever Tennessee scored a bucket. As time passed, the infatuation with Tennessee continued to grow. I remember the first telephone that I had in my room at home was bright orange. As the years passed, I became an even bigger fan of both Tennessee basketball and Tennessee football. My love for Tennessee sports peaked with the 'Ernie and Bernie Show' and the hiring of Johnny Majors as head football coach.

"I think that truly my feelings weren't a love for Tennessee sports but actually a great respect for their program. Tennessee was the one team in basketball that never seemed intimidated by playing the Cats in [Memorial Coliseum and] Rupp Arena. They seemed to thrive on being the antagonist, and Coach Mears did a lot to fuel that. Obviously, my feelings for Tennessee have changed over the years, and now I only see one color, and that is blue."

Unlike many other coaches, Mears competed really well against the Wildcats, posting an even 15-15 mark from 1962 to 1977. Mears was 8-12 against Rupp and 7-3 versus Joe B. Hall. The Vols were a force to be reckoned with when they had All-Americans and future NBA standouts Bernard King and Ernie Grunfeld during the mid-1970s.

"Ray Mears had the best Tennessee teams in history when he was there," Hall said around 1990. "I guess his team with King and Grunfeld was probably as good a team as I ever competed against."

Mears is among the SEC's winningest coaches of all time with an overall mark of 278-112.

Chip Rupp graduated from West Virginia, but that doesn't mean he cheers for the Mountaineers against Kentucky when both schools meet. He is too close to the Wildcats and has too many connections in the Lexington community.

During John Calipari's era, WVU and UK have met in the NCAA Tournament at least three times as well as one regular season game in Morgantown in 2018.

When John Calipari's first UK team – which had freshman superstars such as John Wall, DeMarcus Cousins and Eric Bledsoe, along with junior standout Patrick Patterson – faced West Virginia in the 2010 East Region finals, Rupp really had mixed feelings. The Mountaineers came out on top, defeating Kentucky 73-66, as they earned a Final Four trip.

"I was feeling all kinds of emotions as I watched the game," said Rupp. "I have fond memories of the time that I spent at WVU, and I'm grateful for the education that I received from there.

"WVU has waited a long time to make a return trip to the Final Four [since 1959]. And, if anyone was going to beat the Cats, I'm glad it was them. It makes for a really nice story with Coach [Bob] Huggins returning to coach his alma mater and having Jerry West's son on the team. It almost seems like destiny was on their side. I'm happy for them."

Despite his WVU degree, Rupp left no doubt that he is a Big Blue fan. "Having grown up in this family, there's no way that I can ever pull for any team to win against the University of Kentucky," he said. "[But] as the final minutes wound down and it became evident that WVU was going to advance to its first Final Four in 50 years, I was happy for them and proud that I had been a Mountaineer. At the same time, I had this hollow, empty feeling when I realized the season was over with the Cats. I reflected back on the great year and the fact we probably wouldn't get to see Wall, Cousins, Patterson and others to play again."

By the way, one of Chip and Cathy Rupp's three children graduated from UK in 2019. Frederick, who started as a varsity baseball player at Lexington Christian Academy, had a double major in finance and management. The couple also has two daughters, Elizabeth and Anna (who captured the 2018 and 2019 cross country state championships in Class A as a high school freshman and sophomore).

As mentioned earlier, Rupp is a faithful UK fan who has seen many games from his front-row seat. He remembers a special moment during the December portion of the 2001-02 campaign when Tubby Smith was guiding the Wildcats. UK's leading scorer that year was All-American Tayshaun Prince, a 6-foot-9 senior forward from Compton, California.

"One of my favorite memories is from the North Carolina game in Rupp Arena when Tubby Smith was coaching," commented Rupp, whose Lexington area-based company handles the sales and distribution of orthopedic and neurosurgical products. "That was a nationally televised game with a sellout crowd between the two winningest programs in college basketball history. The atmosphere for that game was electric.

"I remember Tayshaun Prince going on an incredible run, knocking down five straight three-pointers to blow the game wide open, with the last one coming from just a few steps inside of the midcourt line. I don't think that I have ever felt the energy stronger than it was in Rupp that day, and I've never heard the crowd louder. It was awesome."

In one of the school's greatest individual performances in history, Prince finished the exciting contest with 31 points with 7 of 11 three-pointers as 11th-ranked Kentucky pulled away for a 79-59 win over second-year coach Matt Doherty and his UNC squad, which later finished the year with a poor 8-20 mark.

December 10, 1977.

That was the date that 76-year-old Adolph Rupp died of cancer, among other complications, just over five years after he had retired from coaching in 1972. Ironically, Rupp died just minutes after his alma mater, Kansas, had lost to top-ranked Kentucky 73-66 at Lawrence, Kansas. While Rupp's death made the national news, it was one of the very few lowlights during the 1977-78 memorable campaign when the Wildcats later won the NCAA title.

On a cloudy day of Rupp's funeral, former Kentucky Governor and ex-baseball commissioner Happy Chandler and team physician Dr. V. A. Jackson rode together in the same funeral vehicle, serving as pallbearers, and they recalled a Rupp moment in a hotel room from previous years.

In a 1998 memoir, titled *Beyond the Baron* by Dr. Jackson and his wife Marie Jackson (which was published after his death), the authors tell an entertaining story that took place during a road trip in Baton Rouge, La., when Rupp half-jokingly talks about his death.

"When you start to the cemetery with me, I want you to have a fifth of bourbon and enjoy that trip," Rupp told close friends Dr. Jackson and Chandler in the book.

And Chandler asked, "Adolph, do you want us to drink that bourbon going to the cemetery or coming back?"

"Hell, Happy, you drink it going to the cemetery. I won't be with you coming back."

During the Joe B. Hall era, Dr. Jackson and his wife, Marie, also served as the house parents at the now-demolished Joe B. Hall Wildcat Lodge, a dormitory where the Wildcats stayed.

And several UK coaches later after Rupp's death, John Calipari was chosen as the new basketball coach at Kentucky on April 1, 2009. Herky Rupp was one of many folks, along with the news media and school officials, invited to attend the televised news conference which announced the hiring.

Moments after the press conference ended, I asked Herky if his dad would be pleased. "Oh yeah, absolutely," said Herky with a smile after he had met with the new UK boss.

Eight months later, Calipari – along with Joe B. Hall and Herky Rupp – paid a visit to the grave of Coach Rupp with Christmas flowers at the Lexington Cemetery as UK was approaching its 2,000th victory in school history.

Needless to say, Chip's grandfather – the Baron – was a true coaching legend who started UK's tradition-rich hoops program, spanning many generations of Big Blue fans who faithfully follow the team year after year.

Chapter Two

The PR Man Who Gave Me
My First Media Pass

*I*t was 1975 when President Ford attempted to heal our wounded country after the Watergate scandal that had led to President Nixon's resignation from the White House.

During that time, I stayed pretty busy with college work and making good grades, as well as writing sports articles for a campus newspaper at Somerset Community College. Unlike today, we even had a basketball team competing against several other community and junior colleges throughout the state. On SCC's schedule, the Cougars were slated to play against the UK junior varsity team at Memorial Coliseum in mid-February in a preliminary matchup before the Kentucky-Ole Miss varsity game.

I needed a media pass to cover the Feb. 17 games but as you'll find out later, it wasn't easy to get one.

Two weeks earlier, my friend and I had gotten UK student tickets as the community colleges back then were part of UK system and watched Kevin Grevey firing long downtown jumpers in leading Kentucky to another victory. During a break, I approached Russell Rice, who was standing near the press row. He was the man that I was told to contact about getting a media credential.

Well, he looked at me funny. As you can imagine, I was very young looking. His body language sure wasn't friendly. The former sportswriter who took the UK post as sports information director (SID) was an intimidating man with graying hair. In a deep gruff voice, he said, "Why do you need one?" He didn't want to give me a pass, and the conversation wasn't going anywhere. And Rice slowly walked away.

I refused to give up. I politely followed him, saying I need to write a story about that game. Rice was getting exasperated, and he finally walked toward his SID office, not far from the hardwood floor, under the Memorial Coliseum seats.

"Okay, here's the pass," said Rice, not smiling, and I walked back to my seat and watched the rest of the UK game.

Like I said, it was a struggle to get one. He probably thought my campus newspaper wasn't big enough to warrant a pass, and he didn't even know me. Oh, well, it sure was a very odd encounter, but that was my first media credential.

As it turned out, Rice and I slowly became friends throughout the years when I wrote for the UK student daily newspaper, *Kentucky Kernel*, and then *The Cats' Pause*. Interestingly, we eventually even wrote stories about each other and stayed in touch. Many years ago, I even visited him in Daytona Beach while on a vacation.

If you follow UK, you probably have heard of Rice, a native of Paintsville, Ky., who was popularly known as the historian of UK sports during his retirement days. He was the man to ask if you had a question about UK basketball or football history.

Rice, who passed away in 2015 at the age of 90 in Florida, had written several UK books, including one on Adolph Rupp. You still can find his out-of-print books on Amazon.

In an interview with the author in 2006, Rice recalled a Rupp story when he rode a small airplane with the Baron. "We were on an old bi-plane flying to Kansas where the university was to present him an honor," he said. "I had borrowed an old tape recorder from Joe Brown, the trainer. As we neared our destination, I got up my nerve and popped the question, 'Coach, I would like to write a book about you.'

"He clapped both hands together and said, 'By Gawd, let's get started.' It was like I had died and gone to heaven."

Before coming to work at UK, Rice had a successful journalism career, including stints at Whitesburg, Hazard and Lexington. A U.S. Marine Corps veteran from World War II, the UK graduate worked for the old *Lexington Leader* as a general reporter for eight years before serving as sports editor of that afternoon newspaper in 1962.

Rice said he could tell that Rupp sometimes didn't like his stories in the Lexington paper. "Rupp never criticized me while I was sports editor," Rice pointed out. "Instead, he would say, 'My wife, Esther, didn't like what you wrote about me.'"

During his last year as the sports editor of the *Lexington Leader*, Rice covered all of UK's games in 1965-66, the year of the famous Rupp's Runts. He also attended their practices. Rice shared some of his memories of the ailing Wildcats, ranked No. 1 in the nation, who played in the 1966 NCAA Four in College Park, Md., and defeated Duke in the semifinals before being upset by Texas Western (now Texas-El Paso) in the title game.

"I recall going to Larry Conley's room after the Duke game, and he was in a croup tent [with a bad cold]," said Rice. "Trainer Joe Brown, [assistant coach] Harry Lancaster and [athletics director] Bernie Shively also were there.

"Next, after the [Texas Western] game, I was the first person in the Wildcat dressing room while Rupp was in a media session. I knew Harry would lock everybody else out, which he did. Dr. V.A. Jackson examined Pat Riley's big toe, which was red and swollen. Rupp later said, 'I took a bunch of sick boys to College Park,' but he didn't use it as an excuse."

Years later, the UK-Texas Western showdown was popularly termed as college basketball's *Brown vs. Board of Education* with all-white Kentucky battling Texas Western, which had five African-American starters.

During his newspaper days, Rice also covered agricultural hearings in Washington, D.C., and spent three months as the traveling companion to a gubernatorial candidate in Kentucky.

Rice then took a position in the UK sports information office during the late 1960s, becoming an assistant to sports information director Ken Kuhn and later as the top media relations guy. And Rupp offered a simple advice to Rice. "The barber cuts my hair, Chester takes care of the farm, Charlie runs the [Kentucky] Hereford Association of which I'm the president. I don't tell them how do their jobs; they don't tell me how to coach basketball," Rupp told the new publicist. "We get along just fine. You're the publicity man. Take it from there."

Russell Rice (Photo by UK Athletics)

Rice became a witness to one of UK's most significant events in basketball history, and he has written about it. In June 1969, as the school's publicity man, Rice joined Rupp and assistant Joe B. Hall on a trip to Louisville to record a special moment for UK basketball program as the Wildcats were preparing to sign 7-foot-2 high school star Tom Payne at his Louisville home. It was big news at the time as Louisville Shawnee High's Payne was set to become the first African-

American to get a basketball scholarship at UK as a sophomore. (At the time, freshmen were not eligible to play varsity basketball due to NCAA rules.) Rice took photos of Payne and his parents along with Rupp and Hall. By the way, according to Rice, during that 80-mile trip to Louisville, Rupp even talked about investment opportunities in restaurants like Jerry's. Pretty interesting, huh?

Unfortunately, Payne – who later helped the Wildcats to a 22-6 record in 1970-71, earning first-team All-SEC honors, during his only varsity season at UK – didn't stay long in Lexington. He left for the NBA after his sophomore year.

Former Wildcat standout Mike Casey, who was Payne's teammate at the same time, told the author in an interview many years ago that he thought Payne had made a wise move to attend UK because of his strong family background. "His daddy was a captain in the Army. His dad was very strict on him. So, he kept his thumbs on Tom," said Casey, who also saw racial abuse especially when the Wildcats traveled on the road.

Casey, who passed away in 2009, remembered an incident in Oxford, Miss., where UK played Mississippi. "I look back a lot of times at some of the torment he had to go through – the name-calling – and I remember this just like it was yesterday," he said. "Down at Ole Miss they had an old theater, upstairs and downstairs. [After] we all ate together and practiced, we went to a movie. We went upstairs in the balcony. Now this was 1970-71 [season], and you don't think that is that far back. But they came up there and told [Payne], 'You are not allowed up here.' So, we all left. We said we were all one on the team."

Rice, who saw racism especially in the South when he covered the Wildcats on the road as a sportswriter during the early 1960s, has written about Adolph Rupp and alleged racism, but the author didn't have a chance to ask him about this sensitive topic more in-depth. However, many observers close to the UK program believed Rupp was treated unfairly when it comes to racism.

Grover Sales, who was a UK basketball student manager from 1969-72, said, "Rupp was no racist. He helped many blacks with no credit [of getting recognition or publicity]. He recruited my high school teammate Westley Unseld [at Louisville Seneca High], but he could not guarantee his safety on southern road trips."

Sales played basketball and football at Seneca, but he added that he was too small to play in the SEC. So, he became a student manager through the help of then newly-hired UK football assistant Ron Cain, who had guided Seneca to the Class AAA state football championship in 1965. But Sales only lasted two weeks with the football program. "Coach [John] Ray dismissed me, so I was out in the cold," said Sales, who eventually joined Rupp's varsity basketball team as a manager.

Recalled Sales, who very briefly worked with Rice for a week before joining the hoops program, "Rupp was not user friendly. He was arrogant, set in his ways. Very superstitious. [He wore] the brown suit and had a fixation with bobby pins. He thought they were a sign of good luck. In 1969 women had quit using them, so [equipment manager] Bill Keightley had me go to Woolworth's and buy a card of them.

"We ate our team meals at Student Center and I usually walked Rupp over to the Coliseum. Earlier I salted the sidewalk on Avenue of Champions with bobby pins. Adolph would find one and would be filled with glee. He would tell [then-assistant] Joe Hall, 'We are going to roll tonight!' He never caught on."

Sales pointed out that "Rupp kept his distance from the players. His methods would not work if they thought he was their friend. One statement I remember is based on the farm Adolph was raised on in Kansas: 'Before you can milk a cow, you must have her gawd damn attention or you may be at the ass end of a bull, and there ain't no cream back there. Don't waste your time.' Rupp had a 400-acre cattle farm in Centerville in Bourbon County. I drove him there often. He had an eight-foot wide oil painting in his office of his champion stud bull. I asked him, 'Why do you have small pictures of [his wife] Esther and [son] Herky on your desk?' He replied, 'She can't do what he can do....'

"I heard stories driving Adolph to places that no 19-year-old should hear.... I owe much to Coach Rupp and Bill Keightley. I visit their graves before every season. I pay my respects to both.

"I speak several times a year to sports groups and am asked about Rupp and [the] Texas Western [game]. I tell the truth and will go to my grave defending him."

With current coach John Calipari and Rupp both in the Naismith Memorial Basketball Hall of Fame, Rice was asked to compare the two UK legends. How are they different?

"Rupp was arrogant and overbearing as a coach," said Rice. "Prior to the [Rupp's] Runts' era, he was aloof to the players. Instead of coddling them, he would put them to work on his farm. His sarcasm was biting and effective. Nobody talked back to him without suffering the consequences.

"Calipari seemed much closer to his players. He was more prone to pat a player on the back or rub his head for a job well done.

"The similarity ended there; however, both coaches were masters of their craft, with Cal getting a nod as a recruiter. Rupp wanted the boys to come to him while Calipari recruited far and wide in a more competitive era. Segregation was downhill for Rupp, a situation not all of his making, but one that presented him with problems that Calipari didn't have to face.

"Who was the better coach? Toss a coin!"

When future UK head coach Joe B. Hall was Rupp's top assistant during the mid-1960s, Rice was working for the *Lexington Leader* as the sports editor. They became friends and later worked together as Rice joined the university in 1967. And they often traveled together on recruiting and fishing trips, even when Rice was working for the Lexington newspaper and Hall was an assistant at the time. They once rode together to Dayton, Ohio, to sign future Wildcat Mike Pratt. Rice also did a book on Hall which was published in 1981.

"Those recruiting trips were not always successful and at times downright boring," Rice wrote in *The Cats' Pause* as part of his Big Blue Memoirs in 2008. "I remember more fondly the fishing trips to his native Harrison County, where Joe knew every pothole and submerged rock in the creeks and small rivers of that area. Our first trip to the South Fork of the Licking River near Shawhan, a small farming community where his Uncle Ofal Harney lived, was unforgettable; both for the number of small-mouth bass we caught and for the experience of crawling up a cliff on all fours after dark with no flashlight."

On Hall's personality, Rice, in that same column in *The Cats' Pause*, wrote, "While people seemed to gravitate to Rupp, Joe B. gravitated to people. He was the mainstream type; when he dined in a restaurant, he talked to the waitresses, the busboys, the folks seated at the next table. He touched an amazing number of people in all walks of life, but he seemed to enjoy most those types that he encountered in the small groceries or on the farms during his hunting and fishing trips. His annual parties during the Christmas tournament [UKIT] were gala affairs, featuring some of the best seafood flown directly from New Orleans for the occasion. The guest list included coal operators, political figures, doctors, lawyers, professors, horse breeders, tobacco farmers, warehousemen, and faculty and staff members, along with various other types loyal to UK basketball.

"Joe B. the fisherman-farmer-friend-outdoorsman was a different person from Joe B. the coach. He could be a warm, charming, fun person in the former roles, but as a coach, he was unbending, a person who would tolerate no breach of the rules that he had set for himself, his staff, and his team. He was a low-keyed, almost 'good ole boy' away from the basketball wars, but in the heat of battle, he would lash out at officials, players and staff members. His angry coaching baton was a rolled-up program that sometimes had all the pages shredded during a game. There were times when he sent the program sailing through the air. Joe B. was best described as an overachiever who coached best when driving himself against an opponent of great strength."

In addition to basketball, Rice also ran the publicity machine for UK football.

A longtime sports columnist for the *Lexington Herald-Leader*, John Clay remembers that Rice did a remarkable job without a lot of resources when compared to the current UK media relations staff has today. "When covering UK football [as a beat writer], his book *The Wildcats: A Story of Kentucky Football* was essential reading," added Clay, who also graduated from UK.

Tony Neely, who is the assistant athletics director for Athletics Communications and Public Relations at UK, also praised Rice's work. "Russell Rice meant so much to University of Kentucky athletics," he recalled. "His work as a sports information director put him alongside many of the greatest moments and people of UK sports history. He was always generous with his time and was an invaluable source for historical questions. His skill as a writer and careful attention to detail have made his books invaluable reference points of UK athletics history."

When you think of UK football history, you probably would mention big-name players/coaches like Paul "Bear" Bryant, Tim Couch, George Blanda, Randall Cobb, Sonny Collins and Jerry Claiborne, to name a handful.

Rice got to follow and work with Collins and Claiborne during the 1970s and 1980s. Collins, who was the 1973 SEC Player of the Year, saw his all-time rushing record of 3,835 career yards at UK broken in 2019 when running back Benny Snell Jr. became the school's top rusher in history during Kentucky's 27-24 victory over Penn State in the VRBO Citrus Bowl on New Year's Day.

For press releases to be sent to the media, Rice often wrote about Collins, who had been a star at Madisonville-North Hopkins High School in becoming one of the state's leading rushers. He also did a piece on Collins in his 1975 UK book, *The Wildcats: A Story of Kentucky Football*.

Even before Collins entered college football, the youngster became concerned about his future after he had injured his ankle in the second game of his high school senior year, missing the remaining games. As pointed out in Rice's book, he took a long time to recover from the injury.

"I had to have an ankle operation, and a lot of people thought I could come back from the operation and play, but the doctor told me just to relax and not worry about trying to come back," Collins was quoted as saying in Rice's book.

"Well, I started getting phone calls. Rumors began spreading about, and my daddy worried that I wasn't going to get into college with that kind of stuff going around. I could see myself in the coal mines. I worked one summer there. Both of my grandfathers, or at least one of them, died of black lung. I'd always heard about it, but I didn't know how it actually was until I was old enough to go down. Man, it's spooky. You go about two miles down and then you level off for a while. Then you go through a 36- or 42-inch high hole for maybe a half-mile more. There's no way you can stand straight up. You either bend or crawl.

"Probably the best thing you can find down there are rats. I mean big rats. Bigger than basketball shoes. There's a lot of natural gas around coal, and if you see them you know the air is pretty safe to breathe. But if you see them start running or going in one direction, then you'd better start running behind them because something is going to blow.

"With all that worrying, it wasn't too long before I lost all my hair. I wear a 'fro' off the field now, and I am a different person on and off the field."

Rice also reported that Collins, after his outstanding performance against Mississippi State in 1973, gave his Afro wig to his offensive linemen. A two-time All-American, Collins was drafted by the Atlanta Falcons, who picked him as the No. 8 selection of the second round in the NFL Draft in 1976.

On squeaky clean Claiborne, a former Bear Bryant disciple at UK who returned to the Bluegrass after the 1981 season, replacing coach Fran Curci, Rice had this to say in the revised and updated edition of his UK football book:

> To say that Jerry Claiborne was a different kind of coach would be an understatement. He was a 'dang it' good ole boy who didn't smoke, drink, chew or chase women. He was more at home tending a garden than mixing with the elite at the Kentucky Derby. Claiborne was honest almost to a fault, which was unusual in the competitive world that is college football. He was also extremely loyal to his coaching staff and players.

Claiborne, who was elected to the College Football Hall of Fame in 1999, coached at Kentucky for eight years and earned two bowl trips.

Rice also shared a fascinating memory with the author when Curci's Wildcats blanked Georgia 33-0 in Athens during their 10-1 campaign in 1977. "The 59,100 fans that jammed Sanford Stadium in Athens had little to cheer about except for the halftime appearance by Prince Charles, the Prince of Wales," recalled Rice. "The Wildcats were leading 10-0. I joined Curci and [All-American] Art Still at the end zone where we were standing. The Prince and his escorts walked the length of field. The Prince was introduced to Curci, who presented him with a UK T-shirt and introduced him to Still.

"Gazing up at the 6-foot-7 Still, the Prince looked amazed and said, 'You're a tall one, aren't you?' "

Former longtime UK broadcaster Ralph Hacker recalls a time when Rice took him to Big Easy, where the football Wildcats were facing Tulane during the early 1970s. "First time I ever went to New Orleans was with Russell," he said. "He took me into The Delight Oyster Bar on Bourbon Street and introduced me to raw oysters, one dozen at a time."

During his retirement days in the Daytona Beach, Fla., area, Rice, who had four children, kept himself busy when he's not writing or watching the Wildcats on television. He enjoyed researching, reading, gardening and fishing, according to his daughter, Kimberly Rice. She added that "he loved to see egrets that came by every morning to see him at his home in Daytona."

Through her dad's UK job, Kimberly got to travel, meeting all kinds of people, during her younger days. "My favorite memory of my dad when he was working at UK would have to be all the Sundays I went to work with him at his basketball or football office, whichever season he was in. It was the coaches and players who reviewed the tapes from the previous games, and sometimes I got to listen in. And I thought I was one cool kid."

Another fond memory she remembers is eating lunch in the press box before the football games on Saturdays and getting to meet the media folks.

Russell Rice during his retirement days in Florida. (Photo by Jamie H. Vaught)

"Dad took us so many trips with him to NCAA and SEC tournaments, and to the Sugar Bowl, even if Kentucky wasn't playing, where he worked alongside [well-known SEC media relations guy] Scoop Hudgins," she added. "I could go on and on about all the players and coaches I've met in the past and all the festivities surrounding the games. I think the best memory of all the trips was a feeling that everyone was family. We've always been a Big Blue Nation."

She also pointed out another wonderful memory of going to "Adolph Rupp's house and sitting there listening to Dad interviewing or just chatting with him."

When Rice died in 2015, my young daughter and I paid our respects in Lexington and met some of his family members. We saw Joe B. Hall, *The Cats' Pause* founder Oscar Combs and other UK friends doing the same thing, and they shared old stories. And Combs pointed out a little-known interesting tidbit: Rice was also a lay Presbyterian minister. After his retirement from UK, Rice worked for *The Cats' Pause* (then owned and operated by Combs) where he was the managing editor and a columnist.

Rice, by the way, was inducted into the UK Athletics Hall of Fame in 2011 as a former administrator. Guess what? He was not the only Hall of Famer in his family. Just ask his cousins – Kentucky-born country music singers Loretta Lynn and Patty Loveless. They are members of the Kentucky Music Hall of Fame. Well, as you can see, Rice is sure in pretty impressive company, huh?

Chapter Three

Mr. Hook Shot

*I*t was a beautiful Sunday afternoon in early October 2018 when the author arrived at Cliff Hagan's Lexington home, which isn't very far from the UK campus, where he was a basketball star and the athletics director many years ago. During this book interview, the 6-foot-4 Hagan still had his movie star looks despite his youthful age of 86 years old. This was my second lengthy interview with Hagan, who was wearing shorts on this very warm day. As for the first interview, it took place over 40 years ago at his office at Memorial Coliseum. It was during the late 1970s when I worked as a young student reporter for the *Kentucky Kernel*, the daily campus newspaper at UK, and Hagan was serving as the school's athletics director.

When you ponder about UK's storied basketball history, you'd think of a small collection of elite players or coaches such as Adolph Rupp and Dan Issel. And Hagan, a native of Owensboro, Ky., would be on that exclusive list, too, joining fellow Naismith Memorial Basketball Hall of Famers like Rupp, Issel, Frank Ramsey, Pat Riley and John Calipari. Hagan in 1978 was the second UK player or coach in history to be inducted into that prestigious Hall of Fame. Rupp was the first one, as he was selected in 1969.

Despite his All-American and All-Star status as a UK and NBA performer, respectively, you may be surprised to learn that Hagan's most memorable and thrilling moment of his hoops career was winning the 1949 high school state tournament held in Louisville even though his other teams won NCAA and NBA titles. The prep All-Stater pumped in a then state-record 41 points in the championship game, helping the 29-3 Owensboro Red Devils roll past Lexington Lafayette in a 65-47 victory. (Clay County High School's Richie Farmer now holds the state tourney's championship game scoring record with 51 points in 1988).

It was really a special time for the young Hagan and his teammates who had gone through the district and regional tournaments, and four games in the Sweet Sixteen to capture the state title.

"I guess that was the greatest success that I'd ever had at that time, 1949," recalled Hagan. "The two years before that, 1947 and '48, we had gone to the state tournament. I was a sub on the team, and Maysville beat us both those years. And the first year, '47, Maysville went on and won the state championship. The next year, some real small school beat them after they beat us. Then I'm the starting center in 1949. We had a tough time getting out of the [3rd] Region. We played the Purple Flash of Henderson, and they were a big rival of ours in football. Played them every Thanksgiving in football. And we'd beaten them by 35 points earlier in the year.

"They came to the [newly-opened 5,000-seat] Owensboro Sportscenter, and we played them. And it's before the shot clock. They just held the ball. They didn't take a shot. They just dribbled the ball, dribbled the ball. We just sat back and let them just stay. Got over half court and just dribbled the ball. And we stayed back. The score at halftime was 10-5, our favor. We were up five points, so we felt pretty good.

"Lo and behold, the second half starts, and it's nip and tuck, nip and tuck. They tie up the game, and they got possession of the ball. They're just holding and holding and holding it. And lo and behold, with, I don't know, 15, 10 seconds to go, they take a shot and they miss it. We get the rebound and go down, and pass to Bill Cook, one of our forwards. He takes a two-hand set shot from about 25 feet and it goes in. And we win in the last second over Henderson (21-19) to win the regional tournament. That was the 3rd Region.

"We go off to the state tournament, and the big deal about that was riding the train. L&N, the Louisville & Nashville train, picked us up, the cheerleaders and the coach. We rode the train and got off, and it seemed like we walked to the hotel from the train station. Maybe we didn't, but it seems like that's what we did those days. It was a big deal in riding the train.

"[We] played in the old Louisville Armory [which opened in 1905 and was also the site of many SEC tournaments]. That was a big place. It must have held 6,000 people or something. It was so big, overwhelming. I just remember that we couldn't see the scoreboard very well because of all the smoke. Everybody smoked in the '40s. We're talking about 1949. We had played four games in three days, and on Saturday we played, like at noon, and won. And had to come back that night [for the championship]. We were going to play Lafayette, the big school in Lexington. Of course, they were favored. [Lafayette was led by All-Stater Bob Mulcahy who later played at Eastern Kentucky University and eventually became the head coach at his alma mater during the early 1970s.]

"I remember, after playing that Saturday morning game and coming back to the hotel, I was having cramps in my legs. I couldn't get up. I was laying around on the floor playing cards, rummy or something. And every time I tried to get up, I'd get a cramp. I thought, 'My gosh, I'm not going to be able to play tonight.' They actually had to lift me up to put me on my feet without my legs knotting up on me. I was really concerned.

"But anyway I played that night. And [it was] one of those kind of nights where you're in the right place at the right time. And I was shooting a hook shot then in high school. Not many people were shooting the hook shot. I could get a good shot off, and I had a little jumper too, [along with] some quickness and jumping ability. And lo and behold, we were ahead at halftime. Don't remember what it was, but I think that I may have had more points than Lafayette had. Somebody told me that. At [the] end of the game, we won 65-47. They had 47 points, and I had 41 points. Only six points less than their entire team.

"So, that was the greatest success that I had ever had. And then winning the state high school championship in 1949 is the biggest thing that could have happened to any high school kid, ever. I had had such a strong performance, 41 points. Those are your first thrills, your first big excitement, athletically. Just imagine what that could mean to you. And there's only one state tournament champion. That was very special. And to this day, it's still very special."

Moments after winning the championship, Hagan got a nice surprise from William "Big Six" Henderson, a timekeeper who worked in law enforcement and became a federal marshal in Louisville. "He was out chasing people making moonshine and had all kinds of stories about that time," he said. "Big Six Henderson brought the game ball to me and says, 'I want you to have this. I may get fired. I don't have the right to do this. I want you to have the game ball.' So, we began a close relationship from that.

"He was a Notre Dame graduate and talked me into taking a trip to Notre Dame. And I went up there and met Moose Krause, then basketball coach at Notre Dame. And Frank Leahy, the football coach, says, 'Hey, how about coming up here for football? You'd make a great tight end, wide receiver or whatever.' Of course, I had no interest in football at all. But I did get to meet the basketball coach."

Because of Big Six's memorable gesture with the game ball, Hagan decided to wear No. 6 on his Wildcat jersey, instead of No. 18, a number he wore in high school. Kentucky later retired Hagan's jersey.

Interestingly, a couple of Hagan's future teammates at UK also participated in the 1949 state tournament. All-State performers Frank Ramsey and Gayle Rose played for Madisonville and Paris, respectively. Both schools met in the second round with Paris advancing to the semifinals.

By the way, UK dedicated Owensboro Sportscenter, the city's new arena, in early February 1949 when the top-ranked Wildcats faced No. 18 Bradley in a non-conference game. Kentucky later made four more trips to Owensboro, including Hagan's three varsity years at UK. In 1952, Kentucky blasted Ole Miss 116-58 with Hagan, then a junior, gunning 37 points before his hometown crowd, which also saw UK's All-SEC senior guard Bobby Watson, a native of Owensboro, pump in 18 points.

After that state tournament championship, Hagan and the team went back home for a celebration at the Owensboro Sportscenter, but he didn't stay there very long as he flew on an airplane for the first time.

Remembered Hagan, "One of my friends said, 'Hey, you're off to New York City. You're going to see the Eastern [Regional] finals of the NCAA. Kentucky's up there playing.' I said, 'My gosh.' So, he drove me over to Evansville, and I got on a plane and flew all night, getting into Manhattan about 7:30 in the morning at the Paramount Hotel, where the Kentucky Wildcats stayed."

And the first thing Hagan did was come to coach Adolph Rupp's hotel room and knock on the door. "He came to the door, bleary-eyed in his red silk pajamas," Hagan commented. "He said, 'What do you want?' I said, 'Well, w-w-w-w-well.' And they had given me the *Courier-Journal* [which mentioned Hagan's 41 points] so I gave that to him. He says, 'Oh, come in, come in, come in.'

"And lo and behold, Frank Ramsey was up there also [at the hotel]. I never played Frank in the regular season. But we played him in the state tournament the year before. And we'd beaten them by 35 points [actually 68-34 in the first round of the 1948 state tourney]."

It was that time in New York City when Hagan had decided to expand on his hook shot after watching Yale All-American Tony Lavelli score 27 points, many of them on his one-handed hook shots, against Illinois before losing in the first round of the eight-team NCAA Tournament. And eventual national champion Kentucky, led by 6-foot-7 senior center Alex Groza, was facing Villanova in the other opening round matchup. As it turned out, UK advanced and later captured its second straight national title.

"Anyway, we were up there for three or four days together, being taken around town by somebody, seeing shows, eating out, and going to the game," said Hagan. "One thing I remember about being up there is we were watching

Yale in the Eastern [Regional]. Tony Lavelli was a forward for Yale. And he took a hook shot from the forward position, 20-some feet, shooting a hook shot. That opened my eyes because I was really into my hook shot at that time. Left hand, right hand, and maybe even from the free throw line. But I thought, 'My goodness.' So, I went home, and I started with left hand, right hand, and shooting that hook shot from 17, 18 feet on the fast break.

"And this leads me to telling you the secret of basketball. The secret of basketball is the ability to get a shot off. A lot of people are good shooters, but they can't move. They can't put the ball on the ground, drive around.

"But I could. I developed a little 18-foot jump shot and could put the ball on the ground. Then I could pull up with a shot fake, go by somebody – didn't have to go in too much, just always fade. Go across the free throw line, fade with that hook shot, and get the shot off.

"And people say, 'Why don't they shoot the hook shot anymore?' It's so different because you're not pushing the ball. It's almost like a finger roll where it's rolling off the ends of your finger. It's so contrary to anything else you do. It takes rote and rote, time after time. So, you develop the same feel of the ball rolling off the ends of your fingers for a hook shot as you do for a free throw. As soon as

you shoot your free throw, or a little jump shot, you know whether it's going in or not. Well, you have the same feel with the hook shot, that kind of thing. Period."

Hagan was asked about his first meeting with the Baron, who at the time had the 1947-48 Fabulous Five squad of Alex Groza, Ralph Beard, Wah Wah Jones, Kenny Rollins and Cliff Barker. That 36-3 team won the national championship and represented the U.S. in winning the gold medal in the 1948 Summer Olympics in London.

"During a break in high school or something, a teach-

UK teammates Frank Ramsey (left) and Cliff Hagan. (Photo by UK Athletics)

er in our high school was coming up here to Eastern Kentucky, brought me up to Lexington, and dropped me off at the Alumni Gym," Hagan said. "They knew I was coming. There was an invitation, I guess. It wasn't like a trip now where you're winding down, that kind of thing. I was just riding up here with somebody. I was in the Alumni Gym [which had a seating capacity of less than 3,000]. I remember going out on the floor. And [it was the] first time I'd seen the Alumni Gym. It was a big place.

"The Fabulous Five were practicing, and I met Alex Groza, the center, a 6-foot-7 guy. I talked to him about shooting the hook shot. He says, 'Well, I think it may be a little late for you.' Well, I was already shooting the hook shot, left and right. So, I didn't pay any attention to him at all. But I did meet Coach Rupp, and he said, 'Well, when you get ready to come to college, we want you to come here,' and shook hands. So, that was about five to 10 minutes with him. I think I did go down into the office where you had to duck to go under because [the doorway] was 6-2 or something and I was 6-4 at the time. So, I made up my mind [about coming to Kentucky].

"I did take a trip to Louisville, and I did take a trip to Notre Dame. Those were the only places I visited at all. And got letters from Hawaii and all over places. But the place to go was Kentucky. It was the right decision then; it's still the right decision now, maybe 70 years later."

Hagan was a mid-termer throughout his student days. He had started his education in January because his birthday fell on December 9. That's why he came to Kentucky in January 1950, joining the UK freshman team, which obviously had already begun its season. In addition to Hagan, the members of the freshman team, coached by Rupp assistant Harry Lancaster, included Ramsey, Lindle Castle, Lou Tsioropoulos, Dick Pikrone and Dwight Price, among others, and they ended the campaign with a 15-1 mark.

"We didn't lose any games. Although before I got there, they had lost a game," said Hagan. "So, I always kid Frank that 'You lost more games than I did in college' because we were on the same varsity team."

Hagan and Ramsey were the freshman squad's top scorers.

Earlier, when Hagan arrived at UK campus in the winter of 1949-50 after graduating from high school (and playing for Owensboro) in the middle of the school year, the university already had begun the construction of its new 12,000-seat hoops facility named Memorial Coliseum and its new gym opened in December 1950.

"I had to sit out till the following year, January '51, to become eligible [for varsity competition]," Hagan said. "I didn't play that first semester when we won the [national] championship. I sat on the bench and led cheers, and all that kind of thing. Come January '51, there's a big scene, and they redshirted me. They never discussed it with me. But Harry [Lancaster] and Adolph talked about it, and they decided I would go ahead and play that second semester. So, I was a substitute on that team, actually. I didn't start because [senior] Walt Hirsch was a starting forward on that team. He was the captain, and [junior] Shelby Linville was on the team, 6-foot-6, and I'm a 6-foot-4 college center. They had Bill Spivey, a 7-foot center. They weren't really looking for a 6-4 [center].

"So, I played off and on, and did fairly well. Then we got in the tournaments. Another interesting thing: The SEC Tournament was always held in Louisville at the old Armory. And, lo and behold, in the final game [of the SEC tourney], Vanderbilt beats us for the SEC championship. Normally, the conference [tournament] champion goes to the NCAA. But for some reason earlier in the year, they decided that the regular season champion would represent the Southeastern Conference. So, we went in the place of Vanderbilt.

"We go out east and play, over in the Carolinas [against Louisville in the first NCAA Tournament game], and end up in Minneapolis for the championship. I caught the flu. I wasn't well. I had a temperature, and I was sitting on the bench. Spivey doesn't have a good first half, and Coach Rupp keeps turning around to [assistant] Harry, 'How's Hagan? How's Hagan? What's his temperature? What's his temperature?' After he said something, 'Well, I think that's about right. Put him in.' So, I went in."

And Hagan finished with 10 points to go along with Spivey's 22 points and 21 rebounds as the top-ranked Wildcats – who only had six healthy players – overcame No. 4 Kansas State's two-point halftime lead before winning 68-58 for the 1951 NCAA crown. All-American Spivey was named the Final Four's MVP and Kentucky finished with an 32-2 overall mark, including a perfect 14-0 SEC record.

In the following season of 1951-52, Kentucky had another great year, ranking No. 1 most of the winter, but dropped to Coach Frank McGuire's St. John's club in NCAA Eastern Regional finals, finishing with a 29-3 mark, including another 14-0 worksheet in the SEC. Hagan, Ramsey and Bobby Watson were the team's top scorers, with all three receiving All-American honors.

After the NCAA suspended UK for the 1952-53 season for various rules violations, partly brought on by a gambling scandal involving several schools, the Wildcats returned to action for 1953-54 with three key seniors: Hagan, Frank Ramsey and Lou Tsioropoulos. An individual highlight of that season was Hagan's record-shattering 51-point performance against Temple in the season opener won by UK, 86-59.

On his UK single-game scoring record, Hagan added, "It's against Temple University, a good basketball school up east. In that game, I scored 51 points. No one said anything about a record. I wasn't put back in the game to break a record or anything, but I ended up with 51 points and the team carried me off the floor on their shoulders. Later I found out that was a record until Dan Issel came to school, and Adolph Rupp said, 'Hey, we're going to put you back in there to break Cliff Hagan's record.' So, he put him back in at the end of the game to break my record."

For the school record, Issel poured in 53 points against Ole Miss in Oxford in 1970, a mark he held until 2009 when 6-foot-4 junior guard Jodie Meeks gunned in 54 points against Tennessee in Knoxville.

One of Hagan's close friends at UK was Frank Ramsey. Both hailed from western Kentucky and played against each other in the state tournament with Ramsey from Madisonville High. They were also roommates. And they sometimes argued about the room temperature. Ramsey liked it cool, while Hagan liked it warm.

"I liked the window open with the heat [turned] off, and I slept next to the window. Cliff liked the window closed and the heat on," smiled Ramsey in a 1995 book *Still Crazy About the Cats*, which was the author's second book about UK basketball. "Whoever went to bed first would fix it like he wanted it, and whoever went to bed next fixed it the way he wanted it. If you got up during the night to go to the bathroom or something, it was changing all the time. We had one of those old steam radiators. That was just the way it was."

Even though they were good buddies, Hagan and Ramsey were ultra-competitive at UK and later in the NBA. "We were such nose-to-nose all the time," Hagan said. "He had run down, getting the pivot every once in a while, and I'd get out of there. Coach Rupp would say, 'Throw the ball into the hay' because I'd shoot over 50 percent. And he would check your shooting percentage. That's one of Adolph's big things. Shooting percentage. And mine was all over 50 percent because they were all short shots, short hook shots, or little jump shots.

"We're playing one game and I said, 'Frank, Frank! Get the ball in to me!' He says, 'I will after I get my average.' That's a true story. That's the way we really felt. We were both competitive, we were after our own game, and doing the best we could. But we were good teammates and did pass the ball. And I later led the NBA in assists as a top forward. Leading the league in assists, not guards, but forwards. So, I was a playmaker."

Another good friend of both Hagan and Ramsey was Bobby Watson. "He [Ramsey] roomed with Bobby Watson, an Owensboro teammate of mine, and a UK guard," said Hagan. "So they roomed together, I think one year, maybe two years. Two years, I think, I roomed with Frank Ramsey."

Primarily from the 1940s to 1960s, many college basketball players, including Wilt Chamberlain and Bob Cousy, would flock to the Catskill Mountains in southeastern New York for summer jobs and play competitive basketball with other hotels in the area. Even Red Auerbach, before he became famous as an NBA legend, served as the athletics director at the Kutsher's Country Club. UK standouts Cliff Hagan, Frank Ramsey and Lou Tsioropoulos would spend some time there. And many top entertainers and movie stars such as Jerry Lewis, Don Rickles and Bob Hope would visit the resorts.

On playing summer basketball during his UK days, Hagan recalled, "When I came up here as a freshman and played that one semester of spring basketball, there was basketball in the Catskill Mountains. Frank Ramsey had a new Pontiac so I rode up with Frank and Bobby Watson. We drove up to Monticello, New York, where Kutsher's Country Club is a Jewish resort. It's called the Borscht Belt. All these Jewish resorts had basketball teams.

"But we had to wait tables. Breakfast, lunch, and dinner. Which means you had to get up at 6:00 in the morning, at least to wait tables. And then we played basketball at night up there. Well, when we got up there, who was our coach? Red Auerbach was our coach. He didn't know us or whatever. But he got to know us. That's how he later drafted us [for the NBA in 1953]. We played for him, so he knew all about us."

In the 1953 NBA Draft, the Celtics picked Ramsey as the league's overall fifth pick in the first round before selecting Hagan in the third round (No. 13 overall) and Tsioropoulos in the seventh round, but all three Wildcat players returned to Kentucky for their senior year of 1953-54. The trio wanted to win another national championship after winning the NCAA title in 1951. But, as it turned out, the Wildcats decided not to participate in the 1954 tournament even after a 25-0 mark and a No. 1 ranking because NCAA had ruled the "Big Three" ineligible since the players were graduate students.

"We were a big part of that team – the three of us," Hagan said. "Coach Rupp did not want to go to the NCAA without us playing, so Kentucky declined the invitation. That always bothered me a little bit, and it bothers me more now than it did then because we placed such a great effort in getting our student-athletes to get a degree while they're at school. We didn't know that those were the rules of the game. It was too late when we discovered that the rules said if you enter graduate school, you can't participate in the NCAA championship."

In the previous year, as mentioned earlier, the Wildcats didn't play a regular schedule as they were suspended for the 1952-53 season by NCAA. "It was disappointing," said Ramsey, who added the squad "practiced maybe two or three days a week" and played in several exhibition games.

But, in Hagan's three varsity years at UK, his teams won 86 out of 91 games, winning nearly 95 percent of the time, with a national championship title in 1951 and an undefeated 25-0 squad in 1954.

As a student at UK, Hagan was also involved in school activities other than basketball. He excelled in the classroom, twice ranking among the College of Education's Top 10 students. Hagan was a member of Sigma Nu Fraternity, Student Government, Baptist Student Union and Fellowship of Christian Athletes.

After his college days, since he had been enrolled in the Reserve Officers' Training Corps (ROTC) program at UK, Hagan had to serve two years in the Andrews Air Force Base near Washington, D.C., as a commissioned officer. He also guided the base to two Worldwide Air Force championships.

Some of Hagan's UK teammates also served in the military at approximately the same time. "C.M. Newton was at Andrews Air Force Base before I got there," commented Hagan. "Bobby Watson was at Andrews Air Force before I got there. There was a General [Blair] Garland, head of headquarters at AACS [Airways and Air Communications Service] at Andrews Air Force, who was a big basketball fan. He had an aide called Captain Scott. And all they had to do was get your serial number, and they could get your orders changed to report to Andrews Air Force Base when you got your initial orders.

"Well, I got my orders and was on my way to Georgia to a base down there somewhere. And Scott said, 'Don't report, don't report, turn around, come right to Andrews Air Force Base!' which I did. When I got up there, C.M. Newton was already up there, and Bobby Watson was up there. Later they got

Lou Tsioropoulos to come up there. Already up there was Bob Kenney, who was an All-American at Kansas, and another player from Kansas, a 6-6, 6-7 player. So, we won the Worldwide Air Force championship both years that we were there."

After satisfying his military obligations, Hagan, who had been drafted by the Celtics before his Kentucky career ended, began his NBA career in 1956. But he did not play for Boston as a rookie, as he and 6-foot-8 All-Star center Ed Macauley were shipped to the St. Louis Hawks for the overall No. 2 NBA Draft pick Bill Russell, a 6-foot-9 All-American center from two-time NCAA champion University of San Francisco. Hagan wasn't too thrilled about going to St. Louis. He had wanted to play with Ramsey and the Celtics.

"In my first year in the NBA, they wanted me to play guard," said Hagan, who was actually a 6-foot-4 center at Kentucky. "I got a call from the coach when I was in the service at Andrews, Red Holzman, who was our coach at St. Louis at that time. He said, 'Hey, you've been traded to the St. Louis Hawks along with Ed Macauley.' I was just thrown in on the deal. I think they wanted to get rid of me, a 6-4 college center. Who needs Cliff Hagan? Seriously.

"So, they really didn't know what to do. [Holzman] said, 'Well, we want you to play guard.' Here I was, a college center, a high school center. I said, 'Well, Red, I thought I might play forward,' and I'd always likened myself to [former UK All-American] Wah Wah Jones because he was my size, but he had a two-hand set and all that stuff. But [they want me] to play guard. So, we go to Galesburg, Illinois, at Knox College to work out (in a training camp).

"We started exhibition [season] against the Minneapolis Lakers [now Los Angeles Lakers]. And [I was] trying to play guard. Well, hell, I didn't know how to play guard. A center trying to play guard? That kind of thing. I chipped the bone in my knee at one point in exhibition, so I was on the bench and didn't get to play for six weeks or something.

"That may have saved my life because they can't get rid of you when you're injured. We didn't have no-cut contracts. I was making so little money, least money of anybody on the team. Embarrassed to tell you how little it was and that they wanted to keep me because they didn't want to pay somebody else more money to replace me, and the other teams were cutting players all the time. They were coming [to the Hawks], trying out with us, and not staying very long."

Nevertheless, St. Louis' plan to convert Hagan to backcourt as a point guard fell apart with the Hawks struggling on the floor, and Holzman was fired in the middle of the season. The Hawks found a permanent replacement in 6-foot-7 forward Alex Hannum, who was named player-coach after point guard Slater Martin stepped down from coaching after a 5-3 mark. Even though St. Louis finished with a losing record of 34-38 in the regular season, the Hawks advanced to the 1957 NBA Finals before losing to the Celtics in seven games.

By the middle of that 1956-57 campaign, Hagan began to show promise as a pro when he saw more playing time at forward – not in backcourt – due to an injury to 6-foot-9 Bob Pettit. As a rookie, Hagan had finished with a 5.5-point per game average, while playing an average of 14.5 minutes per game before he exploded in the next nine seasons, becoming a five-time NBA All-Star Game participant.

"We won the Western Division my first year ([in a playoff tie-breaker involving three teams with identical records]," added Hagan, who earned his master's degree in education at Washington University in St. Louis while playing for the Hawks. "But we had to get through Detroit [then Fort Wayne Pistons] and Minneapolis [for division title]. The Celtics won the Eastern Division. They had never won anything [at the time]; the Hawks had never won anything. The Celtics had Bill Russell, Bob Cousy, Bill Sharman, Frank Ramsey, Jim Loscutoff, Tommy Heinsohn, all those kind of guys.

"We went up there [in Boston] to play the first game in the playoffs, and we beat the Celtics. The Boston Garden was only half full. That was on a Saturday. We had to come back and play Sunday; the place was packed. They beat us in the second game. So, we go back and forth, and we ended up in the seventh game at Boston, beating us in a double overtime for their first [NBA] championship."

Boston's 1957 title, as it turned out, marked the beginning of the Celtics' dynasty which won 11 NBA championships in 13 seasons during superstar Bill Russell's playing career.

"The next year, we got the same thing going again [in the championship series]," recalled Hagan, who was the league's seventh-leading scorer with 19.9 points in his second pro season. "And we got the [title in the] sixth game. Now Russell sprained his ankle in the third game. We got the sixth game in St. Louis for the championship. And Bob Pettit scores 50 points in that championship game. I had 15. Nobody else had double figures."

And that would be Hagan's only NBA championship. On his 10-year NBA career with St. Louis, Hagan said it was very unusual to stay in one place. "And [I] got a chance to play that first year after I hurt my knee twice."

Also, for the 1957-58 season, Hagan, a smooth jumper, had the second-best field goal percentage in the NBA with 44.3 percent.

Cliff Hagan and the author at his Lexington home in 2018. (Photo courtesy of Jamie H. Vaught)

In 1966, Hagan's NBA playing career ended. "I had my 10 years, you know, and I could've played another couple of years, but the owner wanted me to retire," Hagan commented. "I think I was making maybe three, four or five times what I had signed for by that time but still under $30,000 a year, and I had been a five-time all-star. [The team said] it's time for me to retire, and part of that is they were gonna have to fund your retirement. And one less player would have saved him many thousands of dollars probably in retirement in which [the NBA] Players Association got started years later."

But he stayed with the Hawks for another year in a different role, serving as a radio and television commentator for the St. Louis franchise (which later moved to Atlanta in 1968). It wasn't an easy job for the former Wildcat.

"I wasn't a natural at that," Hagan said of his TV job. "It was hard to criticize players that you'd just played with. Had I not played with these guys, I think today I would have done a much better job than I did then. I was a little bit shy about all that. So, after that first season, I realized I wasn't a natural color guy. Some people are. As much as I'm talking now, I'm not a verbose person. I'm really not, I'm a quiet guy."

However, 36-year-old Hagan received a call from the Dallas Chaparrals of the new American Basketball Association, which began play for the 1967-68 season. It was a new league that had 11 teams, including the Louisville-based Kentucky Colonels. It was the ABA that introduced the new three-point field goal, the red-white-blue basketball (some called the beach ball) and the sexy bikini-clad ball girls at Miami.

"I flew down there, talked to them, and they wanted me to be a player-coach," he said. "Well, I had sat out a year. I'd retired for a year. I had all the glory, you know, five-time all-star. Anyway, I decided to take the job. As I got into practicing with them, leading practice, I started playing with them. Well, I found out I knew how to pass the ball on a fast break. I knew how to play unselfish. Pass this way, go set a screen, then wait for the ball. Most players want to pass, they want to go toward the ball, and that's not basketball. It's passing, going away, setting a screen for somebody else. Well, I could do that and get some movement going on the court. Lo and behold, I still didn't want to play, but I did. The first game we played a California team [Anaheim Amigos, who later became the Los Angeles Stars before moving to Utah]. They had a 7-foot center. I scored 40 points [actually a game-high 35 points] in the first game. How can I not play after that? Of course, they want me to play. I can still fade and get the hook shot, and I still had some quickness."

A gentleman off the hardwood floor, Hagan was a physical competitor on the court when it came to basketball, becoming one of the league's leaders in personal fouls. Hagan also played in the first ABA All-Star Game in Indianapolis, scoring 10 points and becoming the first professional to participate in All-Star Games in both the ABA and NBA. Representing the Colonels in that game were ex-UK star Louie Dampier, former Western Kentucky University standout Darel Carrier (whose son, Josh, later played for coach Tubby Smith's Wildcats) and Randy Mahaffey.

The Dallas franchise, which eventually became the San Antonio Spurs, did well under Hagan's leadership in the first year, posting a 46-32 mark for second place in the Western Division while the player-coach averaged 18.2 points in 56 games. The Chaparrals finished behind the first-place New Orleans Buccaneers, who were coached by former Mississippi State boss and future Kentucky Colonels coach Babe McCarthy. In 1968, Hagan was named the Texas Professional Coach of the Year. He stayed with Dallas until the midpoint of the 1969-70 campaign when he resigned from his coaching job and was replaced by general manager Max Williams.

One of Hagan's ABA memories was the assassination of civil rights leader Rev. Dr. Martin Luther King Jr. on April 4, 1968, in Memphis. Hagan's team's playoff matchup with New Orleans was one of many major sporting events throughout the country that were canceled or postponed at the time.

During that time, he also recalls one of his players didn't make the team's (returning) flight. "We start practicing the next day, and he's not there. And the second day, he shows up. What do you do with a player that just doesn't show up? And [he was] a little bit of a controversial player anyway. So, I asked the team, 'Should we take him back?' 'Yes, yes, yes,' [said his teammates]. Well, I had trouble with that player the rest of the season [playoffs]."

Several ABA clubs had financial troubles. Not the Chaparrals, who had a strong ownership group. Hagan said he never had to worry about his paycheck bouncing. He couldn't remember his exact salary, but believed it was for a three-year pact at $30,000 each. "The Dallas Chaparrals had 20 owners and each of them had put up $200,000," said Hagan. "So, that was enough for the program."

In the early 1970s, Hagan – who had some business interests, including his several restaurants which bear his name – eventually returned to his alma mater and became the assistant athletics director under AD Harry Lancaster for a couple of years. One of Hagan's early responsibilities as assistant AD was to develop and implement the Blue & White Fund (now called the K Fund) for the new Commonwealth Stadium and then Rupp Arena.

"I was the first assistant athletics director the university ever had," said Hagan. "And now they must have 30 [actually around 23 at this writing].

"I was the fundraiser. I started the program where you donated for the rights to buy season tickets. We were the first school in the Southeastern Conference to start charging extra for the right to buy basketball tickets in the conference. If you did football, you got basketball because basketball wasn't all that big for some of them. But here we had a double whack at people, collecting money for the Blue and White Fund."

Before Hagan became the school's assistant AD in June of 1972, there was lots of talk about Adolph Rupp's possible retirement as the Kentucky coach after the 1971-72 season. The Baron didn't want to quit after 41 years. He wanted to continue coaching despite the school's mandatory retirement age of 70. So, he and his friends fought with UK president Dr. Otis Singletary. It was a difficult time for the university. Hagan was asked if he felt bad about his coach being forced to retire.

"I went to a dinner once at Dr. Singletary's house at Maxwell Place," Hagan said. "Another alumnus was there, his wife, and my wife [Martha] and I. And the [Rupp] subject came up. This alumnus thought it was time for Coach Rupp to retire, [saying] he was old, didn't know what he was doing, that kind of thing. Apparently, he had made a verbal contract with Singletary that he would retire at the age of 70. At that time Dr. Singletary was going to call him on it, but this was the time.

"He didn't want to retire. Most people don't want to retire at 70, although most people should, probably. I recall [former Gov.] Happy Chandler getting involved in it, as he was a big friend of Coach Rupp and thought he should continue as coach. You know, age is a relative thing. But when I came to school there as an 18-year-old in 1950, Coach Rupp was probably in his 40s. I thought he and Harry were both old guys. Really, Harry was younger, and we were a little afraid of him because he was a physical kind of guy. And he was the backup guy to Adolph.

"So, I can understand the players maybe having a little concern and maybe getting around somebody [who is] 65 and then 70. It was a touchy subject and still is, I think."

After his retirement, Rupp was allowed to keep his office at Memorial Coliseum. According to one of Russell Rice's books, *Kentucky's Basketball Baron*, the Man in the Brown Suit also drew an annual salary of $10,000 for consulting work. Rupp and his family later had four front-row seats at Rupp Arena for lifetime. "He was very impressed with that," Hagan said of the Rupp Arena tickets.

And, in 1975, Hagan became the school's AD, replacing Lancaster.

Speaking of Rupp, the younger generation of Wildcat fans may be surprised to learn that the Baron had once agreed to coach basketball at Duke during the pre-Mike Krzyzewski days. That was right before the 1973-74 season, and Rupp actually wasn't ready to give up coaching.

"Daddy got a phone call from the president of Duke University [Terry Sanford]," ex-UK player and son Herky Rupp once commented. "He said, 'Coach, we need a coach. We've dismissed [Bucky Waters] and we want you to coach.' "

In amazement, Coach Rupp said, "Are you sure? These people around here in Kentucky thought I was too old to coach. And here you are wanting me to coach?"

"Age makes no difference to us," replied Sanford. "We want a person we know can coach. We want a person of your stature, and you are the one for the job."

But an introductory press conference at Duke that was scheduled did not take place. Rupp's 500-acre cattle farm manager had died suddenly, and the former Wildcat boss was forced to give up his new coaching opportunity.

Added Hagan, "Duke then isn't what it is now, but he was wise not to take the Duke thing. Just to go ahead, retire and enjoy his great life that he had, his farm and his cattle."

In his post-coaching days, Rupp also spent time in the old ABA as an executive for the struggling Memphis Tams franchise (which at the time was owned by controversial Charles Finley of the Oakland A's) and the Kentucky Colonels.

It was national news when Kentucky coach Joe B. Hall decided to retire in 1985 after an NCAA Tournament loss to St. John's in Denver, finishing with an

18-13 mark. A former Rupp player who grew up in Cynthiana, Hall completed his coaching career with a 297-100 mark at UK, including three Final Four trips and a 1978 national title.

With the national media converging in Lexington for the 1985 NCAA Final Four, the vacant UK coaching position became a media circus. School president Dr. Otis Singletary, Hagan, and a search committee searched for a suitable replacement and had to deal with tons of speculation from the media and the fans. Hagan said the job wasn't that difficult, as the university had one of the nation's most coveted head coaching positions.

"I know the papers were rampant with stories at that time with things that were going on in the basketball program," said Hagan. "We talked to Dave Bliss who was the SMU [Southern Methodist University] coach at the time. [He] had been Bobby Knight's assistant at Indiana. He came in and made a very nice presentation, very impressive. And the coach at Arizona, Lute Olson. We flew him in to talk to him, and we would've hired him. [But] he was settled out there. I don't remember what the problems were, I think there were some family problems or whatever. So, that was the coach we would have had. And then Eddie Sutton. I got a call from Eddie Sutton wanting the job. So, we ended up with Eddie Sutton as it turned out.

"It's a good job, and a well-paying job at the time. It isn't what it is today, that's for sure. None of our salaries were. We contacted Pat Riley of the [Los Angeles] Lakers [where] he was coaching and highly successful at the time. I said, 'This is a courtesy call to you. I know you're involved with that [the Lakers].' So, that's all it was, you know, because the reporters ask, 'Well, have you contacted so-and-so?' 'Well, yes, I have.' That kind of thing. I'm sure there were others at the time, whoever was popular at that time, we would have contacted. But we ended up with Ed Sutton, who had a reputation as a fine coach, an extremely fine defensive coach at the time."

Hagan, who became the first UK player in history to be inducted into the Naismith Memorial Basketball Hall of Fame in 1978, left Kentucky in 1988 under the dark cloud of an NCAA investigation of its basketball program. It was a sad time for Hagan and UK.

"I felt like he had to take the rap for everything that happened there," said former teammate Frank Ramsey during the early 1990s. "Nobody else left [immediately]. I think he has been hurt. We don't discuss it. We talk about children, grandchildren, things like that."

Several months later, coach Eddie Sutton resigned in mid-March 1989 after a 13-19 season, UK's first losing season since the 1926-27 season.

Vanderbilt coach C.M. Newton, who was Hagan's basketball teammate at UK, and Rick Pitino soon took over as AD and basketball coach at Kentucky, respectively. A few years later, Newton, by the way, honored Hagan by recommending to the UK Board of Trustees that they rename the school's newly-remodeled baseball park. It was called the Cliff Hagan Stadium, which was the home of the baseball Wildcats until 2018. "I thought it was wonderful," commented Ramsey. "He deserved it. He did a lot of good things for UK. [It's] a well-deserved honor."

After leaving UK, the Hagans spent their winters in Florida where they had a second home. "We've been down there, I guess, since 1988," he said. "We've had a home in Vero Beach, and we come back for Christmas. We come back the first of May, and we're here [in Lexington] five months."

One of his tennis partners in Florida was Jeff Mullins, a former Duke hoops star from Kentucky. They lived in the same area. They even had their picture taken together for a local newspaper article in Florida.

"I still have quickness to this day, believe it or not," smiled Hagan. "I still have the first step. I'm playing tennis and staying in shape. It's weird [for my age], but I do. We won't talk about that because it sounds like I'm crazy."

Another hobby for Hagan – who has four children, and many grandchildren and great-grandchildren – was collecting antiques. His interest in antiques actually began while in college. "I knew a family here that were interested in antiques," said Hagan, "and in St. Louis, [while playing] pro ball, I'd visit antique shops. On the road, I'd visit antique shops in different cities we played in. Driving from Kentucky to Alabama where my wife's folks moved from Owensboro after we got married, I had to stop at an antique shop and take a look at things. So, I started out sort of interested in glass. Then got interested in silver, that kind of thing. [I] started out with unfinished furniture, finishing some furniture. Cheap way to go, you know.

"Now, I don't go into antique shops anymore. I got over that and don't buy anything anymore because I [would] have to get rid of something. I don't have room for anything."

As we were nearing the end of our fascinating interview, Hagan commented that he had just watched a documentary film *Student Athlete* from HBO Sports.

The documentary discussed the hardships endured by college athletes. One of several athletes profiled is high school star Nick Richards, who later signed with Kentucky.

"Have you seen it? You ought to see it," Hagan said of HBO's program in late 2018. "It's all about how they [prep or college players] think they ought to be making money. You know, getting paid now instead of [waiting for NBA] and how many of them went through school, not taking good classes, don't have a job, don't have any money. It's a real interesting program. You ought to watch it. I'm taping it. I was watching it before you came."

Chapter Four

Basketball Court to Courtroom

*F*or most of his life, James "Jim" Duff has worked and lived in the Washington, D.C, area, a very lively place for politics and American history. And it is the home of our national treasures – Supreme Court, White House and the Capitol – which house federal government's three branches (judicial, executive and legislature).

But he faithfully follows the Kentucky Wildcats. A former member of coach Adolph Rupp's basketball program during the early 1970s, Duff bleeds blue and occasionally flies to Lexington with his childhood friend and ex-Wildcat star Kevin Grevey, who also lives in the D.C. area, to watch a UK basketball game at Rupp Arena. Duff once showed the author his Kentucky Wildcat mementos during a visit to his Washington office in 2010.

Duff – whose parents were from Owsley County in the Eastern Kentucky mountains – grew up in the Cincinnati suburb of Hamilton, Ohio. Even though Duff currently lives out of town, he still has strong roots in the state of Kentucky in addition to UK. He and his brother Kevin inherited one of their grandfather's farms in Owsley County.

While Duff, a consummate gentleman, is better known for his successful legal career, including two stints as the director of the Administrative Office of the U.S. Courts, a federal post he still holds, he played basketball as a walk-on member of one of the nation's top freshman teams ever during the 1971-72 season. Back then the first-year players weren't allowed to play on the varsity team. The baby Wildcats had a perfect 22-0 record and were chosen as the top freshman team in the nation by the *Basketball News*. It was argued that the rookies, coached by Joe B. Hall, were even more popular than UK's 18th-ranked varsity team, which featured All-SEC performers Jim Andrews, Tom Parker and Ronnie Lyons and finished with a 21-7 mark in Adolph Rupp's last year as Kentucky coach. The Kittens – who had standouts like leading scorer Kevin Grevey, Jimmy Dan Conner, Mike Flynn, Bob Guyette, G.J. Smith, Jerry Hale and Steve Lochmueller – were very well-known and popular throughout the state. They even had a medium-sized poster of them available to the public.

Duff, who roomed with G.J. Smith of old Laurel County High School during his freshman year, managed to see some action. The 6-foot, 155-pound backup guard played 15 games, scoring a total of 14 points. But that is okay. Playing for the Kentucky Wildcats was a lifelong dream. "I spent much of my childhood dreaming of playing for UK," commented Duff, whose favorite players were UK All-Americans Pat Riley and Louie Dampier.

But Duff almost didn't suit up for UK. All seven scholarship players from the freshman team had to encourage him to try out for the Kittens' squad. "Kevin, Jimmy Dan Conner, and Mike Flynn were particularly helpful," recalled Duff. "The day that Coach Hall told me I had made the team was one of the greatest feelings I have ever had."

There was a small problem, though. Duff had long hair, and straight-laced Hall didn't like it. "Duff, do you know what a barber is?" asked Hall, who several months later took over Rupp's head coaching post in 1972.

"That was Joe B's way of telling me I had made the team," added Duff, who got his haircut.

Jim Duff (left) and Joe B. Hall at Rupp Arena. (Photo by Jamie H. Vaught)

As mentioned previously, one of Duff's close friends was Kevin Grevey. They had both attended Taft High School in Hamilton, Ohio, where Grevey was a highly-regarded prepster who became one of best shooters ever in Cincinnati-area history. "Some of my enthusiasm for UK may have encouraged him to choose to go there, too," remembered Duff, who once served as the administrative assistant to U.S. Supreme Court Chief Justice William Rehnquist for several years during the late 1990s. "Kevin and I have been in the same town our entire lives and are the best of friends."

Duff had a memorable moment as a Wildcat player. "In my first game at UK, my parents were given seats with the other players' parents, and one of the proudest moments of my life was looking in the stands and seeing my mother and father in the good seats at Memorial Coliseum," he said. "That was a great team. We were undefeated, and we averaged 100 points a game as team. I averaged one point a game, and I've told my teammates if it wasn't for me, the team would not have averaged 100 points a game."

As a sophomore, Duff declined an opportunity to play for the new junior varsity squad to concentrate on academics. "I was invited to play on that team, but I decided to buckle down on the studying and felt that nothing could ever surpass the joy of playing on that undefeated freshman team," explained Duff, who graduated from UK Honors program in 1975 with a degree in political science and philosophy.

During his younger days, Duff's father Cecil – a former All-Stater who briefly was the basketball coach at Owsley County High School during the early 1950s – took him to UK games in Lexington, driving from Ohio where the family lived. They often attended the old University of Kentucky Invitational Tournament around the Christmas holidays. "Our seats were in the last row at Memorial Coliseum," quipped Duff, who attended his first UK game when he was about five years old.

Even several years before arriving at UK campus as a freshman, Duff got to meet legendary Adolph Rupp. "I first met Coach Rupp when I was about 12 years old at UKIT and I went up to him to get his autograph," he said. "My dad had encouraged me to go up to him before the first game of the tournament, and he had handed me a beautiful Cross Pen he had received at his job to commemorate his years of service there. When I returned with Coach

Rupp's autograph, Dad asked for his pen back, and I had to tell him that Coach Rupp kept it.

"Dad said, 'Well, maybe someday if you play for him, you can ask him for it back.' Of course, I didn't when I made the freshman team. I was awestruck. I loved listening to him coaching the varsity practices. They were as quiet as a church service. He hated dribbling, so the ball moved quickly by passing."

Duff has several Joe B. Hall stories. "There have been many great moments with Coach Hall, from the moment he selected me to be on the team, to attending his induction in the College Basketball Hall of Fame, to our 40th-year reunion, to introducing him to Chief Justice [John] Roberts last year, to right up to today.

"But my favorite is one that he says is one of his favorite stories, too. It was over the Christmas break and we were having two-a-day practices. The campus was dead, but we managed to go out and unwind a bit in the evenings. And someone was always missing curfew, which meant the whole team had to run extra the next day.

"We were getting a little tired of the night watchman turning us in every day, so we decided to scare him one night. Ronnie Lyons had some fake vampire blood left over from Halloween or from Big Time Wrestling events, so we put that blood all over me, coming out of my ears, my eyes, my nose, and we had the biggest guys on the team – Jim Andrews, Larry Stamper, Bob Guyette, Steve Lochmueller, maybe a few others – chase me down in front of the night watchman and act like they were beating me to death. It was about 2:00 in the morning, and the night watchman, in a panic, called Hall at home and said in a very quivering voice, 'C-c-c-c-oach, you've got to come down here, they're beating one of your boys to death!' "

"I can't believe that!" Hall said.

"It's true. You have to get down here," said the night watchman.

"Go get Duff and put him on the phone," said the coach, who has said Duff was one of the more trustworthy and dependable players in the program.

"I can't," said the night watchman.

"What do you mean you can't?" said a concerned Hall.

"Cause he's the one they killed," explained the night watchman.

Well, this prank didn't turn out very well for the players at the end. "We had to run extra the next day too," said Duff.

On a serious note, Duff said he is "so grateful to Coach Hall for giving me the chance to play on that team. I learned so much from him, my teammates, and

Bill Keightley [who would officially become the team's head equipment manager in 1972] – a work ethic that I apply every day. Hardly a day goes by that I don't think about that great year."

Duff said the 2003 showdown between No. 6 Kentucky and No. 1 Florida was probably the most exciting UK basketball game he has seen in person over the years. At the time, Tubby Smith was coaching the Wildcats, while former UK assistant Billy Donovan was leading the Gators, who later would capture national championships in 2006 and 2007. UK won that 2003 contest 70-55 before a then-record Rupp Arena crowd of 24,459.

"I was sitting with my father and one of my sons at the UK-Florida game in 2003, and my other son was sitting with Kevin Grevey at the announcer's table on the floor, when Florida came into Rupp ranked No. 1 in the country," he said. "My dad and I had been telling my sons that we had never heard Rupp Arena get as loud as it used to get in Memorial Coliseum.

"But in that game Rupp may have topped Memorial. We upset Florida and sent a message that UK was not conceding its perch at the top of the SEC and the country. It gave my sons an experience they'll never forget, and it reminded me of when I was their age. I only wish my daughter could have been there too, but she went to a game with me the following year and had a great experience, too."

Duff and his wife, Kathleen Gallagher Duff, have three children – Matthew, Kaitlin and Scott – who were active in athletics. Both of his sons have attended basketball camps at UK, and Kaitlin was a two-time All-American lacrosse player at the University of Virginia.

Duff's boss is Chief Justice John Roberts of the U.S. Supreme Court. In January 2015, Roberts appointed Duff – for the second time – to the same post of top federal courts administrator. And two years later, Duff took the Chief Justice for a visit to UK, and Roberts was selected as the first speaker for the school's newly-established John G. Heyburn Lecture Series, which would give the students an educational opportunity to hear from the nation's leading judges and lawmakers.

While in Lexington, they also attended the 2017 Kentucky-Georgia contest at Rupp Arena. An avid basketball fan, Roberts loved the game atmosphere and had a great time. "The Chief Justice enjoyed his visit to Rupp and to UK," said Duff. "It was an overtime game against Georgia, so it was a competitive and exciting game. He is very familiar with college basketball and is an Indiana fan, having grown up in the Hoosier state." For the record, Kentucky, led by rookie Malik Monk's game-high 37 points, edged coach Mark Fox's Georgia club 90-81.

With the help of former UK teammate Jimmy Dan Conner, who had arranged a pre-game meeting with Kentucky coach John Calipari, Roberts and Duff had a pleasant chat with Coach Cal.

Calipari was so pleased to meet Roberts that he discussed the meeting on Twitter the next morning. "Chief Justice John Roberts came to the game last night, and I got a chance to meet him," he tweeted. "When he walked in the office, I had the TV on. He and I watched as President Trump nominated the new Supreme Court justice [Neil M. Gorsuch]."

And Roberts, who was nominated by President George W. Bush and took his seat in 2005, invited Coach Cal to visit him in Washington.

In 2018, *Sports Illustrated* featured an interesting piece about the Supreme Court justices and their clerks playing hoops. You wonder where? In a regular high school or college gymnasium? Nope. They played in the top floor of the Supreme Court building where a storage room had been transformed to a basketball floor many years ago.

Duff was quoted in that *SI* article about playing with Justice Byron White, who was an All-American halfback at the University of Colorado and played in the NFL. Duff was asked by the author about playing basketball at the Supreme Court building.

"I have played there quite a bit, and still go over and shoot around on Friday evenings by myself," Duff told the author. "I've spent many wonderful hours playing basketball in the gym at the Supreme Court and have great memories of games with Justice White there.

"One of my fondest memories there is taking coach Tubby Smith and the [1998] NCAA champions from UK up to the gym after they had visited the White House and shooting around a little with them. I also had a chance to visit with the UK women's team with [athletics director] Mitch Barnhart and Coach [Matthew] Mitchell at the Supreme Court when they were in town for a game against GWU [George Washington University]. And, yes, I have taken Kevin Grevey and his family up to the gym a couple of times over the years, but we just shot around a little and didn't play a game." Duff added Jimmy Dan Conner also shot with him on that floor.

In his current job, Duff is mainly responsible for the management of the Administrative Office, which has about 1,000 employees, and for providing administrative support to 2,400 judicial officers and about 30,000 court employees. Until January 2015, Duff had been working as the president and CEO of the Freedom Forum, and CEO of the Newseum and Newseum Institute in Washington for several years.

Why did he come back to his current post after a somewhat less-stressful professional career at Freedom Forum, a nonprofit organization which supports the First Amendment as a cornerstone of democracy? "I was honored when Chief Justice Roberts asked me to return [to the post of Director of the Administrative Office of the U.S. Courts]," said Duff. "It is a wonderful opportunity to conclude my career where I started 41 years ago, working then for Chief Justice (Warren) Burger.

"The timing was also good at the Newseum where I truly enjoyed my work – our revenues and attendance were up, our expenses were down, and our endowment had risen by $100 million from the time I had started there. I felt comfortable leaving at that time." (The Newseum, unfortunately, closed its doors several years later.)

While attending law school at Georgetown University, Duff had started his career as an office and courtroom assistant to Chief Justice Burger.

Needless to say, Duff – who also has taught constitutional law at Georgetown University for years – is very thankful to be a part of the Big Blue Nation.

"I've been blessed with opportunity," he commented. "I worked with three Chief Justices, including Chief Justice Rehnquist during the [Clinton] impeachment trial and was a pallbearer in his funeral, but putting on that Kentucky uniform remains one of the greatest thrills and honors in my life."

Chapter Five

Joe B. Hall's First All-American

*T*he Big Blue Nation will agree that Kevin Grevey is one of the greatest players ever to wear a Wildcat jersey. No argument here.

The southpaw from Hamilton Taft High School in Cincinnati was that good, pumping long and smooth downtown jumpers at Memorial Coliseum during the early 1970s before the days of three-pointers. After helping the UK freshman team, popularly known as the Super Kittens, to a stunning 22-0 mark in 1971-72, the 6-foot-5 forward starred the next three years and finished his varsity career with 1,801 points while earning All-American honors twice.

As a sophomore, he was chosen the 1973 SEC Player of the Year, co-sharing the award with Alabama's Wendell Hudson before winning the same honor again as a senior. The three-time All-SEC selection (first team all three years) was the league's top scoring machine in 1974 during his junior year, hitting an average of 21.9 points.

And Grevey's last game as a Wildcat was the 1975 national championship game in San Diego before the NBC-TV cameras, with the announcing crew of Curt Gowdy, Billy Packer and Jim Simpson calling the matchup. It was UCLA boss John Wooden's last game, too. The legendary Wizard of Westwood was retiring.

Despite second-ranked Kentucky's 92-85 setback to No. 1 UCLA, Grevey scored a game-high 34 points. The showdown loss was one of the most heartbreaking ones in UK's NCAA Tournament history, even though Joe B. Hall's club did complete its remarkable campaign with a 26-5 mark. And Wooden's UCLA program won its 10th national crown in 12 years.

Many observers have said Kentucky likely would have won the national title if Wooden hadn't made the surprising announcement during the Final Four Easter weekend that he was retiring. Shortly after UCLA's 75-74 overtime win over coach Denny Crum and his Louisville Cardinals in the national semifinals, the

64-year-old Wooden had revealed his decision to step down, shocking the sporting world. Ironically, Crum had served as an assistant under Wooden at UCLA.

After learning of Wooden's plans, Hall joked at a press conference that he should be the next UCLA coach because he followed Adolph Rupp for the coveted Kentucky post.

Afterwards, for many years, Grevey had not been very happy about Wooden's so-called Final Four gimmick. "I held a grudge against him for a long, long time and had a chance to meet him," he said in a 2017 interview.

After Grevey and Wooden had exchanged pleasantries in that meeting, the former Kentucky star said he told the ex-UCLA mentor that his team's NCAA championship banner would have been hung at Rupp Arena, not at Pauley Pavilion, if Wooden hadn't famously announced his retirement. As Grevey recalled, "He [Wooden] looked at me with a smile. When the kindness came off his face, [he] said, 'If you [had] played a little defense, you would've won.' He turned and walked away from me, so he got me back again."

Grevey, however, admitted he was flattered that Wooden remembered him and recognized his accomplishments. Grevey, who lives in the Washington, D.C., area, recalled Wooden saying, "Kevin Grevey, lefthander, 34 points in the championship game. You were terrific, and you had a good NBA career, Kevin."

Kevin Grevey (left) and Jim Duff at a recent Kentucky game. (Photo by Jamie H. Vaught)

One of Grevey's close friends is Jim Duff, a Washington, D.C., area resident who played on the UK freshman team with Grevey. Duff has some stories about the Wildcat great, and they both grew up in the Cincinnati area.

"Kevin and I have been in the same town our entire lives – 62 years – and are the best of friends, so I have many stories about him," said Duff. "I guess one of my favorites is that years after the 1975 national championship game which UK lost to UCLA, Kevin met Coach Wooden at a banquet and had the courage to say to him, 'Coach, I think if you had not announced your retirement right before that game, we would have been national champions....'

"And he was right. We had beaten Indiana's undefeated team, and it was not one of UCLA's better teams. But Coach Wooden timed his retirement announcement to elevate his team's play. And he was also very clever about how he got on the refs – he waited until the cameras were off during commercial breaks to work them over. In that game, though, he actually got a technical foul, and he even went out on the floor yelling at them when Kevin was shooting the technical foul shot, which disturbed Kevin's shot.

"We would have won nine out of 10 games against that team, but that isn't how the tournament works. And just think, if we had won that one, we would have nine championships (total) and UCLA 10. I hope we pass them in our lifetime."

Grevey agreed with Duff's comments.

In 2010, Wooden passed away at the age of 99 at the Ronald Reagan UCLA Medical Center.

Kentucky's 1974-75 team had an unusual makeup. The Wildcats had six seniors and five freshmen on the 15-man roster. Because of that, there had been some concerns about the squad's chemistry. Besides Grevey, the UK seniors were 1971 Kentucky Mr. Basketball Jimmy Dan Conner, Bob Guyette, Mike Flynn, Jerry Hale, and G.J. Smith. The rookies for the Wildcats included Rick Robey, Mike Phillips, James Lee, Jack Givens and Dan Hall.

The 6-foot-10 Robey – who along with 6-foot-4 Givens were the team's top freshman scorers that season – commented that both groups got along very well.

The relationship "was real good," recalled Robey. "Those [senior] guys were probably some of the better friends that I had. You know Grevey went on to play with the [Washington] Bullets. When I went to pros, he and I were buddies. In the summertime, Kevin would come back and we would rent a house – Grevey, Jerry Hale, and myself. So we stayed close friends.

"They were a group of seniors that came in with all the hype of being the next great Kentucky team [after being called the Super Kittens]. You know the year before they struggled (with a 13-13 mark in 1973-74). I think they realized that a real good freshman group came in and, if we were able to nurture all of that together, we could really have a great team. It ended up being a season that probably wasn't expected."

Before reaching the 1975 Final Four, that Kentucky team upset the then top-ranked Indiana Hoosiers in an exciting 92-90 win in the regional finals held at Dayton, Ohio, ranking among one of UK's most memorable NCAA Tournament games. The Wildcats had five players scoring in double figures with Jeffersonville, Ind., native Mike Flynn hitting 9 of 13 shots for a team-high 22 points against his home state school. Grevey and Jimmy Dan Conner each added 17 points. For his remarkable performance against the Hoosiers, Flynn made the cover of *Sports Illustrated*.

"One of the finest [memories] was in 1975 in Dayton Arena in the finals of the Mideast Region against Indiana, which at the time was undefeated and ranked No. 1 in the nation," said ex-Kentucky mentor Joe B. Hall. "They had beaten us by 24 points in Bloomington earlier in December.

"That comeback win, which put us in the Final Four in San Diego, was probably the most exciting game I've ever been a part of, even the national finals."

By the way, it was Kentucky's December 98-74 loss to Indiana that saw Bobby Knight famously slap at the back of Hall's head near the Wildcat bench.

Adolph Rupp was still at UK, entering his last year of 1971-72 as the Wildcat coach, when Grevey became a freshman at UK. Grevey remembers his first meeting with the Baron while in high school.

"I was definitely in awe of Coach Rupp," recalled Grevey. "He was the Baron, someone that I read about, saw him on the cover of *Sports Illustrated* when I was in high school. Then [I was] a bit intimidated in my first meeting. It occurred at the Memorial Coliseum on my recruiting trip. Coach Hall brought me into the Coliseum, and there I was in a meeting with Coach Rupp in his office. I was in [a] 'Yes, Sir/No, Sir' kind of thing. I was very much afraid of him, but he smiled big and made me relax and said he knew of me and knew I was a big-time player from Ohio. That certainly broke the ice. I was glad he even heard of me, wished me well, and hoped I had a good visit at Kentucky, and I certainly did."

Grevey finished his first season at UK on a high note, averaging team-high 22.2 points in leading the freshman team, coached by Rupp assistant Joe B. Hall, to an undefeated campaign.

Rupp didn't want to retire, but he was forced to step down due to the university's mandatory retirement at the age of 70. UK would have a new head basketball coach for the first time since 1930 with Hall taking Rupp's job. Hall's Wildcats did fairly well during the 1972-73 campaign, finishing with a 20-8 mark, including 14-4 in SEC, with 6-foot-11 senior Jim Andrews and a pair of sophomores in 6-foot-5 Grevey and 6-foot-4 Jimmy Dan Conner reaping All-SEC honors. Andrews led the team in scoring with 20.1 points with Grevey following at 18.7 points. Nevertheless, it was a difficult time for the university and its storied basketball program. There were hard feelings among the Rupp and Hall factions.

"That's right. Those were trying times, very political," said Grevey. "I worked the Rupp basketball camp after my freshman year, and Coach Rupp was there and kept telling me all the great things that I could be. He felt I could be an All-SEC player after my freshman year. Coach Hall, on the other hand, was telling me I had a lot to work on and that I wasn't as good as I thought I was, so I was getting a little negative from Coach Hall, a little positive love from Coach Rupp.

"But my dad was like, 'Kevin, you can't take sides in this thing. Whatever happens, happens. You're a good enough player to play for either coach,' and I loved them both, I really did. But I had to let the more important people in the university make the decision of who was going to be the next coach."

Hall's first two seasons as the UK boss weren't easy with the Wildcats compiling 20-8 and 13-13 records. "We all know he was replacing the legend Adolph Rupp," said Grevey. "There was a lot of pressure on him, and that first recruiting class that he had went undefeated. I think he went little over the top with his discipline, bed checks, curfew, and making sure we ate our meals. It was like the military for that first year, and one night [in 1974] we had a bed check after a road trip to Mississippi [where the Cats had defeated Mississippi State 82-70]."

And it was Grevey who missed the curfew at Holmes Hall, a dormitory where the players stayed, getting himself in big trouble with Coach Hall. G.J. Smith, a 6-foot-7 string bean from Laurel County, was Grevey's roommate.

Coach Hall, who himself actually did the bed check, asked Smith, "Where is Kevin?"

Smith said, "He isn't coming back, Coach."

"I'm going to wait for him to come back," said Hall, who ended up spending the night on Grevey's bed.

Added Grevey, who was a junior at the time, "I never made it back. I spent the night out with my girlfriend, and in the morning, there was a note that said, 'Kevin, come see me.' I had to go and see him. I found out and didn't believe it, but he spent the night in my dorm waiting for me, so I learned a hard lesson and never missed another curfew after that."

Since Grevey committed a curfew violation, Hall suspended the player for one game against LSU, which was the team's next opponent. Without Grevey, the Wildcats escaped with a three-point victory over second-year coach Dale Brown and his LSU Tigers at Memorial Coliseum.

As mentioned earlier, Grevey finished that season as SEC's No. 1 scorer with 21.9-point average.

Toward the end of the 1972-73 season, Kentucky was battling three other well-coached SEC teams – Tennessee and coach Ray Mears, Alabama and coach C.M. Newton, and Vanderbilt and coach Roy Skinner – for the conference championship before the Wildcats came out on top after beating the Vols 86-81. After that regular season finale against UT, Grevey said that was the happiest moment he had ever seen of Coach Hall.

"We shared many wonderful moments with Coach Hall during his first three years as a varsity coach," said Grevey. "The happiest I ever saw him was the first time when we clinched the SEC championship at home against Tennessee. It was a do-or-die game. We had to win to win the SEC. We won a very hard-fought game at the Coliseum by just a few points, and when the buzzer sounded, we carried Coach Hall off the floor on our shoulders. That was certainly a big moment for him as a first-year head coach at Kentucky and a big moment for us players, wanting to create some legacy and identity for ourselves."

During his playing days at Kentucky, did Grevey see Coach Hall as a father figure? "Definitely. [Coach Hall's wife] Katharine Hall and Coach Hall together were mama and pop for us young freshmen," Grevey commented. "I remember I got the flu, and Coach Hall said, 'You're staying at our house.' He had a bedroom downstairs, and Katharine brought soup down and nursed me back to health. Whenever there was a problem, either in school or health, on or off the court, Coach Hall did have an open door [policy] and instead of being the coach became more of a mentor or a father. You could see the transformation when you went in there for something. It was personal. He was always there for us players, and I knew not just for myself, my teammates, he was very accessible."

Well, what about his classes on campus? Did Grevey purposely miss any academic work? "I had a General Studies degree," he said. "I wasn't sure what I wanted to be. When I came to Kentucky, I thought that I might be a coach, [that] I might go into education. My dad was more of a businessman, attorney businessman, and he was the most important person in my life at that time. So, I majored in business my first two years and then transferred to the Arts and Sciences and got a General Studies major.

"Most of the time that I had to deal with Coach Hall when it came to academics was missing a class, missing an early class, missing breakfast, doing something I wasn't supposed to do. So, he had a way of making sure that only happened once."

During his Wildcat career, Grevey saw plenty of SEC battles on the road. He played in gyms like Tennessee's 12,700-seat Stokely Athletics Center and Florida's 7,000-seat Alligator Alley

"All of the SEC venues were tough at that time," he said. "The one that was the toughest was Stokely at Tennessee. It was their fans, it was the atmosphere, it was the dark gym, it was the Tartan surface – it was like a rubber surface, it wasn't hardwood floor. The balls bounced differently; the rims were tight. Orange is one of my least favorite colors. Everything about Tennessee was tough. We struggled down there. It was a very, very difficult place to play. That stands out as No. 1.

"Number two happened to be when we would play Mississippi State. They had an old gym [Mississippi State Gymnasium or the New Gym]. The fans were close to the floor. They were angry, nasty, hated Kentucky. I was like, 'Wow, what did Kentucky ever do to Mississippi for them to dislike us so much?' Maybe it was because we beat them all the time. But when we would go down there, they would circle the schedule, like all the SEC teams were, and they were ready for us.

"I remember always struggling early on the road in SEC competition, but we eventually knew that we could wear down the other team. We were in better condition, we were a little stronger, more disciplined. Coach Hall and Coach Rupp always wanted us to execute perfection, not to beat ourselves, and that really played well on the road. We rarely missed free throws, turned the ball over, beat ourselves. If someone beat us, they had to play one of their best games, so it really prepared me for the NBA, playing in those conference venues in SEC play."

Grevey also faced Tennessee stars Bernard King and Ernie Grunfeld, who were two of the best SEC players in the mid-1970s. King and Grunfeld later became NBA standouts.

"I got to know both of those guys quite well after my stint at Kentucky, playing against them in Tennessee," said Grevey. "I played against both of them in the pros, and I could actually say Ernie Grunfeld is one of my closer friends and Bernard King is the same. Ernie Grunfeld [was] the general manager of the Washington Wizards. I live in Washington, so I see him all the time. Bernard King actually played for the Bullets at the end of his career after a really wonderful NBA career. He had those 50-point games with the Knicks. I remember those guys as friends now but foes then.

"They were not fun to play against. Bernard King was a dirty, nasty, tough New York guy. I remember the first time he came to the [Memorial] Coliseum, he was giving it to the fans and walking off the court. There's [some people] saying that he spat on the fans. I don't know if that's true, but I heard that and didn't think much of him when I played against him. Now I can call him my friend. It's weird how this game is, but the 'Ernie and Bernie Show' was legit, let me tell you. They were as tough a one-two combination as there'd ever been in the SEC. I saw them when they were young. I was a senior and they played like seniors (when King was a freshman and Grunfeld was a sophomore). No wonder they had great Hall of Fame careers at Tennessee.

"I heard that he [King] had a tough time with them [at UT]. But he had a chip on his shoulder, too when he was a young man, and he brought some of that on himself as well. I know he would be the first to admit it because he's really turned his life around. I'm glad to see it because he's a good human being."

Many reports have pointed out the three-time SEC Player of the Year had faced racism and other personal problems while at Tennessee and in the NBA. He also claimed that a Kentucky fan threw a lit cigarette at his head after a Vol setback to UK at Memorial Coliseum, and an emotional King got motivated and helped Tennessee beat the Wildcats in the next five games before turning pro in 1977. By the way, during a 2007 halftime ceremony of the Kentucky-Tennessee matchup in Knoxville, King became the first men's player at UT to have his jersey retired by the university.

After a successful run at Kentucky, Grevey became a Washington Bullet. An NBA first-round draft selection in 1975, he joined the K.C. Jones-coached Bullets, which featured a couple of veteran teammates – Wes Unseld and Clem

Haskins – from the state of Kentucky. Unseld had starred at University of Louisville, while Haskins had played at Western Kentucky. Washington also had an assistant from Kentucky on the coaching staff by the name of Bernie Bickerstaff, who grew up in Harlan County. Bickerstaff later became head coach for five NBA franchises.

As a backup, Grevey had a decent rookie season in the NBA, averaging nine minutes of playing time and 3.8 points. Eventually, he worked his way up and later helped Washington, then coached by Dick Motta, capture the 1978 NBA championship, averaging 15.5 points and 26.2 minutes. In the NBA Finals, the Bullets, down 3-2 in the series, had to bounce back to win the sixth and seventh game to defeat the Seattle SuperSonics (now the Oklahoma City Thunder). It was a surprising season for the Bullets, who posted a 44-38 mark and finished eight games behind division leader San Antonio, a second-year NBA member which came from the American Basketball Association. Two of Grevey's teammates that championship campaign were future Hall of Famers Elvin Hayes and Unseld.

For Grevey, 1978 was a very special year. In addition to winning the league crown, he closely followed Hall's Kentucky club that season and saw the 30-2 Wildcats win the NCAA crown. He was so excited to see his former 1975 freshman teammates at UK – Jack Givens, James Lee, Rick Robey and Mike Phillips – helping the Cats win it all as the heralded seniors when they beat Duke 94-88 behind Givens' stunning 41-point performance in St. Louis. In addition, Grevey met his future wife, Sandy, who was working in the office of U.S. Senator Lowell Weicker of Connecticut, that year.

"Probably the best year of my life other than when my children were born," said Grevey with a smile. "It doesn't get much better than that. I don't know if I'll have a year that will be near that one in 1978."

Grevey retired in 1985, finishing a 10-year NBA career with the last two seasons coming at Milwaukee, and hitting for an overall average of 11 points in 672 games. He also ran and owned his popular restaurant in Falls Church, Va., a Washington, D.C. suburb, for many years before closing at the end of 2016.

There were stories when Grevey was a rookie for the Bullets that he had to carry beer in ball bags for the team while on a road trip. Asked if that was true, Grevey replied, "I don't know where you heard that but, yes, it's somewhat true. Back when I was a rookie in the 1975-76 season, I was the only rookie on the team, so I had to carry the projector for film. I had to carry the ball bag, and I had to pick up tabs for the veterans. There was a little bit of fun hazing, if you want to call it that.

"One particular story I'll tell you is I'm a rookie, and our captain and our best player on the team was Wes Unseld. Of course, everybody remembers Wes and his great career at Louisville. He was the boss on the team. He made you earn your stripes. When I got there, I was told by some of the veterans that 'Wes is going to test you. Just bear in there, and do your job, and win him over with your play.' Well, he never once called me Kevin, he called me Rook, so my name was Rook.

"Talking about Wes Unseld and the beer in the bags. For our first road trip he said, 'Hey, Rook, we're going to the West Coast. After the game, put some beer in the ball bags, so we'll have some beer for the road trip.' Every refrigerator was stocked with beer in the NBA at that time. The biggest difference in locker rooms for me was the fact that when I was playing in college we had Gatorade and fruit; in the NBA, we had beer and cigarettes. So, it was a big change.

"Anyway, we played the Lakers in L.A., and after the game I stuffed the ball bag – six balls and bottled beers – and I must've put in 20 bottles of beer with the ball bag.

"Then we got on a flight to Portland. When we landed, we had practice that day. We went to Lewis & Clark College in Portland. From the airport, we went on the bus and went to the gym. We opened up the ball bags, and they were soaking wet with beer and glass. K.C. Jones was my coach my rookie year, and he said, 'Grevey, what the hell is this?' I said, 'Oh, Coach, I'm sorry. I put beer in the bag, and they broke.' He said, 'Well, we can't practice with these balls. Let's get back on the bus.' So, no practice. Wes Unseld was so happy. He got on the bus and said, 'Hey, Grevey just got fined $200 for breaking bottled beer on the balls, and we didn't have to practice. Let's pay his fine.' He said, 'That was a great veteran move, Kevin!' and it's the first time he called me Kevin. He said, 'Kevin, that was a hell of a move you just made there, buddy. We don't have to practice.' So, I kind of won him over that way."

Unseld, who was a two-time All-American at U of L during the late 1960s, often joked with Grevey about playing at UK. Now a member of the Naismith Memorial Basketball Hall of Fame, Unseld liked to call Kentucky the Kitty Cats.

"He teased me because I went to Kentucky," Grevey said. "He was always on me, and he called them the Kitty Cats. He had a bias against Kentucky, he did not like Kentucky. I didn't like Louisville, so it was a bit of a tough couple months to start the season my rookie year with Wes.

"But I learned that the big fella, he had your back, man. After my rookie year he became one of my closest teammates and one of my best friends to this day. Wes was a warrior, a leader, in every sense of the word. He played with bad knees. By the time I was playing with him, he was in a lot of pain but never complained. Back then you used to shoot up your knees and your ankles. He wanted to play and he did, and he's paying a dear price for it now. He's had his knees, his ankles fused, his hips replaced. I feel sorry for him, but I love him in spite of his Louisville background."

Grevey said Unseld also shared stories about Coach Rupp's unsuccessful recruitment of the 6-foot-8 star from Seneca High School in Louisville, where he had led the school to two state championships. Had Unseld picked the Wildcats, he would've been the first African-American to play basketball for Coach Rupp at Kentucky.

Added Grevey, "He said, 'Kevin, you don't understand what it was like back then, being African-American in Louisville' and Kentucky had not broken the racial barrier. I said, 'Well, did he recruit you?' He said, 'Yeah, kind of. I think he was pressured, and it was a token recruit.' I said, 'What do you mean?' He said, 'I'll tell you what it was like. Coach Rupp, he was getting a lot of pressure to recruit me, so he called my family and said he wanted to visit. My mom and dad both said, 'Come on down. You can visit, and let's hear what you have to say.'

"So, Coach Rupp, along with several other dignitaries from Kentucky, came to Louisville and met him in his home, and they were together for about a half-hour, 45 minutes. Coach Rupp made his presentation, and Wes said that he didn't want to be the first. He thanked him for coming, visiting and recruiting him, but he was going to go to Louisville. But he told Rupp, 'I know there's a lot of pressure on you to recruit the first African American, and I appreciate your courage in coming here to talk with me, but I'm not prepared to do that.' "

By that time in 1964, U of L already had broken the color barrier in signing the first African-Americans – Wade Houston, Sam Smith and Eddie Whitehead – to the hoops program in 1962. (Also, Houston later became the first African-American head basketball coach in the SEC in 1989 when Tennessee hired him.)

Grevey had many famous customers who came to his successful restaurant and sports bar, Grevey's. They enjoyed the festive atmosphere and delicious food. What are some of his favorite memories there?

"Wow, you surprised me with that question," he smiled. "I've had some really, really wonderful times at my restaurant. I was just talking to [former North

Carolina star and current Charlotte Hornets executive] Mitch Kupchak on my way driving over here, how I missed the restaurant, especially on [NFL] game day Sundays. We were the home away from home for the Buffalo Bills. That was really a wonderful time. A lot of Buffalonians would come to my restaurant, and we've had senators, congressmen, various people come. Unbelievable.

"We've also had some legendary fans come to our watch parties. Having Tubby Smith with the [UK] championship team [was unforgettable]. My nephew, Ryan Hogan, played on that [1998] championship team. When they went to visit the White House, they came to Grevey's restaurant. That was a very memorable moment.

"[NFL legend] Bart Starr came into my restaurant. Coach Cal came and had lunch. He was recruiting in DeMatha [Catholic High School area] and asked one of the assistant coaches, 'Hey, Grevey has a restaurant somewhere here in northern Virginia,' and they happened to be right across the street when they Googled it, and they came in.

"Every day was a new day, and that's what was so exciting. So many fans, friends, customers, and I love people. I found the right business. I can't tell you how much joy I had running that business in northern Virginia. I miss it dearly, but I'm 65 now and it's time to move on. The restaurant will always hold a special memory in my life."

In recent years, Grevey has worked as a scout for the Los Angeles Lakers, and he is now with the Charlotte Hornets in a similar capacity. He is having more fun than usual since the NBA is now loaded with former UK stars who played for coach John Calipari during the one-and-done era.

"I love my Kentucky Wildcats," said Grevey, who has attended games at Rupp Arena several times a year to scout the prospective pro players.

But that could be a little bit of a problem when the Kentucky players are included in Grevey's scouting reports. According to Grevey, the Lakers organization sometimes believed he may have been too close to the Wildcats to remain objective when preparing his reports involving collegiate prospects from UK.

"I'm a little biased when we were in the conference room with the Lakers in the front office and the Buss ownership," admitted Grevey, who also works as a radio broadcaster for a national network. "Every time I speak positively for a Kentucky player, there's like 'Oh yeah, right. Grevey bleeds Big Blue. You know we have to temper his positive comments about these guys because he is biased.' Maybe I am [biased] but daggone it, these Kentucky kids have done so well in the NBA, and Coach Cal has done a magnificent job since he's been here, bringing in these kids and preparing, making them ready for the high-level game in the NBA.

"So, it is a lot of fun to watch them play, and I'd make a point try to get out and say, 'Hi,' to every player that played at Kentucky."

On Calipari, "I call Coach Cal about players all the time. He doesn't need any help from me recruiting, trust me. He's one of the best recruiters the college game has ever seen in its history. John Wooden, Coach K, Roy Williams, Bobby Knight, Bill Self, and Jay Wright, right now, are probably in my mind the best recruiters that's ever been in college basketball.

"Coach Cal has been very forthcoming and very honest to me about his own players and about other players. I'm a scout, obviously. I need to get background and intel on players before the draft. I've been a scout 17 years with the Lakers. I'm now with the Charlotte Hornets. I hope I continue to have that open door policy … when I call Coach Cal. He's so willing and able to give me some good intel on players."

It is not a surprise the NBA has a lot of ex-Calipari standouts. For the past several years, UK has led the nation with the most players on NBA opening-day rosters.

In addition to scouting, Grevey works as a radio broadcaster for a national outlet, covering different games throughout the country. He has been doing both for a long time. He really enjoys his part-time work assignments. And he loves to drive, instead of flying, when he has the assignment.

"Part-time has become full-time since I don't have a restaurant anymore, but the best part, for me, it's been a lifelong love and passion of the game of basketball," he said. "I've had it since I was a little kid. My dad played basketball at Xavier. He put a basketball goal in the garage as early as I can remember, maybe when I was three or four years old, shooting at a basket that was about four or five feet high. Then he would raise the basket as I got older and older, and then I was shooting on a 10-foot basket when I was about six or seven years old. I was strong enough to get it up there. I loved going out in the backyard and shooting with my dad and my brothers, and by myself. Here I'm 65 years old, and I still have that same love of the game as I did when I was a little boy. What a gift this game of basketball has been."

Interestingly, Grevey also has three brothers who earned NCAA Division I basketball scholarships with Bryan at South Carolina, Scott at Pittsburgh, and Norm at Dayton. The former Wildcat added that he is very thankful how basketball has helped him over the years.

"I'm able now, at my age, to really give back to the game that I've loved and that has been so dear to me and has really helped form everything that I am today. I wouldn't have had a restaurant if it wasn't for basketball, being in the Washington area and playing for the Bullets. It's been a passion. All my kids have played the game. I taught my wife how to shoot and play sports. So, here I am now, a scout, and I'm able to contribute to a team to rebuild teams.

"I'm working with a great friend, Mitch Kupchak, now with the Hornets, and I guess it's just a gift that keeps on giving. The love and passion of basketball is still in my blood, and I'm able still to give. As long as I'm healthy and able and to drive all over the country like I do – I'm a little crazy – I don't know another scout that probably drives as much as I do. Most people fly, but I like to drive. I'm at peace driving and thinking, reflecting. I turn the radio off, and it's just a wonderful thing. So, as long as I like to drive, as long as I'm healthy, and [there's] a team that wants me there, I'll continue to do this."

If and when Grevey is driving to Lexington for UK games, he will often stop by and visit his mom, Michaela Grevey, in Cincinnati. "My mother just turned 84," he added.

But Grevey points out when the weather is bad, he won't drive. He occasionally will fly on an airplane, adding, "I fly to Chicago. I fly to L.A. I'll fly some to the Midwest, but everything on the East Coast and [in the] South, I drive. I drive to Ohio and Indiana. I drive to the Carolinas, and I drive up to New York and Hartford. I try to plan my schedule so that I can see as many games in as few days. I'm lucky to be based out of Washington, D.C., because I have the Big Ten with Maryland and Penn State right there. I have the Atlantic 10 with Richmond and George Washington University, the ACC with Virginia and Virginia Tech. The Big East. I'm naming a lot of conferences here that are all in my circle in D.C. But, of course, I still have to see the Pac-12 and the Big 12, but I go to West Virginia to catch Big 12. So, I don't have to get on a plane as much as most people."

While he's pretty busy with basketball these days, Grevey certainly is enjoying his "retirement."

Chapter Six

LSU Coach Who Has Beaten UK
More Than Anyone Else

*E*x-LSU basketball coach Dale Brown has been a pretty popular guy in Kentucky in recent years even though he had beaten the Wildcats many times during his career and hasn't coached since 1997.

The fans of the Big Blue Nation still remember the outspoken Brown's coaching success along with his upbeat and engaging personality. He was often called the "Billy Graham in Sneakers." Whenever he comes back to the Bluegrass and visits Rupp Arena to watch his former team battle the host Wildcats, he gets a nice reception. The now-friendly folks like to swarm around him near the hardwood floor and talk hoops as well as have their picture taken with the charismatic Brown, who guided his Tigers to two NCAA Final Four appearances during the 1980s. In 1985, Brown appeared on the cover of *Sports Illustrated* magazine with the headline "Crazy Days at LSU."

The colorful Brown, now in his early 80s, said the "most knowledgeable fans in the country are [at] University of Kentucky for a combination of reasons. High school basketball in this state is a big-time deal. Most of the time it's not. So, they [the fans] know the game, they appreciate it, and they're interested. They've [UK] got a great fan base.

"A little old lady, like a little peanut almost, grabbed me and said, 'Coach Brown, excuse me. I've got to admit something to you. I hated you. But I forgive you. I like you a lot now.' I said, 'Why'd you hate me?' She said, 'You always beat Kentucky.' "

Keith Stephens, a longtime press row observer who works with the media at Rupp Arena, commented, "Coach Brown is still a great guy. He still does have the ability to make everyone think he is their best friend. I think his secret is that he really does like everybody."

At recent UK-LSU matchups in Lexington, Brown, who lives in Baton Rouge with his wife Vonnie, would visit and chat with former Kentucky coach Joe

B. Hall and the ex-Wildcats. The coach even made a side trip to see ex-UK standout Tom Payne, who was in prison at the time, in 2011. (Brown had corresponded with Payne and sent Payne numerous books that the former coach thought might help the prisoner.) "The fans were most gracious, and I was very appreciative," said Brown of that Bluegrass trip. He also saw Kevin Grevey and Jimmy Dan Conner, saying they "look like they can still play."

By the way, the author – who has exchanged numerous emails with Brown over the years – would like to share an interesting gesture that the ex-Tigers coach had made. The LSU legend and I had made arrangements to have a brief interview scheduled during the halftime of the 2016 Kentucky-LSU game at Rupp Arena where Brown would be attending. It would be our second face-to-face interview that we've had, and he has said he enjoyed my columns. Before the game, we exchanged pleasantries and confirmed our incoming halftime interview, and he knew I'd be on the floor, taking photos at the game.

However, during the intermission, Brown couldn't get away from his Kentucky friends, as well as the fans. He was busy. So, I let it go. It was no big deal, I thought to myself, since both of us could do the interview at a later date via email. At the start of the second half, I went back to the hardwood floor and sat with the other photographers near the press row to resume my picture-taking duties.

About halfway through the second half, I felt a tap on my shoulder. I looked up, and it was none other than Dale Brown, who had walked through the photographers to reach me from his front-row seat behind the LSU bench. I'm sure some folks at the game were surprised to see the coach there, too. I was stunned that he remembered our little agreement.

So, I got up, and we had our interview in an empty media room while the contest was going on. It's the same room where Kentucky's John Calipari and then-LSU coach Johnny Jones, a former Coach Brown player, would face the news media under the bright lights for their postgame press conference. Nevertheless, Brown certainly was courteous, and he has become one of my favorite sports personalities. That shows what kind of man Coach Brown is. He kept his word.

And he is the same guy who has defeated UK more times than any other college basketball coaches in history, including Ray Mears (Tennessee), Billy Donovan (Florida), Dean Smith (North Carolina) and Bobby Knight (Indiana). Against UK, Brown won 18 times and lost 33 games before retiring in 1997. (By comparison, LSU's record against the Wildcats was 2-32 before 1972-73.) By the time he retired, Brown finished with a very productive 25-year tenure at LSU, a 448-301 record overall.

When Brown arrived at Baton Rouge in 1972, the program was in shambles, and he had to rebuild it by overcoming the school's big-time football reputation and limited resources for hoops. There was very little interest in LSU basketball after the departure of legendary "Pistol Pete" Maravich, who holds the all-time scoring record with 3,667 points in NCAA Division I. The new coach tirelessly began promoting and recruiting, and eventually found success.

Looking back, Brown still marvels at UK's winning hoops tradition. "After coaching 25 years in the SEC and being a coach for 44 years, I think that Kentucky, year in and year out, has the best basketball program in the nation and the best fans," he commented. "While I was coaching at LSU, they were the beacon light in our conference.

"It is a shame this great [UK-LSU] rivalry has been cut to one game a year during the regular season because it was one of the very best in the nation."

Elected to the National Collegiate Basketball Hall of Fame in 2014, Brown was asked about his best moment against the Wildcats. "It would be almost impossible to pick the most memorable moment that I had against Kentucky," he said.

"I felt it was truly one of the best rivalries in all of college basketball. [Legendary Kentuckian] Happy Chandler singing 'My Old Kentucky Home' brought tears to my eyes. I respected and loved him very much. We became good friends. Out of respect for him, I took our team to his house [in Versailles] to meet him and had him talk to our team one year about making a difference in the world, which he did."

Former coaching rivals Joe B. Hall and Dale Brown at Rupp Arena. (Photo by Jamie H. Vaught)

Brown – who had replaced Press Maravich, the father of Pete Maravich, at LSU – knew if his Tigers were going anywhere special, they had to beat Kentucky somehow. There are many great or memorable UK-LSU games in the series involving Brown, and some of them include:

♦ A controversial, foul-plagued 1976 game at 11,500-seat Memorial Coliseum when an angry Brown got emotional and threw his sports jacket to the midcourt with the Wildcats bouncing back to win in an 85-71 decision. One of Brown's players at the time was Owensboro's Kenny Higgs, who had gunned in a team-high 32 points. The game's top scorer was 6-foot-10 sophomore Mike Phillips, who had 35 points. (It was Higgs, by the way, who finished second behind Jack Givens in Kentucky's Mr. Basketball voting in 1974.) Brown, a four-time SEC Coach of the Year who won four conference regular season titles, remembers an emotional second-half episode in that wild contest when he received two technical fouls.

"Probably my favorite story [of Joe B. Hall] is when we were playing in the old Memorial Coliseum," said Brown. "Joe hit his [rolled-up] program and hollered out at the referee. I don't want to say he swore but could have sworn. I stood up and hollered [at the officials], 'Call them same at both ends.' I got a technical foul.

"So, I made up my mind, thinking you know what. Nobody knows who I am. I understand that. Kentucky's the king. They were the beacon light for me. I had great admiration for Kentucky basketball, and I wanted to mimic them. I called timeout and the referee came over. I said, 'Listen, the game's almost over, but let me tell you something. You've already stolen everything from us, so here, take my sports coat.' "

Said official Reggie Copeland, "Coach, sit down [or] I'm going to call a technical foul."

"You're going to call a technical foul on me?" commented the coach who was getting irritated, looking at the referee. "I'm not hollering at you. Take this coat, or I'm throwing it out on the court."

Brown added, "And lo and behold, I threw the thing [sports jacket], and it was like a discus. You know, it wound up spinning around and around, and it landed right on the K [jump circle]. Of course, I wasn't too popular."

After the game, Brown stormed into the officials' dressing room and accused them of being intimidated by Hall, according to late UK sports historian Russell Rice's *Kentucky Basketball: Big Blue Machine*. Along with two technical fouls drawn by Brown in the second half, Hall and Wildcat guard Larry Johnson each also got hit with a technical in the opening half.

In 2016, Brown said of Hall, "He's really a good man and a great coach. I'm not sure he got as much publicity as he should've at the time for the coaching job that he did."

♦ The 1978 game at Baton Rouge when the Tigers, who had all five starters foul out, edged the eventual national champion Wildcats 95-94 in overtime. As it turned out, it marked one of only two setbacks suffered by top-ranked Kentucky that season.

♦ The 1980 game-winning jumper by senior All-American Kyle Macy to spark No. 3 Kentucky to a 76-74 overtime win over No. 5 Tigers at Baton Rouge, clinching a regular season SEC title for the Wildcats. One week later, Coach Brown's club bounced back and stopped the Wildcats 80-78 to capture the first and only SEC Tournament championship in LSU history with 6-foot-8 star DeWayne Scales of LSU getting the tourney MVP honors.

♦ The 1986 showdown in the NCAA Southeast Regional finals when underdog LSU finally stopped UK 59-57 after losing to the favored Wildcats, who finished at 32-4, three straight times during that campaign. The No. 11-seed Tigers, led by undersized 6-foot-6 sophomore Ricky Blanton, who was forced to play at center, won without having three big men who were out for various reasons. And LSU advanced to its second Final Four in five years.

♦ The 1987 matchup at Rupp Arena when LSU rolled past coach Eddie Sutton's Wildcats, embarrassing them with a 76-41 win. It was Kentucky's worst home setback since 1926. (During the late 1960s, Sutton and Brown also clashed against each other when their teams met. Sutton was leading College of Southern Idaho, a junior college, and Brown was the freshman coach at Utah State. Brown respected Sutton, saying he was "one of the good minds in coaching.")

♦ The 1994 contest in Baton Rouge when coach Rick Pitino's Wildcats stunned the college basketball world with a 99-95 win after being down by 31 points in the second half. "Rick Pitino masterfully convinced them the game was not lost. They made a miraculous comeback and beat us," recalled Brown of his most disappointing moment against UK. *USA Today* in a 2013 article also rated this comeback as the greatest ever in sports history in a ranking of Top 10 comebacks.

Before coming to LSU in 1972, Brown – who was born on Halloween in 1935 and grew up in Minot, a small railroad town in North Dakota, during his poverty-stricken childhood – coached at several places, including high schools, the U.S. Army, and a junior high (now middle school). He also served as an assistant at Utah State (five years) and Washington State (one year). "My upbringing in North Dakota has given me a work ethic and [taught me] to never give up," said Brown.

A star athlete at St. Leo's High School and Minot State University in North Dakota, Brown said he doesn't miss coaching. "I loved my 44-year coaching career but do not miss coaching because I'm in contact with all of my players and my new career as a motivational speaker along with directing the nonprofit Dale Brown Foundation that helps those in need has been most fulfilling," he commented.

During the late 1950s, Brown's first salary after college was $4,500 as a high school coach and teacher in North Dakota. Brown said his first-year salary at LSU was $23,600, which included income from television and radio, for the 1972-73 campaign. "Coach [John] Wooden's salary when he retired [in 1975] was $32,500," Brown said. "Coaches during that time loved coaching, and money was never a factor." Rupp's last year at Kentucky, by the way, was in 1971-72, when he earned a coaching salary of $29,000.

After Brown got the LSU post, he called Wooden at UCLA, whom he knew personally while at Utah State as an assistant under LaDell Andersen (who later became the head coach for the ABA's Utah Stars). They first met at the 1970 NCAA Western Regional finals when their teams clashed, with the Bruins winning 101-79 in a comfortable fashion. The new head coach wanted to learn everything from the Wizard of Westwood, and Wooden invited Brown to his home in Los Angeles. Then, over the years, they became good friends, with both often calling each other several times a month before Wooden passed away at the age of 99 in 2010. Brown said Wooden was a special gentleman.

Said Brown of Wooden, "My favorite story on Coach was every time someone would complement and praise him, he would always say, 'Thank you but I am still a work in progress. I am not what I could be, ought to be, or should be, but am glad I am not what I used to be.'

"Every time we were at a restaurant and the waiter would pour water in his glass or bring our food, he would always say, 'Thank you very much,' no matter how many times [the] waiter did something."

When Wooden passed away, Brown wrote a fitting tribute about the college basketball legend, and the author received permission from Brown to include the excerpts of his piece in this book. "My dear friend John Wooden is truly an American treasure," Brown wrote. "He was kind, caring, highly intelligent, vibrant, strong-willed, principled, humble, and one of the most fascinating men of this or any generation.

"Why was the greatest coach that ever lived like this and not egotistical, selfish, arrogant, and greedy like so many that reach the pinnacle of what the world often defines as success?

"It is because he firmly believed in what the first Webster's dictionary ever printed in 1806 describing success as fortunate, happy, kind and prosperous. And not how dictionaries define success today, which is, attainment of wealth, fame and rank.

"He is indeed a legend in basketball but more importantly he was a legend in serving mankind as a master teacher.

"Now that Coach has left this earth, I ask myself how can I ever thank him for being my friend for 40 years. And, as usual, my answer comes from the words of Coach himself. In the last letter I received from him, he said, 'Although <u>thanks</u> is a rather simple one-syllable word that too often is used without true feeling, when used with sincerity, no collection of words can be more meaningful or expressive.' Thanks, Coach!"

Said Wooden, who was quoted in a recent LSU basketball media guide, "I will remember Dale for his enthusiasm. There are those who say he is a put-on – they just can't believe that he can be what he professes. But I never questioned that. He amazed me because there is a lot more depth to the man. He was much more than a basketball coach."

Another friend of Brown's was Adolph Rupp, who once was the winningest college basketball coach in history with 876 wins at Kentucky before the other big names like Mike Krzyzewski, Jim Boeheim, Bob Knight and Dean Smith came along and passed the Baron. The new LSU coach had spent some time with the retired Rupp in Lexington. They were good friends. "The Man in the Brown Suit" gave the new coach some pointers. They talked about having discipline for the players and dealing with their parents and the news media, in addition to hoops.

"I think probably my favorite memory [of Rupp] was when I was first getting started at LSU. I was a no-name guy, came from North Dakota and had no credentials," said Brown, who is conference's third winningest coach of all-time with 448 victories (at SEC schools only), behind Rupp and Florida's Billy Donovan. "I developed a friendship with Adolph Rupp through Happy Chandler. So, we put on a banquet in Baton Rouge for these two legends, Adolph Rupp and

John Wooden. He [Rupp] got up there [to speak]. This is funnier than heck. He was still pretty spry. Rupp said, 'Dale Brown called me and told me he could have a banquet for my friend John Wooden and I. When I finally agreed to doing it, they laid off three postmen [from the post office]. He had contacted me so many times by mail.' Adolph, I think, is misunderstood outside of Kentucky."

As for Kentucky coach John Calipari, Brown admires him and has been a huge fan of Coach Cal. When Brown left coaching in 1997, Calipari was in the NBA, serving as the head coach of the New Jersey Nets after a successful eight-year tenure at UMass.

"When I was in early years in my coaching career, I got a call from a young coach from Massachusetts that I've never heard of," recalled Brown in 2016. "John Calipari said he was coming down and playing University of Louisiana Lafayette [then called University of Southwestern Louisiana]. Could he bring the team by to watch [LSU] practice and come to a game and visit with me? He came to my office, and I had no idea who he was. Nothing about him.

"But the immediate thing I noticed, he connected with people and he was interested in learning. I also think that John does so many behind-the-scene things that people never realize. Today I already think he is the greatest recruiter in the country, bar none. He's also the master at mastering a stupid rule of one-and-done. He gets criticized for it in Kentucky. It's not Kentucky that did this. So, he's taking advantage of it properly, and I thought last year's [2014-15] team reminded me so much of the UCLA teams. There wasn't one punk on the team. There was nobody [who was] selfish. They put the team above themselves. I think he is going to go down in history as one of the greatest coaches of all time.

"He is the most misunderstood coach in college basketball.... He truly loves his players. He also shows great respect to the old-timers that no longer coach. He is a great coach. Many are jealous of his success. I have seen how kind he is to the common folk."

Brown appreciates the fact that Coach Cal has tried to look out for the former coaches. Calipari once "found out there were some old-time coaches that were saving their money to come to the Final Four [sitting] up in the rafters, high as you can get in a Superdome. He found out about it, got a hold of me, and said, 'Dale, find out who those guys are. I want to buy them good tickets. They can sit behind our bench if I come to the NCAA Tournament.' So, he does a lot of good things. He's a good motivator. He's got a good personality. He loves the kids, and he's tough love."

Ex-NBA standout Shaquille O'Neal is one of Brown's many star players from LSU. O'Neal earned All-American and SEC Player of the Year honors twice (1991 and '92). Brown shared his impressions about the 7-foot-1 O'Neal, who later earned his doctorate degree in education in 2012.

"He was a good student and very conscientious," he said. "[For the] first speech he had to give in his speech class, he came to my office and asked me to listen and critique it and to go to class with him and listen again. [He was] coachable and disciplined. Education was the first thing his parents talked about when I visited them [on a recruiting trip]." The coach added that he's not surprised about O'Neal's latest degree.

It was Brown who made the national headlines as he got himself in trouble during the 1992 SEC Tournament for trying to protect O'Neal and his players. In a bench-clearing brawl, the LSU boss stormed to the court and ran toward Tennessee's Carlus Groves, who had grabbed O'Neal when the latter was preparing to dunk. Many players from both clubs, including Groves and O'Neal, were ejected from the contest.

By the way, there was a television documentary that looked at the special relationship between O'Neal and Brown. *Shaq and Dale* first aired on ESPN and the SEC Network in 2015. The documentary was shown as part of the *SEC Storied* series.

It is a well-known fact Brown is not a big fan of the NCAA. For a long time, he has fought against the Indiana-based organization that oversees the membership schools and student-athletes. He didn't like the bureaucratic NCAA's hypocrisy and its lack of commonsense rules. He became a compassionate voice and strong advocate for his players.

And Brown was one of many individuals featured in a 2016 book titled *Indentured: The Inside Story of the Rebellion Against the NCAA*. The authors – Joe Nocera and Ben Strauss – told the remarkable story of a loose-knit group of rebels who decided to fight NCAA. "Dale [Brown] is one of a kind," Strauss told the author. "He is passionate, persistent and has been one of the loudest voices for change in college for decades, long before there was much of a chorus around him."

The book discusses two of Brown's former players at LSU during the 1980s – Zoran Jovanovich and Mark Alcorn – and their difficulties in getting medical or related help because of rigid NCAA rules.

Added Strauss, who was a contributing writer for the *New York Times*, "The most surprising thing I learned about him [Brown] was the story about Mark Alcorn. It was one of the most heartbreaking I came across in years of research. He was diagnosed with cancer and returned home to Missouri for treatment. His parents later threw a fundraiser for him and asked Dale to send three of Alcorn's teammates to the event.

"After pouring so much money into treatment for their son, they asked Brown and LSU if they could cover the [players'] cost. It was, essentially, Alcorn's dying wish. Dale said, of course, he would do it. But when he asked the NCAA, he was told paying for the players' transportation violated the association's rules.

"So, Dale called the players into his office and drew the blinds. He handed them envelopes filled with cash, enough to cover a red-eye flight, a hotel room and some food. He told this story and explained that here we were doing this basic act of kindness, and he felt like there were cameras watching him. It's powerful stuff."

When he was coaching, the personable Brown said he followed the rules, but whenever he was confronted with his players' hardship or tragedy, he had to find help somehow. "Only rules I broke had to do with human dignity, and that was after they were already at LSU," said Brown. "I called NCAA first and explained the situations, but they could have cared less.

"I was never afraid of ever losing my job because these things had to do with common sense and dignity, not for any other reason."

Brown – who had been the target of several NCAA investigations – has seen the 369-page hardcover *Indentured*. "I applauded Joe Nocera from *New York Times* for writing the book," he said. "His heart was in the right place. He wasn't writing with emotions. He was writing with facts, and this wasn't a vendetta or anything else. I think the thing he made quite clear, for years, the NCAA has legislated against human dignity, and they practiced monumental hypocrisy. Frank Deford from *Sports Illustrated* said it's the largest legal cartel in the world. So, I admire what he did."

The authors of *Indentured* have argued the NCAA is morally bankrupt in many ways. Its first executive director – a former sportswriter – made up the term *student-athlete* to avoid workers' compensation lawsuits. Its 400-page rulebook basically forbids athletes – poor or rich – from receiving human kindness, such as a ride or a meal. Its investigative methods have been reported as questionable in many cases. Its huge TV money isn't shared with the student-athletes, with exception of his or her stipends that cover extra expenses in college.

Brown feels the NCAA has made progress but still has ways to go as far as dealing with student-athletes, among several issues.

"I think there is no question that they've made progress, but I add an asterisk to that," said Brown, who years ago provided recommendations or improvements to the NCAA and its Division I members in a letter-writing campaign, with many of those suggestions eventually adopted by the organization. "They've come millions of miles, but they've got light years to go and light travel is 186,000 miles a second, so they've got a long way to go.

"But I do think that [NCAA president] Mark Emmert has made himself more available than any other people. They usually go into a cocoon and hide. They have made progress but not nearly enough."

Even though Emmert, a former chancellor at LSU (1999 to 2004), knew the *Indentured* book would unlikely treat him or the NCAA well, he was still gracious to give a lengthy interview and allow the material to be used for the book, according to the authors.

As for the FBI's investigation of alleged corruption in college basketball, which became public in 2017, Brown believes "the FBI may revive the NCAA from the long coma they have been in. College basketball will be better off."

During his LSU coaching career, Brown often sounded like a preacher or an evangelist, especially when delivering powerful messages, and he had catchy nicknames. Some folks called him the "Billy Graham in Sneakers." Asked by the author about that catchy phrase, the coach believed it came from "a nationally televised game that Brent Musburger and Billy Packer were doing. I was not trying to be a preacher."

And the sportswriters enjoyed being around Brown because he was good copy, giving them colorful quotes or comments. An inspiring personality from a poor background, he was never boring. In fact, a video documentary about Brown's fascinating life was made and released in 2012. The fast-paced documentary, *Man in the Glass: The Dale Brown Story*, included interviews with all-star cast members such as actor Matthew McConaughey, and well-known basketball personalities such as Shaquille O'Neal, John Wooden, Dick Vitale, Tim Brando, Joe B. Hall and Kenny Walker. In addition, it featured old clips and photos of Adolph Rupp and Wooden when they were honored at LSU in the 1970s.

Also briefly included in the video were Brown's adventurous travels around the world. He has even climbed the Matterhorn in the Swiss Alps and visited Mother Teresa in Calcutta. "I have been in 90 countries in the world, and none of them compare to this great country, even with its flaws," Brown pointed out. "When I say 'God Bless America,' it comes from my heart and not my mouth."

If you knew him, it is not a surprise that Coach Brown still keeps up with social issues, such as poverty, crime, violence, civility, gun control, race and religion, among others that affect our nation. He has strong moral feelings and is outspoken on various topics, wanting our country to do the right thing. He often sends commentaries about these issues via emails to his friends and followers.

After former President George H.W. Bush passed away at the age of 94 in November 2018, Brown watched ceremonies honoring the former President on television, including the funeral at Washington National Cathedral, and he came away impressed, and it reminded many folks that our country needed to be together, not divided.

"Watching the beautiful tribute yesterday for President H.W. Bush, the first thought that came to me, was how much he reminded me of my mentor coach John Wooden," said Brown. "He was kind, caring, vibrant, humble, honorable, forgiving, loyal, and principled. The second thought was that I hope that President Trump and Congress learned some lessons about how he was a true servant leader and brought people together. There is no I in the word team, never has and never will be. But there are three I's in the word idiotic.

"Teamwork is one of the most essential intangibles for success. The Boston Celtics have won the most NBA championships. They were made up of blacks and whites, Catholics and Protestants, and coached by a Jew. The reason they have been so successful is because they fully understood that the best potential of me is we.

"Watching the President and Congress operate reminds me of two selfish children arguing over a toy. Many civilizations have risen to a dominant position in world history. Some rose quickly, some rose slowly, but without exception they fell because they quit working together. Watching politics today is like watching ourselves self-destruct. If this was a sports franchise, they would not win a game because they have no concept of teamwork. All championship teams always possess the most important factor of success, and that is unity.

"We as citizens must unite as one, forget this nonsense of political parties. We are the United States of America and not the unreasonable shallow Americans. Both start with USA. If we do not unite now, then what Abraham Lincoln said will come true, 'America will never be destroyed from the outside. If we falter and lose our freedom, it will be because we destroyed ourselves.'

"That is exactly what we are doing right now. All this bickering and hatred must be stopped now. Hatred corrodes the container it is carried in. When the power of love and understanding overcomes the love of power, we will then and only then put our country back on the right track before we have a head-on collision with total disaster. We can disagree without being disagreeable.

"Please call, write, or email the people in Congress that represent you and give them your opinion. Also, do the same with President Trump. Do not remain silent because [author] Charles Krauthammer's statement is so very true, 'You're betraying your whole life if you don't say what you think.' Again, I plead with you to take immediate action. Thanks to you that do and to those that do not, remember that people can be divided into three groups, those who make things happen, those who watch things happen, and those who wonder what happened. What group do you belong to? It is not too late to join group one."

In 2003, Brown's health was big news in the nation, spreading like wildfire from New York City to Los Angeles. The college basketball world was shocked to learn that 67-year-old Brown had a serious setback, suffering a near-fatal stroke. The fans were very concerned. But he recovered nicely and is fortunate that he has had no side effects from that frightening episode. A thankful Brown realizes he has been blessed.

And his faith has helped him succeed in life. "Without my faith in God, I would be a lost soul," said Brown, who has one daughter and three grandsons. "I cannot live one day without God."

Chapter Seven

Hoosier to Wildcat

While playing high school basketball at Tell City, located by the Ohio River on the Indiana side and not far from Owensboro, Ky., future Wildcat Steve Lochmueller's coach was none other than his father, Bob Lochmueller, a former U of L star who had played for coach Peck Hickman. (Bob led the team in scoring during his junior and senior years before going to the NBA.) The younger Lochmueller was asked if it was good or bad playing for his dad at Tell City High School.

"That's a great question," he said in a December 2017 interview at his Alumni Coliseum office on Eastern Kentucky University campus, where he was the school's athletics director before resigning his post in October 2019. "As I look back on it now, he's my mentor. I aspire to be the man that he is. He's still alive. He just turned 90. In fact, after Christmas we're going to go down to Tell City and visit. But back in the late 60s when I played for him, I'll tell you a funny story. Being the son of the coach is not easy for either the player or the dad.

"So, when I came up as a sophomore, I didn't start immediately. There was an assistant that coached for Dad by the name of John Jameson. And after about two or three games, he said, 'Bob, you've got to start him. I know you don't want to because he's your son and you think you'll get criticism, but you've got to start him.' So, he did, of course. I started the rest of the season.

"But I was also one of the few players to ever get kicked out of practice. When you're playing and you're playing against someone that maybe isn't as good as you at that particular time, they'll do a lot of fouling. So, when you're in practice, you get the ball and you're going to the basket, they'll always foul you because it's practice, it's not the game. Several times I got upset, and I would get a little rough with who was guarding me.

"And Dad would say, 'You get your tail in the locker room.' So far as I know, I'm the only one that ever got thrown out of practice during my dad's [career] as coach. The funny piece of this is that I came home with Dad because I didn't have a car. I go to the house, kind of throw my stuff in, and go eat dinner. Mom's there [in the kitchen]. She's cooked dinner.

Mom says, 'How's everything going, son?'

'Fine,' said the son.

'Practice good? School good?' asked his mother.

'Well, school was fine,' said the younger Lochmueller. 'Practice went okay. I got kicked out.'"

Added Lochmueller, "She had my plate ready for me, and I sit there and eat my dinner. Dad came in [after] changing some clothes and washing his hands.

'What's for dinner, honey?' said the father.

'I don't know – fix your own,' she replied."

Lochmueller commented, "So, that's a funny thing, but I think about my mother in my memories of a story being kicked out of practice, playing for your own dad. But like I said earlier, he's my mentor. I aspire to be the man that he has been."

Interestingly enough, Lochmueller and his dad are members of the Indiana Basketball Hall of Fame. Not many people will see a father-son duo who are members of the same hall of fame. Any hall of fame, actually. To Kentuckians, one well-known father-son pair in the Indiana Basketball Hall of Fame includes Kyle Macy and his father, Bob.

"There's just a handful where the father and son are members of the Indiana Basketball Hall of Fame. You know, it's such a great honor [to be a part of] history of Indiana basketball, and I'm not talking about Indiana University; they have their own history," said the personable Lochmueller, who also mentioned that IU legend Steve Alford and his dad are in the same hall of fame as well. "As much as I love Kentucky, and I do love Kentucky, this is my home. How does it compare with Indiana basketball? When I get back to Indiana from time to time, I like to go by and just not only see the honor that I received and Dad received but see all the people who've come through that hall of fame. It's really impressive, and to be a part of that is an honor."

The 6-foot-7, 215-pound Lochmueller, who was a three-sport star in high school, signed with coach Adolph Rupp's program at Kentucky in spring 1971, but he almost didn't become a Wildcat. He had some tough collegiate decisions to make. He could play hoops for new coach Bobby Knight at Indiana. He could play at Purdue. He could play at Louisville. He could play at Kentucky. Or he could play football at Tennessee, Notre Dame, or even for coach John Ray at Kentucky. If then-UCLA assistant Denny Crum hadn't come to U of L to take over the school's hoops program, Lochmueller's dad might have been named the head coach at Louisville.

"My senior year, I waited until late in the year to commit to where I was going to college," Lochmueller recalled. "There were several dynamics there. At one time I almost committed to IU. Bobby Knight had recruited me and asked me and [prep star] Steve Green to come and visit at the same time, and we did. Obviously, at that time, going into your state institution was attractive.

"At the same time, [I was] being recruited by multiple schools. I took a look at Purdue University because George King was the coach then. George King and my dad were roommates in pro ball. In fact, previous to moving back to Indiana, my dad was the No. 1 assistant for George King at West Virginia University, so we were there four years. There was a big family relationship between the King family and the Lochmueller family.

"George wanted me to come play for him, and I thought that was attractive. But finally George said, 'Steve, they're going to name me athletic director next week, so I'm going to have both positions – athletic director and coach. I'm going to have to give one up the next year or two, and I want you to know, if I give it up, it'll be the coaching position. I'll be the athletic director.'

"So, he was honest and straightforward to us as family friends, and that 'unknown who was going to come in as coach' was a little bit bothersome to me. I eventually told Coach King, 'Thank you so much, Coach. I appreciate you and the offer that you gave me, but I'm going to look elsewhere.'

"Well, at the same time, Louisville was offering. My dad was [a three-year starter] at U of L. What most people don't understand is that when [John] Dromo decided to retire [after a heart attack], the job came down between Denny Crum and my dad. So, I was not going to make a decision until I found out who was going to be that coach. You had the old guard, Peck Hickman and his folks, who were pushing for Dad as an ex-student-athlete to be the next coach there. And then you had the new guard pushing to bring somebody else in from the outside. For whatever reason, and my dad's never told me, and I'm not saying it would have changed the outcome, he chose to take his name out of the hat, and they offered a job to Denny Crum.

"So, that whole dynamic was playing out because had Dad received that head coaching job, then, you know, 'Was I going to go to IU? Was I going to go to Purdue?' wasn't an option anymore. 'Was I going to go to North Carolina? Was I going to go to Kentucky? Where was I going to go to school?' When he [Dad] withdrew his name from the search, then all of a sudden Kentucky, which I was very interested in all along, became so obvious to me because I had been recruited by Kentucky. I loved the tradition that Coach Rupp had. I got to know Coach [Joe] Hall and T.L. Plain and some of the other coaches at that time, and that relationship was good. I really enjoyed the visit, the institution, the tradition, and [the] greater Lexington area. So, then it was like the door opened, and the light shined in, and I said, 'No, this is where I wanted to go to school,' and I have no regrets. None whatsoever."

Since Rupp in his latter years didn't go on recruiting trips, it was his assistants – Hall, Plain, and Dickie Parsons – who visited the Lochmuellers and signed the promising youngster to a national letter of intent.

What was his first meeting with Coach Rupp like? At the time, Rupp was about to retire. The 1971-72 campaign would be the Baron's last year at Kentucky. His top scorers on the squad, which shared the SEC title with Coach Ray Mears' Tennessee club, were 6-foot-11 junior center Jim Andrews, 6-foot-7 southpaw senior Tom Parker, 5-foot-10 sophomore guard Ronnie Lyons, 6-foot-3 senior guard Stan Key, and 6-foot-6 junior forward Larry Stamper. Three Wildcats – Parker, Andrews, and Lyons – received All-SEC honors, with Parker named SEC Player of the Year. And Lochmueller played for the highly publicized freshman team that season, joining his new teammates like Kevin Grevey and Bob Guyette, among others. The freshman team also practiced with the varsity team. As mentioned in a previous chapter, it was a difficult year for the athletics department as there was tension between the Rupp backers, who wanted to see the Baron continue coaching, and the administration officials.

"I remember meeting him on the recruiting trip when I came to Lexington," said Lochmueller. "Oh yeah, you're starstruck. Plus there's this man sitting behind the desk, and he's the legendary Adolph Rupp. But it was interesting because, even as starstruck as we were, it had been explained to us that this was Coach Rupp's last year, and it also had been explained to us that Coach wasn't necessarily totally in agreement with that. But that was the case because during the recruitment to come to Kentucky, Coach Hall had said that [Dr. Otis] Singletary had made the decision to move forward and that Coach Hall was going to be the coach-in-waiting, per se. So, it was very interesting, especially when we got here and got into conditioning and then into practice [with] the freshman team.

"You could tell that Coach Rupp was supportive, but yet he was kind of bitter about the situation. There was just a little divide there between the team that Joe had recruited versus Coach Rupp's boys. There were some awkward times. It was funny because, at that time, Coach Rupp sat on the side of the court and only got up when he had something to say. Of course, when he got up, everything got quiet, and he said what he said, but during the freshman year, we had to be there at three o'clock. There was a couple of people hurt. There was an open position on the varsity where they didn't have enough people to practice. So, Coach Rupp required the freshmen to practice from three to five against the varsity, and then we had our practice from five to seven.

"Even though it was a great year, it was a very demanding year to have to practice from three till seven and then go eat dinner, and then go back [to your room or study hall] and do your homework. A lot of people, whether it'd be at Kentucky or other places, didn't think we studied. Well, my freshman year, for example, I roomed with Bob Guyette. Bob is a [facial] plastic surgeon now, but he and I were in pre-dentistry, and we studied. It was not easy, but we studied. It was all well worth it. We got a great education at the University of Kentucky."

Lochmueller has lots of memories about the top-ranked "Super Kittens." One of them was helping Frankfort open its new 5,000-seat arena in December 1971, which since has been demolished.

"It was the very first event in that building that we played Furman over there," said Lochmueller of the old Frankfort Civic Center. "We were No. 3 or 4 in the nation at that time, and Furman was ranked No. 1. We, the Super Kittens, were the ones who opened it up, and we beat them [132-73]. I mean we just gave them a shellacking, and that one sticks out because then we [jumped to] No. 1 and maintained that No. 1 [ranking] the rest of the year.

"It also sticks out because not only did the seven scholarship freshmen play but also the walk-ons and the other kids who came into the freshman team. Everybody got to play and had fun. It's not always the case in basketball that you have 13 people [on roster] in today's world. What was so nice was everybody had smiles. We were then No. 1 from there on out."

Lochmueller added the freshman team was very close, and the members do meet in a reunion pretty often. "There's a friendship there that's for life," he said. "It's almost like when we get together that we're back and we're 18 and 20 [years old] again. It's a family for life."

Statistically, Lochmueller's best game took place when he was a sophomore backup during Coach Joe Hall's first year as the head coach at UK. Against coach C.M. Newton's Alabama club at Memorial Coliseum, Lochmueller hit a career-high 18 points, along with seven rebounds, helping UK to an 111-95 win. Grevey took the team's scoring honors with 29 points. Alabama's Wendell Hudson poured in a game-high 31 points.

Added Lochmueller, "I remember that game and another game that sticks out in my memory. I remember playing against Tennessee at home and having a really good game. In other words, I normally shot fairly well from the field. I just didn't throw shots up. I had a pretty high percentage as well as my free throw percentage. Against Tennessee, I remember, after the postgame show, Coach Mears saying that Lochmueller came in the first half and provided such as spark that got them going against Tennessee. It's always refreshing and makes you feel good when the opposing coach recognizes you. Those are great memories. That's what life's about. Memories."

Another memory was in Nashville during the 1973 March Madness when the 20-8 Wildcats overcame James "Fly" Williams and his Austin Peay Governors 106-100 in overtime. A Brooklyn phenom who later played two years in the old ABA, Williams gunned in 26 points, but it wasn't enough to help Lake Kelly-coached Austin Peay. "He was kind of like a version of Pete Maravich," said Lochmueller. "I will say this: He had the free ticket from his coach to shoot when and where he wanted to." By the way, the Governors at the time had a couple of future Joe B. Hall assistant coaches on the bench – Kelly and assistant Leonard Hamilton. Interestingly, it was Hamilton who recruited Williams to Clarksville.

After the victory over Austin Peay, the Wildcats lost in the next NCAA tourney game – a Mideast Regional Final – in the Music City. Kentucky dropped to 32-year-old coach Bobby Knight's Indiana squad, which had 6-foot-5 freshman star Quinn Buckner, in a 72-65 decision. The young Hoosiers would advance to the Final Four, which would be Knight's first of his five Final Four appearances.

1973-74.

That was a really bad year for UK basketball. That was Joe B. Hall's second team at Kentucky with the Cats finishing with a 13-13 mark (9-9 in SEC), just like coach Adolph Rupp's 1966-67 version, which posted a similar 13-13 record (8-10 in SEC).

"That was a very frustrating year," said Lochmueller who was a junior at the time. "We really didn't have a true big man, where Bob Guyette and I were the only two that could play center, and whereas as a sophomore, we had [Jim] Andrews at 6-11, almost seven foot, and we got hurt a lot on the inside. After coming in as freshmen, after having the great sophomore year that we had and just missing out on going to the [national] finals, I think there was a lot of frustration. I know it was a difficult year for Coach. He was under a lot of stress, a lot of pressure.

"In any situation that you have whether it be business, athletics or even your home life, when you insert all that pressure and stress, things have to give and sometimes they don't give in the right direction, they give in the wrong direction. And I think that particular year was just a multitude of stress and events, and they didn't all go very well, and I personally don't think anyone can point any fingers, whether that be at the coaching staff or the players or whatever. Everybody wanted to do their job. Everybody wanted to do well. But obviously, it didn't turn out as good as what we wanted. I know it didn't turn out as good as what Coach wanted. There were tense moments."

It certainly helped when the Cats finished the forgettable campaign with a blowout victory over Mississippi State in an 108-69 fashion, snapping a four-game losing streak and allowing UK to finish without having a losing mark. Had Kentucky lost that game, it would have given the Wildcats their first losing year in almost half a century. Junior Kevin Grevey led the 1973-74 Wildcats and SEC in scoring with 21.9 points. Following him in the scoring department were three double-figure scorers in Bob Guyette, Jimmy Dan Conner, and Mike Flynn, all juniors, in the 12-point range.

Lochmueller, who was majoring in pre-dentistry, didn't play basketball during his senior year. Earlier, he had gotten permission from Joe B. Hall to go out for spring football practice. Since Lochmueller had good size and speed, it was not a surprise that he made the 1974 roster, which listed him as a 6-foot-6, 230-pound defensive tackle. While at Tell City High, he earned All-State honors as a tackle in 1970. Fran Curci, UK's fairly new football boss, liked him. Curci was rebuilding the long-suffering program after two disappointing regimes under Charlie Bradshaw and John Ray. The charismatic coach was coming off his first season at Kentucky with a not-so-bad 5-6 mark, playing its home games at sparkling new Commonwealth Stadium, and there was much excitement in the football camp heading into the 1974 campaign. Lochmueller's teammates

Steve Lochmueller at his former EKU office. (Photo by Jamie H. Vaught)

included standouts like junior running back Sonny Collins, who was selected SEC Player of the Year as a sophomore, and offensive tackle Warren Bryant. Also, Lochmueller's high school teammate from Tell City was on the team – senior running back Rich Alvey. "He [Curci] was in his own way a very dynamic individual and brought a lot of excitement to UK at the time," said Lochmueller.

On his decision to change sports, Lochmueller said, "It was an interesting dynamic. As it all turned out, it probably didn't work out as well as I thought. The primary decision [was] to go out for football, and I was going to go ahead and play basketball as well. The reason that I made that decision going into my senior year was I pretty much knew that there was no next year, so pro basketball was not in my future. At least, the way I saw it. And I still believe that today. And back then, there weren't very many opportunities to go overseas; that had just started. So, I made the decision [that] if I'm going to play beyond this, I've got to do it in football because it's not going to be in basketball [after UK]."

But then he got hurt in a preseason football practice. "I'd actually gotten to the point where I was going to be a starter on defense at right defensive tackle, and about a week before the season started, I got injured," recalled Lochmueller. "I had a blood clot in my thigh, and they didn't get in there and drain it as soon as they should have. So, I had a big blood clot; it has to dissolve. I was out for seven weeks and didn't get to play football games because of that injury."

While he was out, he stayed with the team, cheering his teammates from the sidelines. He began to think about redshirting and returning to school for a fifth year. "What was going through my mind at that time was I wasn't in shape for basketball [for the 1974-75 season]," he explained. "And then reality sets in. I'm getting ready to try and go to dental school. At that time, that's what I thought I wanted to be – a dentist. [But] I didn't do that.

"I started looking and researching, which I should've done in the front end, but as young men, you don't always do what you're supposed to. I started researching this redshirt opportunity [about] coming back and playing, and (perhaps) get drafted. Well, at that time, offensive or defensive linemen made about $50,000 a year. Not bad, but their life span was three years. And more so than that, the rate of permanent injury was almost a given that if you played three years and you would be injured in such a way that you would not be able to continue your career. I just decided [to] graduate and move on. Pro ball was not in my future."

Later, Lochmueller said even though he didn't redshirt, he "had three offers to try out" for the Buffalo Bills, Dallas Cowboys, and Philadelphia Eagles in the NFL. "They were looking at basketball players being agile and being able to convert [to football] at the time. There's less of it going on today. But back then there was a handful of people that did come out of collegiate athletics in basketball and either try out or play professional football. Look at [former UK and NFL stars] Derrick Ramsey and Art Still. Those guys, I mean, you're talking about some of the greats that ever played for the blue and white."

After UK, Lochmueller began his career in the mining, coal, and steel production industries. He eventually rose through the ranks to become a high-ranking executive at several businesses, including startups, over the years, managing multi-million dollar budgets. His strong background in management and telecommunications helped Lochmueller get the AD post at Eastern Kentucky University in 2015 over three other finalists, including his former UK football teammate Derrick Ramsey, who was a freshman signee in 1974.

During his four-year tenure at EKU, Lochmueller enjoyed watching the Colonels face Kentucky in football, basketball, and other sports. He pointed out these matchups were for the players. "The games against my alma mater are not about me, they are about the student-athletes competing at the highest levels," he said in 2017. "It is my job to make sure the student-athletes have all the tools necessary to be successful on and off the court [or field]."

While at Eastern Kentucky, his athletics department saw record averages in student-athlete GPAs and captured four straight Ohio Valley Conference Commissioner's Cup awards as a symbol of overall athletic excellence within the league since 2015.

Although Lochmueller, who stepped down from his AD position in late 2019, said he was "honored to have the opportunity to lead Colonel athletics," he will always be a faithful Wildcat.

Chapter Eight

Golden Goose

*T*he Goose was Golden.

That was the main headline written by the editors of famed *Sports Illustrated* magazine when Kentucky star Jack "Goose" Givens graced the cover shortly after guiding the Wildcats to a national title in 1978 with his stunning 41-point performance against Duke in his last collegiate contest.

How did the smooth southpaw come by that nickname? What's the story behind it?

"Well, there was a Goose who played with the Harlem Globetrotters, so the guys on my high school team [at Lexington Bryan Station] said I resembled him and his style of play, so they started calling me Goose," Givens recalled. "It wasn't necessarily a nickname that I wanted or liked. Of course, that made them call me Goose even more. It was one of those things that just kind of put on me in high school, and it just stuck."

His widowed mother, Betty Givens, didn't mind his nickname. However, she didn't want her son to play basketball during his early days. She even refused to sign the permission slip for the school.

"My mother wasn't really high on me playing basketball to begin with," he explained. "She wasn't in favor of me playing. As a matter of fact, in my ninth-grade year when I really started to enjoy playing, she refused to sign the permission slip for me to play at Dunbar Junior High school at that time. Junior High is what we called it, but she refused to sign it, so I convinced one of my sisters to sign it. So, my sister forged my mother's name on the permission slip to play, and that was good until one day I got hurt and broke my nose. They had to bring me home in an ambulance to pick her up, and she wasn't real happy about finding out that way that I was on the basketball team.

"But my mom never went to a game when I played high school ball. She was just too nervous. She listened to every one of them on the radio, but she never went to a high school game because she knew or thought she knew I was going to get hurt. She could sit at home and listen, and she could turn it off if we fell behind and turn it back on to see if we caught up."

By his sophomore year, Givens didn't have to find someone else to sign the papers for basketball. Mrs. Givens finally relented and gave permission. "Every year you have to sign it, so she finally said okay and signed it to allow me to play after that," he said. "She did sign it my 10th grade year and said, 'Okay, here is the deal, for every point you score, I'll give you a dollar.' Then I started scoring too much, I wouldn't take it, but she said, 'Okay, we'll back off to a quarter.' By the time I was a senior, she backed off to a dime and said, 'I'll give you a dime for every point you score.' Of course, I never took any money, but it was fun. It was her way of saying 'Okay, I encourage you to play and to be good at it.'"

As it turned out, Givens became a prep All-American and a two-time All-Stater, leading Bryan Station to a 76-17 record in three years. In addition, he received Kentucky's Mr. Basketball honors.

While Mrs. Givens didn't see her son play a single game in high school, she did attend a few of her son's games at Kentucky.

Givens, who also went to the 1975 Final Four in San Diego as a freshman, shares several memories about UK coach Joe B. Hall, who won four SEC Coach of the Year awards during his 13-year tenure at UK before retiring in 1985.

"Coach Hall was a better coach than people give him credit for," said Givens in 2018. "He followed a legend [in Adolph Rupp], which is hard to do, so they never really gave Coach Hall the credit he deserved. He was very good at getting players to achieve beyond what they thought they could. It was really fun being a freshman on such a great [1974-75] team with Kevin Grevey, Jimmy Dan Conner, Bob Guyette, Mike Flynn, and all of the other great seniors on that team. You know at times Coach Hall wasn't the easiest person to get along with, and he didn't want to be. He wanted us to know that he was in charge.

"But, coming in as a freshman, it was good playing with a bunch of seniors who had been through it and who knew how to deal with his style of coaching. One of the lessons I learned early was from Kevin Grevey, who would always tell me, 'Sit right up front when in the locker room at halftime or pregame. If you're the leading scorer or if you are the captain or the main guy, sit right up front, keep your eyes right on Coach Hall while he's talking. Make sure you pay attention or at least make him think you're paying attention.'

"But Grevey said, 'Whatever you do, don't listen to a word he says. Just let him talk. He's gonna give you a hard time because you're the leading scorer, you're the captain, but it's not towards you personally. It's just so everybody else in the locker room knows if he's giving you a hard time and he's on your case as the captain and leading scorer, then everybody is fair game.' So, he used that.

"Another story, the night we won the [national] championship, we were out on the floor celebrating, and the NCAA [officials] presented us with our trophy, the watches, and championship stuff. Thirty or 45 minutes after the game, going through all this stuff on the floor, cutting down the nets and all of that, we were walking back to the locker room, and everybody was celebrating. Coach Hall came up and put his arm around me and said, 'Now you see what all of that screaming and cussing I did to you over these years, you see why it finally paid off.' He looked at me, and I looked at him. He kind of laughed and then walked away before I could even answer, but I'm glad I had an opportunity to play for him. He's a good coach."

Hall has fond memories of Kentucky's 1978 NCAA title victory over Duke. At that time, it was UK's first national championship in 20 years. "I think a big thing was Jack Givens' performance in that championship game, and [it was] just a flawless effort on his part," said Hall. "But having the comfort to be able to empty the bench and to have every player on my squad to play in that championship game – that meant a lot to me."

Hall also was asked what was his most fun team that he had as far as coaching, which included stints at Shepherdsville High School in Kentucky, Regis College, and Central Missouri State College. "I had about 30 of them," smiled Hall. "I felt embarrassed when I called it work because I loved every minute of it. Coaching was a blessing to me. I never had a day's work the whole 30 years that I coached and 20 years I was at the university – seven as an assistant coach and 13 as a head coach. I have had so many good kids to work with. They were just a real pleasure. I still stay in contact with most of them."

As a 6-foot-4 star player, Givens – who was named SEC Athlete of the Year in 1978 – isn't sure if he was ever intimi-

Jack Givens (Photo by Jamie H. Vaught)

dated by Hall. "Well, I don't know if *intimidated* was the right word," commented Givens. "There was a respect that you always have for your head coach, so I respected him. I don't know that I ever was intimidated, but I knew he had the power to give me playing time, he had the power to put you in the game, take you out of the game, to use you the way he wanted to use you. He had that power, so I tried to respect that, but I don't know if I was ever intimidated."

By the way, Hall is mentioned as one of only three men to have captured a national title as a player (in 1949) and as a coach (in 1978), joining Bobby Knight and Dean Smith. The former coach smiled about that, pointing out that isn't really accurate, since he actually didn't play in the NCAA finals during the 1948-49 campaign as a sophomore member of the Wildcats during the "Fabulous Five" era. "I transferred in mid-season [to University of the South in Tennessee]," Hall explained, "but I was on the squad as a freshman and up through half of the sophomore year."

Hall, who once toured with the Harlem Globetrotters in Europe back in 1951, later returned to UK as a student and completed his degree requirements.

The Rupp Arena era began in late November 1976 when Givens was a junior, coming off his sophomore campaign when he led the team with a 20.1-point average in guiding UK to 1976 National Invitation Tournament title in New York. (Unlike today, NCAA and NIT only had a combined total of 44 teams in postseason action with 32 in the Big Dance at the time.) After seeing action at their home games at 11,500-seat Memorial Coliseum during his freshman and sophomore years, Givens and his teammates played their first game at the new spacious facility and won, defeating the Wisconsin Badgers 72-64. An ailing Adolph Rupp was there. The Baron – who received deafening standing ovations before the poorly played contest – sat with his grandson Chip in the front row behind the Wisconsin bench. (Interestingly, it was Bo Ryan who at the time was sitting on that bench as a first-year assistant coach for Wisconsin. Yes, it's the same Bo Ryan who coached his Badgers team to a 71-64 upset win over then-unbeaten Kentucky in the 2015 Final Four.)

For Givens, playing in a new arena with no tradition was a little surreal, and he remembers a little bit about that November night, saying that it really didn't feel like a home game for the most part. For the record, he came up with a double-double in getting 12 points and 10 rebounds against Wisconsin in his Rupp Arena debut.

"It wasn't the same atmosphere that we had built at Memorial Coliseum," Givens recalled. "It was big, and there was a lot of people. All of that was great, but at first it didn't feel like home. It was new. Just like any new house. People move in and the new house is great, and all the furnishings and everything brand new and that's all good, but the homey feeling that you get from being in that old house, we're not there yet. [The seats had] all kinds of colors in there. It was no doubt it wasn't Memorial Coliseum. It took us a while to get used to that, but I don't even know how many points I scored or anything like that, but it wasn't home, and it took a while to get comfortable playing there."

Of course, after 40-plus years, Rupp Arena, which recently underwent significant improvements, has now developed its own winning basketball tradition by having marquee games and players as well as big-name concerts. "The atmosphere is totally different [now]," said Givens. Incredibly, the Wildcats, who often led the nation in average home attendance, have won around 90 percent of their Rupp Arena games.

In 2018, the Travel Channel picked Rupp Arena as the nation's top hoops facility for its "The Sweet 16 College Basketball Venues."

While Givens is best known for his 41 points in the 1978 national title game, he also had a memorable performance against Arkansas in the national semifinals. Against the fifth-ranked Razorbacks and Eddie Sutton, the No. 1 Wildcats prevailed with a 64-59 win, with Givens recording 23 points and nine rebounds, both game-highs, and playing outstanding pressure defense. That was Givens' best game of the 1978 NCAA Tournament at that point. He didn't do as much in the previous three tournament games against Florida State, Miami (Ohio), and Michigan State [which featured All-American Earvin "Magic" Johnson].

After the win over Arkansas, the Cats would have a day off – Easter Sunday – before facing Duke on Monday night. Givens certainly remembers what he and his teammates did between the Final Four games.

"I just happened to have some relatives in St. Louis who lived there," he said. "We – James (Lee) and I and maybe a couple of the other guys – went to church on that Sunday between the Saturday's game and Monday's and then ate dinner at my relative's house. Had a good visit. We had to come back and had kind of a light practice. Then we had our team meal. We were going to see a movie after that, which is our normal routine. But we decided we didn't want to go to a movie. We wanted to go back to the hotel and watch video of that Notre Dame-Duke game [in the other national semifinal]. We as a team kind of learned as much as we could about Duke and, you know, to help us get ready to play that [championship] game, so that's kind of how we spent the day that Sunday in between."

Givens was asked if Joe B. Hall, especially if he was younger, was coaching today, would he be able to handle a different generation of players (Generation Z) as well as social media distractions such as Facebook and Twitter, and a larger group of news media outlets.

"He would've adapted some, but there were a whole lot of coaches from back in that day who couldn't coach now," Givens theorized. "Not so much for the social media, but the players are different. Back in those days, it was a coach's game – Joe B and Bobby Knight. Bobby Knight couldn't coach now. John Chaney and all those older coaches. It was about them, and they controlled the players.

"Nowadays only a very few coaches have control of the team. [Mike] Krzyzewski, Rick [Pitino] before he was let go at Louisville, [John] Calipari, and there are some others like [North] Carolina and some of those schools. It's about the coaches, but for the most part, it's about the players. Back in my day, it was about the coaches, and a lot of the coaches from that time period and even later couldn't coach now."

Also, there is the dramatic growth of AAU basketball, which provides the nation's top prep players opportunities to compete at the highest level. "It [the change] is not so much about the social media and all the external stuff," added Givens. "It's about AAU basketball. It's about basketball shoe companies who have made the game about the players. It's not about coaches anymore, and even the places that I named – Kentucky, Louisville, Duke, Carolina – the No. 1 conversation is 'one-and-done.' Guys who are good enough to come in and go. It's not about guys who are going stay for four years and let Calipari or Krzyzewski develop them to be a good or great player. The game is not about that anymore.

"So, if Coach Hall came in now and was a young up-and-coming coach, he would be fine because that's life. That's the nature of the beast."

Following his playing career – including two years with the Atlanta Hawks after being an NBA first-round draft selection and then playing another five years or so overseas in Italy, Belgium, and Japan – Givens spent some time in television and radio broadcasting. For many years, he served as the commentator for the Orlando Magic telecasts during the 1990s and early 2000s. He and Doc

Rivers, who was the head coach at Orlando at the time, once had a conversation about the upcoming NBA Draft. Givens asked the coach if he was going to select a high school player in the draft. And the former Wildcat told Rivers that he shouldn't pick someone out of high school who's never played in college.

Rivers, who was the head coach of the Los Angeles Clippers when this book went to press, didn't agree, saying, "Goose, here is how I look at it. Why would I want a guy who I think is going to be a great player? Why would I want him to go to college for four years? He wears his body out for four years in college and learns a lot of bad habits. I'm going [to] have to change the way he plays either way from all the bad stuff he's done through high school, and now I have to change the bad stuff he's done through high school and then the bad stuff he learned in college, so he can learn my system. Why wouldn't I want to get a guy at 18 instead of 22 whose body is fresh, who hadn't learned all the bad habits that he's going to learn in college? Why would I want to wait? He makes my team better by having him. Even if he doesn't play, he's learning my system a whole lot sooner, a whole lot younger."

Givens doesn't like the one-and-done rule, either, but he can see the arguments from both sides. "I think it hurts the college game, I think it hurts the NBA," said Givens. "Both of them are weaker now because of the players who come out of college after one year. They're not [as] ready to play as maybe some other scenarios if they stayed longer, even two or three years. So, I'm not a fan of the one-and-done, but I'm a realist. I know that for any other student who stays for four years or even longer and they get their degree, there is no degree they can get that's going to pay them the amount of money the players get for playing basketball coming right out of college. There is nothing. I don't care what degree you get; you're not going to make two, three or four million dollars a year as some of the guys coming out do.

"While I would rather see players stay in school longer, I certainly understand that guys have to take the money when they can get it, and if an NBA team would have come to me at that age and said, 'Hey … you know, I'll sign you to a long contract, and we'll pay you X amount of dollars a year,' I probably would've also. So, I see both sides of it. Now having been on both sides, I certainly understand them taking the money while they can."

Speaking of the NBA, Givens added, "It's all about the dollar. The NBA wants these good players. The NBA understands that. That means more TV revenue, that means more people coming to games, so it's all about money. That's why the NBA [Players Association] won't change it because they like having these guys in the NBA.

"Now I think if John Wall comes to Kentucky for four years, he's going to have a bigger following, which ultimately is going to sell more tickets for the NBA as well as [DeMarcus] Cousins, Anthony Davis, you name any of these guys. It's going [to] lead to a bigger following, which is going lead to more mature players, better players, and more dollars, but the NBA doesn't see it that way."

In 1974, when Givens arrived on UK campus as a highly-regarded recruit, Kentucky was already integrating its basketball program as 7-foot-2 Tom Payne became the school's first African-American on basketball scholarship just a few years earlier. Also, during the mid-1960s, coach Adolph Rupp had tried to re-cruit other black standouts such as Wes Unseld and Butch Beard, who won Kentucky's Mr. Basketball honors in 1964 and 1965, respectively, but had no success. By the time the 1974-75 campaign began, the Wildcats already had five African-Americans on the roster, including Givens, James Lee, Reggie Warford, Merion Haskins, and Larry Johnson.

Over four decades later, Givens had a chance to reflect on racial issues at Ken-tucky when he was a student-athlete. He didn't encounter any racial problems personally. "Well, I felt fine," he recalled. "I never had any issues. Fortunately, when I got there, Reggie Warford was there, Larry Johnson was there, Merion Haskins was there. While it was still over 40 years ago and things were less than ideal, I never had any racial issues just simply because I'm from Lexington and that helps. I played all over the state of Kentucky. I don't care if I'm talking about Louisville, if I'm talking about Whitesburg, if I'm talking about Hazard, if I'm talking about the northern part of the state, we were everywhere. I was being recruited every night. Every game. Every gym was full of Kentucky fans. Back in those days, there weren't a lot of black Kentucky fans. I was being recruited by white people every game. They [UK fans] were saying, 'Goose, we want you, please come to Kentucky. Jack, come to Kentucky.'

"So, by the time I got there [at Kentucky], there wasn't a question in my mind whether some guy from Harlan, Ky., wanted me as a Kentucky Wildcat. It didn't matter because everybody who confronted me or everybody who talked to me wanted me to come to Kentucky. So I was very comfortable here [at UK]. Fortunately, I've never had any bad situations; any adverse situations and bad comments that I heard that would've encouraged me to go somewhere else."

When Givens finished his degree in 1978, he joined an impressive club as he is among the first five black basketball players to graduate from UK, joining Warford, Haskins, Johnson and Lee. "That is a source of pride," he said. "I know changes had to be made. We all took a big step in going to the University of Kentucky because there were other schools that we could have very easily gone to that had a track record and history with minority players."

2,038 points.

That's the total number of points Givens accumulated during his Kentucky Wildcat career. When he left UK in 1978, he finished at No. 2 on the school's all-time leading varsity scorers among men, just behind Dan Issel's 2,138 points. Then Kenny Walker came along and joined the duo in 1986 with 2,080 points, surpassing Givens. Now that means they are the only UK All-Americans who have scored over 2,000 points on the men's side [It would be five if you add stars Valerie Still (2,763 points) and A'dia Mathies (2,014) from the UK women's program.]

Because of one-and-done era, it's pretty safe to assume there will be no one else to join them soon. How does Givens feel about that remarkable feat – a membership in the exclusive 2,000-point club?

"Well, obviously, that's a great achievement, with all the great players who have played at Kentucky, to be in the three with Dan Issel and Kenny Walker," he commented. "It's pretty amazing, really. Great achievement. [It] really means that I had a lot of good players playing around me that were able to do a lot of

Dan Issel, Jack Givens and Kenny Walker in 2018. (Photo by Jamie H. Vaught)

different things, which allowed me to focus more on my offense. But it's a great honor, no doubt about it. It's good because now, with the way the game is going and the one-and-dones, it seems like all the really good players who could accomplish that are gone way too soon to score 2,000 points."

Givens, by the way, led the varsity team in scoring every season at UK except for his freshman year when All-American senior Kevin Grevey averaged 23.6 points in 1975, fourth best in the SEC. As a Wildcat rookie, Givens also did very well, averaging 9.4 points, which was fourth highest on the squad. He also led the team in free throw percentage as a sophomore and junior, hitting 82.9 and 83.2 percent, respectively.

Another highlight of Givens' career took place during UK's graduation exercises in 1978 when a surprised Givens received the prestigious Sullivan Medallion from then-university president Dr. Otis Singletary. It is the highest award given to a student by UK. "I was just amazed," said Givens. "That was good. It's a combination of academics and community involvement. It's a number of things that go along with that, but certainly it was an award that was not necessarily only based on athletics. I think, of all the awards I've gotten, that was one of the awards that I'm most proud of because it kind of took me away from the basketball court and into the lives of other people, including other students. So, that was a very, very high honor for me to receive that."

Chapter Nine

A Slam Dunk Champion

Kenny "Sky" Walker, a two-time SEC Player of the Year, played for one of UK's greatest teams that didn't reach the NCAA Final Four. That was his senior year.

After the Wildcats had won the first two games of the 1986 NCAA Tournament, beating Davidson 75-55 and Western Kentucky 71-64, they advanced to face coach Wimp Sanderson and his strong Alabama team in the Southeast Regional semifinals in Atlanta. The other two Sweet Sixteen teams in that Regional were LSU and Georgia Tech. That's three SEC teams at the same place. UK's first-year coach Eddie Sutton said that was like "SEC Invitational" tourney, and Georgia Tech was a former member of the SEC.

It would be the fourth time that both Kentucky and Alabama had played each other during that season. Could the Wildcats stop Crimson Tide and their two big men – Buck Johnson and Derrick McKey – again after winning three times against Alabama, including an SEC Tournament victory in Lexington?

As history records will show, the Wildcats were victorious again in a defensive battle (68-63) over Alabama, advancing to meet coach Dale Brown's LSU squad, which outlasted Georgia Tech 70-64 in the regional semifinals. Against the Crimson Tide, Walker had a good game, scoring a game-high 22 points along with seven rebounds.

Current Tennessee coach Rick Barnes was an assistant to Sanderson on that Alabama team. In a 2016 press conference in Knoxville, Barnes recalled his early days at Tuscaloosa. "I remember was that we lost four times to Kentucky," said Barnes. "I think they beat us by one point [actually two] in Tuscaloosa – I can still see the shot that Roger Harden hit against us [with five seconds left] – then beat us in the conference tournament and met them in the NCAA Tournament.

"Coach [Sanderson] is a great coach. He is a great personality. We stayed in touch through the years and has given me some great advice throughout the years. He has watched us play. He is just a real genuine person, and if you have ever been around him, he is a fun guy to be around. He is a terrific basketball coach. You think about where I have been. Everybody talks about me being at football schools. What he taught me is to just do your job and don't worry about football. He really embraced it. I remember the relationship he had with [Alabama football coach] Ray Perkins. They had a great relationship. He said, 'We've got a job. He has got a job. Let's just do our jobs.' Everywhere I have been, I have never looked at anything but our job. Let's do it the best that we can do it."

After the Crimson Tide game, Kentucky had to meet another team for the fourth time. The Wildcats had already beaten coach Dale Brown and his LSU Tigers three times. But third-ranked Kentucky was not so fortunate this time as LSU, using a balanced scoring attack with four double-digit scorers, won in a stunning 59-57 upset. Walker, a two-time All-American, finished his UK career with 20 points and seven rebounds. After the game, Coach Brown hugged and consoled a heartbroken Walker on the hardwood floor.

Even though Walker's game stats were respectable, LSU was able to limit the Wildcat star's effectiveness. "We mixed up our defenses and at times used the freak defense, which I created as a high school coach to defend Phil Jackson. Yes, the NBA Phil," Brown told the author in 2018. (Brown and Jackson both grew up in North Dakota.)

Brown said the 6-foot-8 Walker is one of the top basketball players he has ever seen. "In my 25 years of coaching in the SEC, Kenny is one of the very best," he said. "My two most vivid memories of him are every time he made a vertical jump, I felt he would go into orbit. The other was his sadness after our victory in the regional championship. I could not resist hugging him and complimented him on his brilliant career and how much I admired him. A class act and I love him."

When Walker came to UK from Georgia in 1982, Joe B. Hall was his coach at Kentucky. Hall and his assistants loved his basketball potential, and he was fun to watch. At Crawford County High School in Roberta, which is near Macon, Ga., Walker had helped his team to two straight state titles. The blue-chipper received *Parade* and McDonald's All-American honors. During his senior year in high school, he also appeared on the cover page of *The Cats' Pause* magazine and was thrilled to death. The black-and-white photo showed Walker soaring for a slam dunk.

Kenny Walker (left), Mike Pratt and Dave Baker during a pre-game show. (Photo by Jamie H. Vaught)

"What was so great about this picture is (then-publisher) Oscar Combs took this picture," Walker said. "It was the first time that he ever saw me play at my high school. He rarely took pictures. He says it is the best picture that he ever took. When I saw my picture on the cover of *The Cats' Pause*, I couldn't believe it. It was the biggest thing that ever happened to me up until that point."

Walker said he came to Kentucky "because of the fans and the great tradition of Kentucky basketball. Coach Joe B. Hall and assistant coach Leonard Hamilton did a great job of selling the program to me and my family."

Walker's parents were enthralled with Hall when he came to Georgia on a recruiting visit. "My parents were impressed with coach Joe B. Hall from day one," said Walker. "To be such a big-name coach he had such a down-home personality and a real people's person. My parents always loved and respected him for that."

After Hall retired following the somewhat disappointing 18-13 campaign in 1984-85, which included a strong finish with two NCAA Tournament victories in Salt Lake City, Utah, before losing to St. John's in Denver, Walker had a new coach, Eddie Sutton, who famously "crawled" to Lexington from Arkansas. Before signing a five-year contract at Kentucky, Sutton had an impressive resume as he rebuilt the Razorbacks program to an 11-year mark of 260-75, including five

Southwest Conference titles and a Final Four trip in 1978. The Kansas native was a two-time national coach of the year prior to his Kentucky days. While at Kentucky, Sutton also captured a couple of national coach of the year awards in 1986 (Associated Press and NABC).

Walker highly respected both of his UK coaches. "Joe B. Hall and Eddie Sutton were two great coaches," he said. "Joe B. Hall is like a father figure to me. He gave me the opportunity to showcase my talents at the University of Kentucky. I think he's a very underrated coach. Joe B. Hall is the only coach to follow a legend and have an outstanding coaching career.

"Coach Sutton was the best defensive coach that I ever played for. It was sad how his career ended at Kentucky [in 1989 due to NCAA investigation on the program]. If we didn't have to play LSU four times my senior year, Coach Sutton probably would've won a national championship here at Kentucky."

One of Walker's teammates was 6-foot-11, 240-pound Melvin Turpin, a "Twin Tower" product from Lexington Bryan Station who earned All-American honors en route to the 1984 NCAA Final Four in Seattle. Turpin, nicknamed "Dinner Bell Mel," was a happy-go-lucky guy who loved to eat, especially McDonald's cheeseburgers. And Walker has a favorite story involving Joe B. Hall and Turpin.

"One funny thing that I remember about Coach Hall was how difficult it was from him to keep Melvin Turpin from eating junk food and gaining weight," he said.

Turpin once poured in 42 points against both Georgia and Tennessee. An overall No. 6 pick of the 1984 NBA Draft by the Washington Bullets, Turpin played six years in the NBA. Sadly, in 2010, he committed suicide.

Walker was one of the main reasons why Kentucky had a Final Four team in 1983-84. The 29-5 Cats had a strong frontline. In addition to Walker, then a sophomore, UK had a pair of Twin Towers in 7-foot-1 Sam Bowie and Turpin. Walker was that squad's second-leading scorer, averaging 12.4 points.

One highlight was Walker's buzzer-beating basket in leading Kentucky to the SEC Tournament championship, defeating Coach Sonny Smith's Auburn club and future NBA standout Charles Barkley 51-49.

"The most memorable night for me at Kentucky was making the game-winning shot against Charles Barkley and Auburn," added Walker, who admitted his last field goal wasn't very pretty. The Georgia native hit six of seven shots for 12 points along with a game-high nine rebounds in that showdown played at Vanderbilt's Memorial Gymnasium.

Walker's former UK teammate was Roger Harden, a 6-foot-1 guard who was Indiana's Mr. Basketball and McDonald's All-American in 1982. The duo played together all four years in college. Harden was asked about Walker.

"My thoughts on Kenny Walker? Those of us who were role players could not have asked to play with a better superstar than Kenny Walker," said Harden, a former third-team All-SEC performer in 1986 who led the team in assists for two consecutive years. "He was humble and hard-working. He never put himself above those around him and never demanded anything from the ball to a saved seat. He could take a subpar lob pass and turn it into a *SportsCenter* highlight. [He] always showed up with effort and attitude."

For many years, it was a Kentucky tradition to have Happy Chandler – a huge UK fan who held major titles such as U. S. Senator, Governor, and Baseball Commissioner – sing "My Old Kentucky Home" on Senior Day (or Night) in an emotional ceremony for departing seniors and the Big Blue fans.

Speaking of 1986, the Wildcat seniors were popular 5-foot-5 backup guard Leroy Byrd, Harden, and Walker. The trio also were on the cover of *The Cats' Pause* preseason yearbook, posing with new coach Eddie Sutton.

Just like the other Senior Day ceremonies, 1986 was no exception. Walker said that was a major highlight of his Kentucky career. "A close second [as the most memorable UK moment] would be my Senior Day 1986, standing at center court of Rupp Arena with my mom and dad while Happy Chandler sang 'My Old Kentucky Home.' "

Harden agreed, "My most memorable experience as a Kentucky ball player was Senior Day vs. LSU. [I was being] summoned through a paper hoop with my image on it while my parents were on the court in Rupp with Happy Chandler singing 'My Old Kentucky Home' and 24,000 [fans], and thousands more on national TV and radio honoring your blood, sweat, and tears you gave to Big Blue Nation. I don't know who started that ceremony, but Hollywood could not have written a better ending to a player's career. Winning that day was icing on the cake."

That was a victorious day for the Wildcats, who defeated LSU 68-57 and finished the regular season on a high note with a 26-3 mark, including a 17-1 mark in SEC games. And Walker hit a team-high 17 points before heading to the bench in the closing seconds, receiving a standing ovation. Even LSU coach Dale Brown walked over to congratulate Walker before the game was officially over.

Earlier in their UK careers, Harden remembers a trip to Joe Hall's farm in Harrison County. "Coach Hall would take every freshman to his farm in Cynthiana as a matter of relationship-building. At least that's what he would say," commented Harden, who is No. 3 on UK's all-time list for assists. "I got a note from [the] basketball office that Coach would pick me and Kenny up on a Saturday at 7 a.m. to go to his farm.

"Well, we thought that was a sign that coach wanted to talk to us about our roles in basketball. It turned out when we got there, Kenny and I ended up weed-eating his whole farm and cleaned out his barn.

"We said, 'I bet Dean [Smith] doesn't do this to his players,' and Coach said, 'Dean doesn't have a farm.'"

During Walker's second and third NBA seasons, Rick Pitino helped rebuild the New York Knicks franchise back to respectability. In Pitino's first season at New York, the Knicks improved by 14 wins and reached the NBA playoffs for the first time in four seasons. In the following season, New York went 52-30 and advanced to the Eastern conference semifinals.

So, Walker – the No. 5 pick overall in the 1986 NBA Draft who later won the Slam Dunk championship during the 1989 All-Star Game festivities – knew Pitino well. When Pitino was being approached by Kentucky athletics director C.M. Newton about the UK head coaching post, the New York mentor had some concerns, so he asked Walker about the Kentucky environment.

"I was a little surprised when he asked me about the Kentucky job because he was doing so well as the New York Knicks head coach," Walker said. "I'm glad that he came to Kentucky because we needed someone like Rick Pitino at that time to help us get back to our great tradition. His wife was a little concerned about the culture in Kentucky because they both grew up in New York. I had several meetings with them and told her that her family will love the state of Kentucky. I think that's the reason why they came back to Louisville [later in 2001 after a four-year stint with the Boston Celtics]. Pitino was a great coach."

After a near-death penalty by the NCAA for breaking several rules, June 1, 1989, marked a rebirth of Kentucky Wildcats basketball. It was the historic day that Kentucky managed to attract young-looking Pitino away from the bright lights of New York City. He was chosen to coach the scar-marred Wildcats – who would face one year of no live television coverage and two years of no post-season tournament action due to NCAA penalty – and to restore Kentuckians' pride in the UK hoops program, becoming the youngest mentor in the SEC at the age of 36.

What was his most memorable conversation that Walker has had with Coach Hall after his UK playing days were over?

"The best memory or talk I had with Coach Hall was after I won the 1989 NBA Slam Dunk Contest," Walker recalled. "I had lost my father two days before the contest, and I talked to Coach Hall after he passed away. He told me how proud he was that I went out in such a difficult time to represent myself and my family and how proud he was of me and he knew that my father would be proud of me also." Remarkably, two former Wildcats later followed Walker's Slam Dunk Contest heroics during the NBA All-Star Weekend. John Wall captured the title in 2014, with Hamidou Diallo winning it in 2019.

Like the good and caring coach he was, Hall gave Walker a valuable advice. "Probably the best advice I got from Coach Hall while I was playing at UK was that he often talked about how important it was to be prepared to do your best and to have a great attitude," he said. "He said, 'If you could do those things, you can accomplish anything in life.' Those words stayed with me until this day."

Walker was asked who was the toughest player that he has ever faced or defended in his overall career?

"The best player that I played against was Michael Jordan [in the NBA]," he answered. "Fortunately for me, I never had to guard him a lot. The toughest player for me to guard was Larry Bird. Magic Johnson and Larry Bird were the two best players in the NBA before Michael Jordan's career took off."

Walker believes he would have been ready for the NBA after only one year at Kentucky if the one-and-done era had been in place during the 1980s. "If I was in college today, I think I could leave and go to the NBA after just one season," he said. "However, I'm glad that I stayed all four years at Kentucky because I needed each and every year at Kentucky to develop mentally and physically. The diet [programs] and technology are much better than it was when I was in school. The best thing about staying in school all four years is I had an opportunity to get my degree, and that is something that you can't put a price on even though these kids make a whole lot more money than I did when I first left UK."

Because he stayed at Kentucky for four years, Walker will remain as the men's second-leading scorer in school basketball history with 2,080 points for the foreseeable future.

Chapter Ten

College Basketball's Mr. Excitement

*T*his is just for fun. Can you picture Dick Vitale and Mark Twain together in your mind?

No, not really, but they are both celebrities from different eras. Twain, whose real name was Samuel Clemens, was a well-known writer whose famed novels like *The Adventures of Tom Sawyer* and *The Adventures of Huckleberry Finn* were published in the late 1800s. And Twain had numerous places named after him, including the Mark Twain Elementary School in Garfield, N.J. That's where Vitale, a television broadcaster for ESPN, got his first teaching job while coaching junior high school football and basketball.

That's where the amusing Vitale-Twain connection ends. And the opinionated Vitale is one of the most enthusiastic and unassuming people that you'll ever meet in your life. The face of college basketball – who, unquestionably, is a huge fan of UK hoops – gets excited when he is covering the games for ESPN, often saying one of his household phrases like "Awesome, Baby!" on the air. And he gets excited when he can raise millions of dollars for cancer research, especially for children who are suffering from this dreaded disease. He has an optimistic outlook about life in general.

In an exclusive interview with the author at the Vitale home in a gated community not far from St. Petersburg, Fla., he was asked where he got his positive or enthusiastic attitude from. "I've had this basically all my life," commented Vitale, who was wearing blue plaid short pants on this hot summer day. "I've been an enthusiastic guy. I was labeled 'Mr. Enthusiasm' growing up, really as a kid, and obviously I developed the passion and love for the game of basketball – the spirit, the competition – and got involved in coaching.

"But I'm always trying [to tell the audience in] my motivational talks about how if you live your life with a lot of energy…. I call it the threes: energy, enthusiasm, and excitement for life. If you have that with you every day, and you try to enjoy life to its fullest, I really believe you'll enjoy life a lot better, and I'm trying to do that. I've tried to have goals each day, things I want to achieve, things I want to accomplish, and I attack them as best I can.

"I control my emotion in terms of my passion, and so many people can do the same, but I want to be around people that are looking at the glass half-filled, not half-empty. Unfortunately, a lot of people will say, 'Well, the glass bottle is half empty.' I would say, 'It's half full' because I believe in being positive. If you think positive, have faith, and make good decisions, a lot of beautiful things are going to happen, and that's the way I've tried to attack life."

Before he became a household name as a sportscaster, Vitale had a very productive career in coaching basketball. After several years of coaching, including a successful seven-year stint at East Rutherford High School in New Jersey, Vitale moved on to the collegiate and pro ranks. "I started out lucky at about age 24 [when] I was named the head coach at my alma mater, East Rutherford High School," said Vitale. "At that time I got the job because, not that I had any ability, nobody wanted it and they gave it to me. And in a matter of seven years that I was there, we won four sectional state championships, we won two back-to-back state championships, went undefeated [at] 35-0, won our last 35 games. And from that, I got a chance to go to Rutgers University as an assistant [for two years]."

On recruiting during his two years at Rutgers, Vitale remembers one special moment. "As an assistant at Rutgers I was thrilled to get a commitment from the best player in the nation, Phil Sellers, who ultimately led Rutgers to the Final Four in 1976," he said. "No one could believe that we would be able to compete with the great schools who wanted him. We knew that we had a great deal to offer him since he was from the New York area and could become a superstar playing for Rutgers, the State University of New Jersey." A first-team All-American, Sellers, at the time of this writing, is the school's all-time leading scorer and rebounder.

Then Vitale became the head coach at the University of Detroit, a post he held for four years during the mid-1970s, posting an overall mark of 78-30, a 72.2 winning percentage. His 1976-77 Titans squad finished with a 25-4 mark, including a victory over eventual national champion Marquette, which was coached by Al McGuire, in Milwaukee and an NCAA Sweet Sixteen appearance at Rupp Arena. While in Lexington that season, Vitale got to meet a very important man who had been out of coaching for five years. That man's name was Adolph Rupp. The Vitale-Rupp encounter was a very short one, though.

"I met Adolph Rupp during that time for two minutes basically," he said. "Certainly [he is] one of the legends of all time. It was one those quick 'Hi, how are you doing' kind of things. Never sat with him, but he was in the gym. I was a nobody back then."

As it turned out, Vitale's last game as a college coach was at Rupp Arena, when his 12th-ranked Titans battled against No. 1 Michigan and Coach Johnny Orr in the Mideast Regional semifinals, losing 86-81. And Rupp passed away several months later on Dec. 10, 1977. (That 1977 Detroit-Michigan matchup, by the way, was replayed on television recently in the Detroit area.) Vitale then became the athletics director at Detroit, a position he held for one year.

Even when Vitale was coaching in college during the 1970s, he looked forward to getting a copy of the highly regarded *Street & Smith's* hoops yearbook when it hit the newsstands. During the pre-Internet days, the publication was a very valuable source of information.

"As a fanatical basketball fan, I always was very anxious to get a copy of *Street & Smith*," recalled Vitale. "It was always fun to see who were projected to be the best players and the best teams, and [I] also enjoyed their coverage of the high school superstars."

Vitale has some thoughts about Rupp's successor, Joe B. Hall, and current UK coach John Calipari. He was tickled when Hall was named to the National Collegiate Basketball Hall of Fame in 2012. While Calipari's Cats were winning the 2012 national championship in New Orleans, Hall and other newly named Hall of Famers were recognized on the floor during the NCAA Final Four.

"I was happy for Joe B. Hall to finally get recognized like he did for the College Hall of Fame because I don't think people ever gave him the kind of recognition he deserves for the years he dedicated himself to Kentucky basketball," Vitale said. "You know he won the '78 national title with [Rick] Robey, [Mike] Phillips and that gang. They did a phenomenal job. I've been on a show with him and [ex-U of L coach] Denny Crum. Lots of fun."

Unlike UCLA, which struggled to find coaching stability after John Wooden retired even though the Bruins had modest success, Hall was able to maintain UK's success after he replaced Rupp, with eight regular-season SEC titles and three Final Four trips.

Dick Vitale at his Florida home. (Photo by Jamie H. Vaught)

Added Vitale, "Well, you know, John Wooden was an amazing story. John Wooden won 10 national titles. To follow that, seven out of 10 years, people in L.A., first of all, not like Kentucky, [have] one thing that they're really thinking about [what to do]. There's so much to do [in L.A.]. You've got the Lakers, you got the movie industry, you got Hollywood, you got the Dodgers, you got the Kings in hockey. If you don't win it all and you don't have a great, great team, they're not coming out.

"In Kentucky it's all basketball. I don't care if Kentucky is 10-18. They are still going to have a great crowd come to their games because people eat, sleep, drink basketball. Certainly, John Wooden was unique to me. As tough as it is, it's going to be tough [at Duke] to follow Mike Krzyzewski. That is going to be another tough, tough situation, but certainly John Wooden was rare and unique. I mean, his winning was off the charts."

At the Wildcat Coal Lodge dormitory near the Joe Craft Center and Memorial Coliseum, Hall has an extraordinary statue in his honor on the UK campus. Commented Vitale, who has seen the unusual sculpture showing the former Wildcat boss in his bronzed seat, "I personally feel the statue is a nice tribute for his dedication to Kentucky basketball. And I have no problem with Joe sitting down [with a rolled-up program in his hand]."

Vitale and Calipari are both members of the Naismith Memorial Basketball Hall of Fame. Over the years, both have shared ideas and teased each other. "I love being around John," said Vitale. "John excites me. We've shared opinions with one another because we made the jump from college to the pros. We've shared conversations about treatment of people, about certain things to do, not to do, or how to handle this.

"[When] John Calipari was winning in Massachusetts, they'll tell you the story. And I called them up. I showed the picture where he was living. I said, 'Come on, John. With all your money you're making now, you can do better than that, man. Go buy a beautiful new house.' Well, he laughs and he says to me when he sees me, 'Did you see my house now in Lexington, Dickie V? Things have changed.'

"Also you'll walk in [to his office or practice], he'll say, 'Boy, we had a tough one today. Oh, man, they're this, and they're that.' I said, 'John, come on now. You're loaded [with star players], man. They're going to be saying that about you. They're all typical, coach, always expecting that we might not play to your ability.'

"He took my wife [Lorraine] and I for a tour of the basketball facilities. I was in awe and teased John that, if he could not recruit the blue-chip stars to Big Blue Nation, he is the worst recruiter in the world. John laughed. He is fun to be around. [He] showed us the new dorm for the players, and it blew us away. He was hysterical when I said, 'This is a little different than your early days in coaching.' " And Vitale probably told Coach Cal, using one of his famous catch phrases, "This place is awesome, Baby!"

With Calipari's NCAA problems at Massachusetts and Memphis, his outgoing personality as well as coaching philosophy, the Kentucky boss has been misunderstood by some folks, according to Vitale. The criticisms of Coach Cal have been mostly unfair. Some people also are just plain jealous of his extraordinary success. There have been many "hate" lists around. For instance, *USA Today* in 2013 published a list of 10 most hated coaches in college basketball. Interestingly, three individuals with UK ties were on that list. They include Calipari, Rick Pitino, and Adolph Rupp. *Sports Illustrated* and *Bleacher Report*, among others, also had Calipari on a similar list.

"I think a lot of that [dislike] comes from the fact what transpired at Massachusetts, transpired at Memphis, which I thought it was unfairly labeled by a lot of the fans because the NCAA totally cleared him from any situation, any involvement," explained Vitale. "But I think he went in on a hill. When you're on the top of a mountain, and you're making mega, mega millions, there's envy out there, and people want to knock you down. They want you down in that valley. They'll help you maybe get up there, but once you get there it's like the

[New York] Yankees. It's like Notre Dame football, Duke basketball, Kentucky basketball. People want to knock them down. It's sad, in a way. It's sad.

"John Calipari is a good person. John Calipari's got a heart of gold. John Calipari obviously communicates a great deal in the media, and some of his comments rub people the wrong way. I think all of that sometimes is the reason that people want to take shots. He has a little bit of that swag about him, and people don't like that. You know what? He's a winner. What he has done has been amazing [in taking] all of those young players [to become a success]. I had somebody tell me, 'John Calipari has ruined basketball with the one-and-done.' And I looked him in the eye, and I said to the guy, 'Do you know what you're talking about?'

"John Calipari is simply better than all the others who want the same kids but can't get those kids. You don't think another school would want a Julius Randle? Who wouldn't want a John Wall? Who wouldn't want some of these greats that he's had over the years? Give me a break! He's just been better. He didn't make the rule. John didn't make the one-and-done rule. All he's doing is going out, trying to get the best players for his program, and they happen to be players, most of the time, who will stay for one year and leave. They see the success that the former guys have had in going to the NBA, and they say, 'You know what? He's right.' He's not just telling a story. Look at the list. I mean, Mike Krzyzewski's got one-and-done with [Jabari] Parker, [Kyrie] Irving, and [Jahlil] Okafor coming in. I mean, I think that's an unfair rap he has about the one-and-done because my argument is, he's just better than the other ones in recruiting them."

If and when he decides to retire from coaching down the road, many observers seem to think Coach Cal has a good future in television broadcasting as a color analyst, and Vitale agrees. "I don't think there is any doubt that Coach Calipari would make the transition from coaching to television when he decides that he has had enough of the sidelines," commented Vitale. "He has all the qualities that the TV executives would look for. He is very quick-witted and has a response to almost any situation. My simple advice to John Calipari would be to not try and be 'Mr. Perfect,' as people can tell when someone is not being themselves."

What is the craziest thing that Vitale has seen about the rabid Big Blue Nation? "What I have seen over the years in Big Blue Nation are fans who are unbelievably loyal and passionate," he said. "They eat, sleep, and drink Kentucky basketball. In my four decades I have never seen any fan base with such a hoops-hysteria attitude. No other college has the fan interest on the road like the Big Blue Nation."

After several years at University of Detroit, Vitale was named the head coach of the NBA's Detroit Pistons in 1978. He stayed there for a little over one year, compiling a 34-60 record. In his second NBA season (1979-80), Vitale was fired when his team got off to a poor 4-8 start. He had found coaching success in the college ranks, winning 73 percent of the time, but not in the NBA, where he won 36 percent of the games. Why? Same thing happened to Rick Pitino and Calipari years later when the duo struggled in the NBA.

"I think a lot of guys in college have had a struggle going through the professional ranks because we have the mentality with practice sessions and all, a lot different than the pros," Vitale explained. "And not being a former pro player, you don't understand their lifestyle or what they're going through. And my superstar, Bob Lanier, used to come in all the time and say, 'Dick, we can't have these two-and-a-half-hour practices. Intensity. We're playing three, four times a week.'

"And I didn't want to hear it, but he was right. And that's why I think I belonged in college. I didn't belong in the NBA. But I went because, you know, ego, dollars, money. Wow, in seven years, I was in the sixth grade as a teacher in 1971, coaching high school [and then] I'm coaching in the NBA. My career was exploding, and I just really made a bad, bad move. I belonged in college. But you know what? That's what life is, though. Life is you have ups, you have downs, and how you battle those downs separates, a lot of times, the person that's the winner and the loser. You got to take those bumps. You're not getting to the top of the mountain without taking some bumps."

Did Vitale miss coaching? "Yeah, I did, in a certain way. I love TV," he said. "But I do know this. Knowing my personality, I couldn't handle losing. Losing tore my heart out. If I would've stayed in coaching, I would've been dead by 50."

Vitale began his new career at fledging ESPN in 1979, shortly after the network's launch in September of that year. He called the new 24-hour sports network's first-ever major NCAA basketball game between Wisconsin and DePaul. And his TV tenure skyrocketed.

"So many things began to happen in my career [along with] books and TV commercials, and I've been playing roles in different movies, cameo appearances, speaking again. I mean it exploded to where coaching was no longer even an option," said Vitale. "But my wife loved this lifestyle a lot better because, when you're coaching, it's 24/7. It's every minute, every day you're worried about losing this player, that player. You're worried about keeping the media happy, worried about winning. It's a nightmare. But let me tell you, they're [coaches] earning it. They're earning it with the pressure they face."

Vitale, as a broadcaster, has seen numerous games at Rupp Arena, and many of them are memorable. Not surprisingly, he had difficulties in picking out his favorite Kentucky contest at Rupp Arena.

"Man, I've seen so many over the years," said the announcer. "Well, my God, there's been so many great ones. The one thing, Rupp's always one of my favorite places because fans are so passionate. I've always said that Kentucky fans are the most passionate fans in all of basketball. Their love sometimes even goes a step too far, but they have such a love. And Rupp, with the Big Blue Nation, is always special. I mean, I can't single out a game. I know there's been so many great ones over the years. Even the Kenny Walker era had some great matchups. I remember one that stood out for me [in 2003]. Florida came in No. 1 in the nation, and they came to Rupp. Kentucky put a beating on them that was unbelievable. It was a blowout [a 70-55 win by Tubby Smith's Wildcats, who had a 45–22 halftime margin]. We were all pumped up on TV [with Florida] No. 1 in the nation. Kentucky laid it on them with a brilliant performance."

His most embarrassing moment on television? "I've had too many, man," said Vitale, who has been broadcasting for around 40 years. "I've had many embarrassing moments. Oh, wow. Funny embarrassing moment because I didn't know about TV. I did the very first game, the DePaul-Wisconsin [contest] on ESPN in 1979. I looked at it [the video] the other day. I couldn't believe it. We did the opening, and the guy Joe Boyle I was working with says, 'Hi, everybody, first game at ESPN, I'm here with Dick Vitale.' I literally went on. If it were today, I would have been crucified. I went on nonstop – if you go to the tape and look at it – over two minutes straight. I hope he [Boyle] didn't get paid by the word because if he did, he would make no money."

As a broadcaster, Boyle, who died in 2017, also covered several sports in Minnesota, including the Major League Baseball's Twins and National Hockey League's North Stars (now located in Dallas).

In 2019, Vitale signed another contract extension with ESPN through the 2021-22 season, working as a game analyst in key matchups each week during the regular season, among other duties.

Unlike the old days, when college basketball had a handful of colorful coaches, a fan today will struggle to find a few in the coaching ranks who are outspoken. Years ago, you would read about or watch well-known coaches like Jimmy Valvano, Al McGuire, Rick Majerus, Bobby Knight, John Thompson, and Dale Brown in their lively interviews. They were good copies for the media. They were not afraid to be controversial and spoke from the heart.

"Coaches [today] are more reserved in their comments," said Vitale. "You can almost project and predict what a press conference is going to be. It's almost blasé. We don't have the characters that we had years ago. I mean these guys, really, were unbelievable. You never knew what was going to come out of their mouth, and they had some flamboyance and charisma. We don't seem to have that. I think a lot of that is because the coaches are protected. I think we live in a day and age today where the social media has really created a nightmare in many cases. Anything you do, it's just bam! It's all over. It goes viral so quickly. We got guys at talk radio [shows] now that we didn't have years ago. On talk radio, [they] say anything they want, ripping guys and never have to face them [or] never look them in the eye. Because of that, coaches, I think, have become a little bit more backed away from sharing what they want to share."

Some basketball fans, including UK, have complained about Vitale's TV presentation on ESPN, basically saying he talks too much about the other stuff, not the game he's covering, but the announcer still has a good share of followers.

"This man is an unabashed supporter of college basketball who has given his adult life promoting the game, its coaches, and its players," said Julian Tackett, the commissioner of Kentucky High School Athletics Association. "And the entirety of his free time is spent on charitable causes such as the V Foundation. Thankfully, he ignores his critics and just does what he is paid to do. For the right reasons. Thank you, Dick, for all you have done and continue to do."

Added John Ferguson, the former student manager who was on Adolph Rupp's last two teams at UK, "Vitale loves basketball – all basketball. I met him when he walked into Coach Rupp's office when his team, Detroit, [played] in the Mideast Regionals. He is a very genuine person."

In his profession, Vitale knows that he certainly "can't please everyone, but I have been blessed that the fans have treated me like royalty over the years. I am proud to say that my career has exceeded any of my dreams, as I just recently received the ultimate honor of being inducted into the national Sports Broadcasting Hall of Fame along with Bob Costas, Jim Nantz, Mary Carillo, and several others. To have a career that has given me so many special moments has been a blessing, and I feel very fortunate that I'm in the Naismith Basketball Hall of Fame and the National Collegiate Basketball Hall of Fame and the Sports Broadcasting Hall of Fame."

Joe B. Hall, who once served as a TV commentator for the ABC network, was asked many years ago if Vitale is too outspoken. "Dick Vitale is probably the most identifiable, controversial person in the media covering basketball in the world," Hall said. "Yes, he is too outspoken, but he always has an opinion and says it very forcefully, and you can take it or leave it. People are interested in what he says. There are people who like him very much and those who don't. He is knowledgeable and has a style and personality that come across in an exciting way."

The recent college basketball mess, which was uncovered by the FBI in 2017, has bothered Vitale. "The FBI scandal that broke initially shocked me, as it did many people in basketball, as it seemed like it was only the beginning of many negative and sad situations breaking out in the game I love," he said in early 2018. "We have not found out much since the initial reports, but what is so troubling to me is to read about coaches who were taking money from agents and representatives. These people are truly sleaze bags. It is sad to learn that coaches who were indicted were taking money to sell kids. To me, this is like a form of prostitution. Anyone who is found guilty of such behavior should be penalized in a most severe manner. Let's make it very clear that the game will survive because, in spite of this scandal, there are a lot of good and honest people in college basketball."

During the 1940s and '50s, Vitale grew up in New Jersey with his loving parents. In addition, he had many aunts and uncles whom he spent a lot of time with. Vitale and his wife returned to his childhood homes several years ago, and it brought back lots of warm memories. What would his mother and father think about their son and his success, including induction into the Naismith Memorial Basketball Hall of Fame in 2008, the highest honor given to anyone associated with the sport?

"My mother and father were phenomenal. I miss them so much," said Vitale, who celebrated his 80th birthday in June 2019. "My mom and dad had a doctorate of love. They were uneducated. They didn't have a formal education, but they taught me in this great country that if you have pride about yourself, passion about yourself, a lot of beautiful things are going to happen. My parents were hard-working, blue-collar people.

"My wife and I just went on a trip on memory lane. When I went to New Jersey, I was honored by my alma mater, Seton Hall, as the Humanitarian of the Year. And when I went back there, we took a trip where I lived in my first house, when I was up until about 14 years of age, at 372 Madeline Avenue, Garfield, New Jersey. I took a picture of the house to show my grandkids. We had like one bathroom, but the house was filled was so much love. And then I took a journey to my second house, where I lived from about 14 to about 30-ish, and that was on 121 Fencsak Avenue, Elwood Park, New Jersey, and we took a picture of that.

"I took a picture of the high school [East Rutherford High] that I coached at where we won back-to-back state championships, and we had a gym that was probably 65 x 35. It was a small bandbox that we practiced in, played our games the last year, all on a roll. What great memories!

"But my memories start at my home. My mother and father had nine brothers and sisters [each]. My mom had five brothers, four sisters. My father had four brothers and five sisters. And they're all gone now, that breaks my heart. All 18 have passed, but I used to learn so much after church on Sundays. All of my uncles would come over, and my mother would have bagels, coffee, and cake. We would sit and argue about sports. That's where I developed my love for sports.

"[As for] all my uncles and all my aunts, they were about one thing: family. Family, family, family. They were blue collar. They were all factory workers. They never missed a day's work. They were out there to take care of their family. They worked in shoe factories. My father pressed coats in a factory. A place where he busted his gut, the more clothes he pressed in a sweatshop, the more money he made.

"And then he'd come home at night, eat for an hour, put a security guard uniform on, and go walk the mall 6 to 12, I can't even imagine the look on my father and mother's face if they saw the house I live in today, and what's happened in my life. But it would've never happened without the love, the direction, and guidance."

Not surprisingly, Vitale loved sports as a kid. Some of his favorite athletes growing up were Mickey Mantle, Yogi Berra, and Oscar Robertson. "The Big O when he played for the Cincinnati Royals," said Vitale of Robertson. His favorite team? "I always rooted for local teams," he said. "My favorite teams were New York Yankees, Boston Celtics and New York Giants, and I have been a lifelong Notre Dame football fan."

While he had a lot of family support and love at home, Vitale's childhood wasn't all that smooth. He had some rough days. And he was a victim of bullying, a serious problem usually involving unwelcome, aggressive behavior among the school-aged children. "A lot of people don't know this. I lost my eye as a kid," Vitale said. "I'm blind in my left eye."

When he was a very little boy, Vitale had a terrible accident. His left eye was poked with a pencil. He recalled his parents trying to save his eye, going from doctor to doctor. So, he ended up wearing a glass eye. Some of the school kids, unfortunately, began to bully him and rudely called him names like "One Eye."

Vitale said these incidents have caused him considerable pain. In his 2014 book, *It's Awesome, Baby!*, he mentioned that he was even too shy to ask the girls for a date during his teenage years because of that bad eye.

"I always thought it was teasing," he told the author. "But it was bullying. I went through a cycle where I would come home and go up to my room. I'd cry because my eye used to drift to the side, and I didn't want to tell my parents. It doesn't do that now. I had an operation. But I could never look somebody straight in the eye, and people would say, 'Hey! Who are you looking at? Can you see us?' And it would hurt because you couldn't control it. Yeah, I faced that. But you know what? I try to advise people now: Please don't hurt people. Be good to people. People will be good to you. I wrote an article about being bullied as a kid, and it became an article that got a lot of attention."

Because of his caring parents, Vitale eventually maintained a positive attitude about his disability. They encouraged him to reach for the stars. A faithful Catholic who rarely misses a Sunday Mass even when he is on the road, Vitale recalls a couple of valuable pieces of advice. He hasn't forgotten them, and his mother called him Richie, not Dick.

Vitale added, "She taught me two things. One, she's always said to me, 'Richie, don't ever believe in 'can't.' This is America. You can be what you want to be.' And the second thing they taught me to always believe: Be good to people. I must've heard that 10 times a day. Be good to people, and people will be good to you. And I've tried to use that in my life, every day of my life. I act and I feel like [I'm] 12 because I get excited about life. I try to take care of myself, I try to do anything I do for people to the best of my ability."

Vitale was asked who is the first person he would like to see in heaven? "Boy, the first person I'd like to see in heaven? My father and my mother. The two of them," said Vitale. "Yeah, I'd love to see them and say thank you. None of this

[his career success] comes without them believing in me, guiding me, constantly telling me to do the right thing, and I've tried to do that. I've tried to live by a very simple formula I learned as a youngster: passion plus work ethic plus good decision-making equals 'W' in the game of life.

"A lot of guys, they don't have passion. A lot of guys maybe have a great spirit or a work ethic, but then they [are] destroyed because they don't make a good decision about drugs, about alcohol, about how to treat people. And they ruined it all. I've been trying to always remember that formula, to let that be part of my life on a daily basis."

Vitale's said his Catholic faith is important in his life. He makes a special effort to attend a Mass wherever he's at – home or on the road. "I don't believe in promoting [it in] people's [lives]. I just try to live my life the best I can," said Vitale, who showed the author his rosaries that he keeps in the drawer of his large office desk. "I will simply tell you this: I cannot remember missing Sunday Mass in over 25 years. If I'm physically able – I'm not sick and I'm not laid up – I will find that one hour to get to church. That's just my [way]. I was brought up that way. My mother had a stroke, and she would drag her leg and walk like a mile and a half, two miles, every day. She wouldn't go to church once a week [but] every day. And I used to watch her, and I'd say, 'Mom, you can go on Sunday. Why you got to go every day?'

"So, Catholic religion was part of my life. My daughters, whom I'm very proud of, both went to Notre Dame, did their masters in Notre Dame. I went to Seton Hall. It's a Catholic university. But again, I respect anybody's beliefs. You have a right. That's why we live in the greatest country of all, to believe the way you want to believe. And I love people."

The Vitales got a thrilling visit with Pope Benedict during their 2011 summer vacation when they journeyed to Italy. Vitale, who is of Italian ancestry, was so excited that he tweeted about his memorable encounter with the Pope afterwards.

Even when there are no college basketball games to cover in the summer, the New Jersey native finds a way to stay really busy. "I'm very active," said Vitale, a friendly grandfather who regularly keeps his fans informed about his daily activities all year around with stories, comments or pictures on social media.

"I'm a very big baseball fan. And obviously I have season tickets with the [Tampa Bay] Rays. So, I go to quite a few baseball games. Then I do a lot of travel, a lot of motivational speaking. Just got back from California and spoke for U.S. Trust [which is a part of Bank of America]. So, I do a lot of motivational speaking, which keeps me busy. I've got five grandchildren who are very active in tennis, baseball and lacrosse, and I go watch them play and have a great time. I work with them a little bit on basketball, and I have a little fun. They're in the area here in Lakewood Ranch. I have a full day [along with daily tennis and exercise]."

Despite his age, Vitale has lots of energy, saying he feels "like I'm 25…. I try to keep myself in good condition. This morning I played tennis, I worked out, I try to walk a minimum [of] at least 45 minutes to an hour every day if I don't play tennis. I try to do a little light weights, I have machines upstairs, Nautilus, all that, and I try to take care of myself. I try to watch what I eat. I think one of the lucky things for me is I've never been a drinker, and I've never smoked, and I don't do drugs. I can, honestly, truly say I don't play those games. And I think all that has helped me get me this energy and spirit. And with that, I have people say how do I get the work? I don't know. God will know that, my bosses will know that, but as long as they want me, as long as I feel I'm able, I'll go on until one day the man upstairs…. See, we all have a clock, and the clock's going to come to an end. I know that. The clock ends for everybody. There's a time the clock stops. Right now, my clock is running. And as long as it's running, I'm going to keep running."

Then the popular college basketball ambassador mentioned that he would be leaving for New York City the next day for two formal engagements when he would receive a couple of honors – Man of the Year by the American Cancer Society and Court of Honor by the National Association of Basketball Coaches Foundation.

"I'm getting one of the highest honors [by the American Cancer Society] – a very humbling effect," added Vitale, who tirelessly has been promoting and raising millions of dollars for cancer research for many years, especially in the area of pediatric cancer.

In addition to Vitale, the past recipients for the Court of Honor Award from the NABC Foundation have included folks like Phil Knight, Jerry Colangelo, Jim Nantz, John Thompson Jr., George Raveling, and Bill Bradley. "To be there in mention with those kind of people just gives me goosebumps," said Vitale.

Along with his family and basketball, fighting cancer has become one of Vitale's biggest passions. Vitale has been on a heartfelt crusade in combating that atrocious disease with his fundraising projects. He gets very emotional when discussing the cancer-stricken kids and about helping them.

A huge event dear to Vitale's heart in waging the war on cancer is his annual gala at nearby Sarasota, attracting big-name celebrities such as John Calipari and Alabama football coach Nick Saban. Former UK assistant Leonard Hamilton was one of three honorees at the 2018 Dick Vitale Gala. Hamilton, now the head coach at Florida State, has had several of his family members pass away because of cancer. He was very pleased to be a part of this cancer-fighting program.

"My grandmother died from cancer, my father, my mother and two of my brothers who I loved dearly have also been taken, so I have had a history of people in my family who have been affected by cancer," said Hamilton.

"There is no doubt that my family has been affected by cancer. We talk about it, care about others who have gone through it, and try to be as encouraging as possible to those going through it. It's life's work and something we are committed to as a family. The time is now to find a solution. We can all play a part in finding the cure."

The annual Dick Vitale Gala has raised millions of dollars for pediatric cancer research with the V Foundation, a nonprofit organization dedicated to finding a cure for cancer and established by ESPN and the late Jim Valvano in 1993.

The spirited Vitale is firmly committed to the war on cancer. "I'm so entrenched now and to my last breath I'm going to plead with people to donate to help me," said Vitale in his nicely decorated home office, which includes a framed Hall of Fame jersey on the wall. "If you look behind my desk, you see all these articles. These articles are all from my gala, my Dick Vitale Gala, we just had. Joe Craft was there, and we got a big donation out of Kentucky. John Calipari gave us a big donation this year. And we dedicate all of mine now to kids, all the pediatrics. I have gotten to know so many beautiful kids over the years. I mean, I'll be honest with you. I was crying this morning, and I met a dad who came to visit me. I got to know him and his family, and he lost his son.

"And I've become so obsessed with raising money. You saw me give my wife a couple of envelopes. What I do is I mail new articles or notes to big corporate CEOs and say, 'If you can help us, man, people can make it,' and they donate through the V Foundation for kids battling cancer. There's nothing dearer to me.

"Cancer's a vicious disease, and tomorrow I'm getting the American Cancer Society's Man of the Year award, but you know what? A lot of people on my team deserve those awards. I have a great team. My team consists of my family, my ESPN family, and my friends. Those three parts really are so valuable to me in where I've gone with my wife. But my biggest mission now is raising money.

"I'm living a life that's exceeded any dream, and I want it to go on and on as anybody does, but I want to be able to raise dollars for cancer, so please just tell people, go to dickvitaleonline.com and make a donation. They might save someone they love, save a child they love. No kid should be doing chemo with radiation. They should be playing. I spoke at a funeral in my area, here, for a little boy [who was five years old] who lost his life, and I've spoken at black-tie events, corporate events. It was the toughest speech ever, watching a mom and dad put their little child to rest. That shouldn't happen."

During the mid-2000s, Vitale had a throat issue. It was an extremely difficult time because he uses his loud voice to make a living. As it turned out, he had a cancer scare in 2007 when he had a vocal cord surgery, sidelining him for a while. "It really gave me a perspective to understand what people go through that are waiting for a biopsy to come back," Vitale said. "You wait and wait till that phone rings because that could change your life. That one little moment could change your life: the way you live, your lifestyle. It was a nerve-wracking time. I ended up having ulcerated lesions on my throat, which were called dysplasia, which is pre-cancer. They're pre-cancerous cells that you have to monitor and take care of, and we've tried to do that, and who knows, [it may] change tomorrow.

"But I constantly try to do the best I can. What I do over the years and all, I've used my throat a lot. Man, I've used it. It's sad, though. At that time, I was really down because I couldn't even echo the words that I wanted to echo. And I had such fear coming out of my mouth. Really. Surgery certainly helped me."

Lorraine Vitale, an attractive and pleasant lady who was at home during this interview, sometimes will travel with her husband when he is on the road for ESPN telecasts or to give a speech at a corporate event. Dick Vitale is thankful he has her to help with his work. They have been married for nearly 50 years.

"My wife, sometimes in certain games, travels with me when I'm going to go away for more than one day," he said. "But if I'm going to go just there and back, she doesn't. But it's family, we do a lot together. To me, there's nothing like family, sharing time with your people. That's important to me. There's nothing more important. There's 11 in my family now. I got five grandkids, my two daughters, their husbands and my wife and I [for a] total of 11. We all live about five minutes apart.

"My wife has been valuable to my family. I'm tell you she's a genuine superstar. I'm lucky that my daughters don't look like their father. I'm happy they look like their mother, and I'm happy they have their mother's intelligence, not their father's, but we're, my wife and I, inseparable, and she's been vital to me. She's been so good to my family, my kids, and she's just a beautiful woman. I've been blessed."

Vitale – who rarely eats his meals at his home because he loves to be surrounded by people – is one of the kindest persons you'll ever meet in the sporting world. As mentioned earlier, he has faithfully raised money for cancer research and awareness. The TV celebrity remembers his humble beginnings in New Jersey. He rarely turns down an autograph request from a fan. He loves people. Where did he get his kindness from?

"I learned at a very young age from my mom and dad, who were not formally educated but had a 'doctorate of love,' to be good to people and people would be good to me," said Vitale. "In my lifetime I have found this to be very true, as so many people have extended a hand to me and assisted me in my career. I pinch myself when I think about the honors and awards that have come my way. I firmly believe that many good things have happened to me because I followed this mantra of trying to be good to others. I do a great deal of motivational speaking and love to share stories about the game we all play. I firmly believe that if a person has passion and a sense of pride in whatever they do, they will be a success in pursuing their dreams."

Chapter Eleven

Cawood's Sidekick

*D*uring the late 1970s, the author was starting out in journalism, writing for the campus newspaper, *Kentucky Kernel,* as an ambitious student reporter and then as sports editor at UK. One of the more friendly media-type folks at Commonwealth Stadium (now Kroger Field) and Rupp Arena at the time was none other than Ralph Hacker, who often had a warm smile for everyone, including yours truly. Before a Kentucky Wildcat game, we the media usually would gather around tables in the press box, having a snack or a pregame meal that was provided by the university, and discuss that day's popular topics. We talked about sports, politics, family or whatever came to mind.

And when you think about UK's broadcasting teams over several decades, Hacker would be on the list, joining other announcers like Cawood Ledford, Claude Sullivan and J.B. Faulconer, as well as the current team of Tom Leach and Mike Pratt.

Before retiring from his radio work in 2001, Hacker had a major role in the UK Radio Network for 34 years. A native of Richmond, Ky., where he began his radio career at the age of 15, Hacker and his partner, legendary Cawood Ledford, were one of the country's top broadcasting teams in collegiate ranks while covering UK football and basketball for 20 years. After Ledford called his last game, the classic Kentucky-Duke NCAA Tournament showdown in 1992, Hacker took over and became the team's play-by-play man and covered UK's 1996 and 1998 national title teams.

"I began covering UK football and basketball in 1966, at that point being a reporter and sometimes play-by-play announcer for WVLK-AM in Lexington," said Hacker. "Being nearly the same age as most of the players, I was able to get to know them in a very friendly way; they learned they could trust me with what to and what not to report. In other words, they learned I was not there to break a story but to tell a story, their story, in a positive way. This served me well through all of my days of covering the Wildcats."

Hacker knew Cawood Ledford well as they worked and traveled together for numerous years. They were good friends and shared stories. To many older generations of Wildcat fans who listened to him on the radio, Ledford was simply a beloved figure who later had his jersey retired at UK even though he wasn't a former player or a coach. He was the radio "Voice of the Wildcats" for 39 years.

"Cawood Ledford was a unique person," commented Hacker. "We were on the air together for 20 years, but in all reality worked together for more years than that. There were many nights, even though sitting right beside him, I would close my eyes and see the game through his eyes. He was amazing.

"There are so many Cawood stories. In Year One, UK was playing Florida in 'Alligator Alley.' There was no real doubt about Kentucky winning, but late in the game, the Gators made a run and the Florida cheerleaders jumped to their feet right in front of us and began cheering. Cawood turned to me and said, 'Ralph, tell those cheerleaders to quit shaking those fuzzy things in my face.' I replied on the air, 'Those are pompoms, Cawood.'

"Perhaps that was a payback from our first season together when I believe it was the Dayton [game] in the UKIT in Memorial Coliseum as the official made what Cawood thought was a horrific call. After much ranting and raving, he turned to me and said, 'What do you think about that, Ralph?' I replied, 'I don't know, Cawood. It was too far away for me to see.'

"With a look that could have killed, he said, 'Ralph the Lionhearted, sitting right next to me and 18 years my junior with perfect eyesight and no guts.' Perhaps that is where the term, 'That's right, Cawood,' was born.

"Cawood was more than my on-air partner. He was my friend, confidant, closest thing I had to a big brother, and I never wanted his job as long as he wanted to work. I knew my job, and that was to fill in the blank spots if there should be any."

Well-known retired broadcaster Jim Host, a former UK baseball standout who later pioneered in the collegiate sports marketing industry, said Ledford had a great understanding of Kentuckians who cheered for the Big Blue. "Cawood was from Harlan and probably understood the Kentucky fans and what UK meant to them all better than any announcer could," said Host, who was honored by the Naismith Memorial Basketball Hall of Fame in 2018 when he received the John W. Bunn Lifetime Achievement Award.

"I heard Coach Rupp tell Cawood one time, 'Cawood, if my boys are not playing well, then tell the fans, "By Gawd, Coach Rupp's boys are not playing well because they are not playing as Coach Rupp told them to."' Cawood would not say that exactly, but he had no problem reporting exactly what was going on on the floor or the field.

"Cawood had a distinct style and knew when to get excited and when not to. Ralph [Hacker] was the right complement to him for 21 years. I contend and will always feel that Ralph and Cawood were the best duo of all time in the college announcing space."

Sadly, Ledford passed away in his hometown of Harlan, Ky., in 2001 after a long battle with cancer. His wife, Frances, died in 2018, also in Harlan.

When he was 15, Hacker began to do some work as a disc jockey at a local radio station in Richmond and covered the local high school games. And the youngster eventually served as broadcaster at Eastern Kentucky Colonels football games when future TV star Lee Majors (Harvey Lee Yeary) was on the squad during the early 1960s. Why did he want to be a radio guy?

"Once I realized I would never be a big-league baseball player, I knew I wanted to be an announcer," said Hacker. "I listened to Claude [Sullivan], Waite Hoyt, Ted Grizzard, Arty Kaye, Nick Clooney, John Sullivan, Jim Brown, and others. I knew I wanted to work at WVLK. One night, after working the six-to-midnight shift on WEKY, I left the studio, turned on the radio and heard, in my opinion, the greatest announcer I had ever heard with the greatest voice ever. I knew I had found my role model. It was Ralph Emery [popularly known as the dean of country music broadcasters] who has remained my role model ever since, in many ways my mentor, and for over 42 years one of the greatest friends a person could have."

When Hacker was asked to cover the EKU game on a short notice, he wasn't ready but had no choice. "At fifteen, I was covering high school games as well as being a DJ, when, by strange circumstances, the play-by-play guy for Eastern failed to show. They threw me in without training or rehearsal and therein begins the story," said Hacker. "The first person I ever met from Middlesboro to my knowledge was Harvey Yeary. He would come to the radio station and hang out with his friend and our program director John Sullivan, shortly thereafter married a friend of mine, Kathy Robinson. [Then] he left for Hollywood to become a star. I have seen him little since those early days, but, like all guys from Eastern, have followed his career with great interest." (Yeary, who was an all-state performer from Middlesboro High School, also had a football scholarship at Indiana University. But he later transferred to EKU, then known as Eastern Kentucky State College, and graduated in 1962.)

Jim Host added that he himself "was doing games as a play-by-play broadcaster for the Kentucky Central Network in 1959 at Memorial Coliseum when Ralph was doing play-by-play of the state tournament at age 15 for WEKY in Richmond. We have been good friends ever since."

For a period of time, Kentucky had more than one Wildcat voice on competing networks or stations that carried the UK games. Besides Ledford, the other well-known radio guy was Claude Sullivan during the 1950s and '60s. In 1967, Sullivan, however, died early in his remarkable career at the age of 42 due to cancer. He was also broadcasting as the Voice of the Cincinnati Reds.

"If Claude had lived, he would have been the Voice of the Wildcats," recalled Hacker. "As good as Cawood was, he was no better than Claude, and Claude was the voice of the small stations out in the Commonwealth, where Cawood was the voice of UK on WHAS, which covered 40 states."

It was Sullivan who had recommended Hacker to start broadcasting on WVLK, telling the management folks he can do the job. "I have been critiquing his tapes since he was 15 at WEKY in Richmond," Sullivan told them.

And ailing Sullivan also gave a young Hacker a valuable professional advice during a meeting at the Phoenix Hotel in downtown Lexington.

"May I offer you some advice?" asked Sullivan.

"Of course," a thankful Hacker replied.

Hacker added that Sullivan "began by telling me to build a wheel for myself, working at WVLK provides you a hub. From there cast your net as far and wide as you can, do every job that is offered. TV will be a big thing, do some TV play-by-play, sell advertising, get into management. If and when one of the spokes of that wheel break, the other spokes will run the wheel until that spoke is replaced."

Hacker said he has followed Sullivan's advice, passing it along to others. Like Hacker, Jim Host was mentored by Sullivan, as well.

With his various roles in covering UK games, including pre- and postgame shows with the coaches, Hacker has worked with many Kentucky coaches and has gotten along very well with them, with many stories to share. "I never had a problem with any UK coach," he said.

Football coach Charlie Bradshaw, who was a former Bear Bryant player at UK, once complained about Cawood Ledford's radio performance during the Wildcats' 48-7 blowout loss to Auburn in 1967. Bradshaw said he didn't appreciate Ledford's critical comments about the team.

Replied Ledford, "Charlie, I don't know how to make a 48-7 loss sound good!"

And Hacker said that Bradshaw once "called me and asked I come and sit in the office while the UK Athletics Board discussed his future. 'I want to see if they have the guts to come to my office and tell me or call.' They called." Bradshaw was forced to step down in late 1968 after a disappointing seven-year tenure at Kentucky.

"Charlie Bradshaw was tough, a great football mind who saw himself in the image of coach Bear Bryant but could not get the players," said Hacker. To replace Bradshaw, UK hired John Ray away from Notre Dame, where he was the assistant head coach and defensive coordinator under legendary coach Ara Parseghian. A *Sports Illustrated* article reported that Ray had declined nine head coaching job offers before coming to Kentucky. He sure was optimistic, promising UK would win in the SEC.

Remembered Hacker, "John Ray suggested they put me on the UK football broadcast because Cawood was living and working in Louisville, and he wanted someone who could attend daily practices, get to know the coaches and players on a personal level, and tell a story. That is what he got."

After 2-8, 2-9, 3-8 and 3-8 seasons, including a memorable UK upset of No. 8 Ole Miss 10-9 in 1969 at old Stoll Field in Lexington, Ray was fired after the 1972 campaign. "John Ray overpromised, could not deliver the players, but helped to reorganize the UK athletics department when he hired Frank Ham, and insisted Russell Rice, the sports information director, be allowed an assistant who would handle basketball, while Russell dealt with football."

After the end of Ray era, charismatic Fran Curci, a former All-American quarterback from University of Miami (Florida), took over the struggling football program and found some success, including a 1976 Peach Bowl season as well as the 10-1 campaign in 1977.

"Fran Curci was the complete package, knew the game, recruited well, hired great coaches, and promoted [the program]," Hacker said. "Recruiting violations were his albatross. In today's world he would have succeeded, and the Kentucky program would be among the tops in the SEC. It was Kentucky's loss."

Then Maryland coach and ex-Wildcat player Jerry Claiborne, and Alabama coach Bill Curry came along as Kentucky head coaches during the 1980s and

1990s, respectively. There have been slightly different versions of how Curry left Alabama for UK, but Hacker has one. If Hacker hadn't encouraged or suggested to top UK officials, including then-assistant AD Larry Ivy, about getting Curry away from the Crimson Tide as a possible replacement for Claiborne, it is conceivable that Curry might not have arrived in the Bluegrass. In Alabama, there were some grumblings about Curry, who hadn't been accepted very well by the Crimson Tide supporters, despite finding success during his three bowl years with 7-5, 9-3 and 10-2 records at Tuscaloosa.

Hacker said, "Later, Bill and I were talking about this, and he said, 'I always wondered where the wild idea of C.M. [Newton] talking to me about Kentucky came about.' If it did not occur this way, at least I have a good story to tell my granddaughters. I was always surprised Bill did not succeed."

After his seventh-ranked Crimson Tide dropped to No. 2 Miami in the Sugar Bowl on Jan. 1, 1990, Curry had discussions with Newton in New Orleans and decided to come to Lexington, creating a stunning excitement about the UK football program having a big-name coach. As it turned out, Curry coached seven years at Kentucky, compiling an overall record of 26-52 with one bowl appearance.

As for coach Adolph Rupp and his UK successors, Hacker said Rupp "was marvelous with me. In the early years, [he] treated me like one of the senior players in many ways. Being the youngest member of the media traveling squad, I was designated by the others to be his driver. [I was thankful] for the opportunity to get educated by the greatest basketball teacher of them all. Coach Rupp brought organization to the college game.

"Coach Hall brought the physicality to the sport; Coach Sutton brought defense; Rick Pitino brought the three-point shot, the running game, and improved upon the recruiting of his predecessors; Tubby Smith continued with this, minus the fast pace. People took it for granted Tubby was a Rick disciple. He was not, even though it was at the encouragement from Rick, C.M. Newton went strongly for him."

After serving as the color commentator under Ledford who retired in 1992, Hacker had a very tough act to follow. He replaced the popular announcer on the broadcasting team, becoming the team's play-by-play man. It was like seeing Joe B. Hall taking over Adolph Rupp's place two decades earlier. And the hard-to-please, demanding fans began to complain about Hacker's broadcasting work after many years of hearing Ledford on radio. Some didn't like Hacker's voice. Some didn't like his style. But he had his share of supporters.

Ralph Hacker waves to the crowd at Kroger Field. (Photo by Jamie H. Vaught)

"It was tough, something like being at the end of a rope and being shot at from all directions," Hacker recalled. "Yes, there were people who complained, and some who complimented. Among the faithful supporters were Bill Curry, Rick Pitino, and C.M. Newton.

"I was no Cawood, never thought I was, never thought I would be. People wanted Cawood, no question. So did I. I don't mean to sound cocky with this statement, but a few years ago, a broadcast friend who has national prominence and I were talking about this very thing, and he said to me, 'The problem is you never had a Ralph Hacker beside you.' "

Host commented it was extremely difficult for Ralph to follow Cawood as the play-by-play voice, but he was "the only person who could have done it. No one else could have ever followed Cawood as well as Ralph did."

What was Hacker's most memorable game as a UK broadcaster? "There were many games that stand out, and I have always been hesitant to say which one was the greatest, as in hindsight they all seemed important to the success of the greatest college basketball story ever," said Hacker, who was selected to the UK Athletics Hall of Fame in 2017 as well as the Kentucky Sports Hall of Fame in 2019.

"Of course, the Duke game of '92 is among the best. In this game I said to Cawood with :02 on the clock, 'Kentucky is moving on the way in the NCAA.' He replied, 'Not so fast, Ralph – this is Duke we're playing.' "

Other spectacular matchups or memories, as pointed out by Hacker, include:

♦ "There is the big comeback in '98 against Duke in St Petersburg, Fla. [in the NCAA South Regional finals]. No one talks about this game even though it was a major comeback win and another step to what would become a national championship [for Kentucky]," he said.

♦ "The come-from-behind win at Baton Rouge when [Gimel] Martinez, and [Jeff] Brassow lit up the scoreboard [in 1994 as the Wildcats won in a 99-95 stunner after trailing by 31 points in the early second half]."

♦ "The win over Arizona in the [1993] Maui Classic with a one-handed tip-in [by Brassow] at the buzzer to beat the higher-ranked team."

♦ "The upset of Auburn in the [1984] SEC championship game in Nashville when the Tigers were led by Charles Barkley and Chuck Person."

♦ "The comeback wins over UNLV [University of Nevada, Las Vegas] and Kansas, two highly-ranked teams. (The Kansas game was) played in Rupp Arena."

♦ "The first NCAA championship I was honored to work when UK lost to UCLA [in 1975], the 1984 game when the shooting went down south and the Cats lost to Georgetown in Seattle. Each championship game has a special place, and as far as I know, no one has as many special memories as do I."

Things, however, weren't always rosy on the UK scene, and Hacker had to report or discuss the not-so-good news during the late 1980s.

"There were occasions when I did have to tell a story when it was not on the positive side, one being when Rex Chapman told me he was going to leave to play pro ball after the season ended. He later denied this. Then when he heard the tape, he agreed that is what he said, and it was the path he would pursue," Hacker said. Chapman turned pro in 1988 after two All-SEC years at Kentucky. The popular standout from Owensboro was a first-round pick – No. 8 overall – by NBA's Charlotte Hornets. And the NCAA investigation was beginning at the time certainly didn't help.

Earlier, during October 1985, the *Lexington Herald-Leader* created a huge firestorm when it published a series of investigative and damaging articles about the alleged corruption in UK's hoops program and college athletics. For that investigative reporting, the Lexington newspaper won its first Pulitzer Prize in

1986. Somehow, NCAA couldn't do much, and Kentucky was hit with "a slap on the wrist."

However, in 1988, the program again was under a cloud of NCAA investigation for other possible rules violations. Not long before Rick Pitino took over the UK coaching post in 1989, replacing embattled Eddie Sutton, NCAA severely penalized the school for recruiting and academic fraud violations.

On Sutton's national television announcement in 1989 that he was resigning, Hacker added, "I sat with Eddie Sutton and his staff during the long days and nights of his ordeal and, in fact, wrote the statement he had delivered to then-President David Roselle and later to James Brown on CBS-TV. This was an interview I arranged through my working with James earlier at CBS Sports. During this time, I was part of many meetings with all of Sutton's coaches, the staff, and his lawyer. It is my belief no one outside of Eddie and Patsy Sutton knew more about what was going on with this 'real life' drama than did I.

"But again, trust came into play, and what I knew and heard was never divulged, until [editor] John Carroll began work on a book about the Pulitzer Prize [that] the *Lexington Herald-Leader* was awarded for the coverage on this matter. The book will more than likely never be published due to the [2015] death of Mr. Carroll, a fine man and brilliant writer. If it were published and stated as I said to him, 'The *Herald-Leader* won the Pulitzer with untrue reporting.' "

After his *Herald-Leader* days, Carroll later became the award-winning editor of the *Baltimore Sun* and the *Los Angeles Times,* where both newspapers won several Pulitzer Prizes.

Hacker, who served as president of HMH Broadcasting Inc., which included then-UK flagship station WVLK, also did some television work, including freelance assignments for ESPN, CBS, and UK networks.

Who was the best college basketball player – UK or non-UK – that Hacker has ever seen in his long broadcasting career? While Hacker understandably didn't want to name the best Kentucky players, he listed Michael Jordan, Lew Alcindor (Kareem Abdul-Jabbar), Magic Johnson, Charles Barkley, and Shaquille O'Neal among the best in the college ranks other than the UK greats.

On not naming the top Wildcat players on the list, Hacker smiled. "See, you get me started, and the memories flow, and I begin to write a book, something Mr. Bill Keightley and I agreed we would never do. Both of us agreed if we wrote one, we would tell the absolute truth, and that would hurt too many of our friends."

In August 1995, when coach Rick Pitino and his Kentucky squad traveled to Italy for a five-game tour, Hacker and wife, Marilyn, had a very special occasion. The couple renewed their wedding vows, with the ceremony taking place at St. Peter's Cathedral in Vatican City. It was Pitino who encouraged them to renew their vows, according to Hacker. "If you all agree, I will take care of all the details," said the coach, who had help from Father Ed Bradley, the team's chaplain.

At the Vatican wedding, Hacker added that the UK coach and his wife, Joanne, as well as Ledford and his wife, Frances, "stood up for us. Nearly the entire traveling party attended, and later we had a very private tour of the catacombs, and we're the only ones in the Cathedral, with the exception of the cleaning crews as they were preparing the Cathedral for the return of the Pope who would say Mass. [It was] quite an experience."

Chapter Twelve

Three Final Four Trips

*I*f you look at UK men's basketball media guide, it would show the Wildcats have had six players who were named NCAA Final Four's Most Outstanding Player. Can you name all six? Probably not unless you are a Kentucky Wildcat fanatic. The first award recipient goes all the way back to 1948 when 6-foot-7 Alex Groza of Rupp's "Fabulous Five" guided the squad to the national title. And Groza won the award again in 1949 as the Wildcats captured another NCAA crown. The other award winners from Kentucky were 7-footer Bill Spivey in 1951, Jack Givens (1978), Tony Delk (1996), Jeff Sheppard (1998), and Anthony Davis (2012).

Sheppard, a 6-foot-3 guard from McIntosh High School in Peachtree City, Georgia, was outstanding in the 1998 Final Four in San Antonio as his clutch play helped Kentucky, popularly called the "Comeback Cats," fight back in the second half and win its second national title in three years in beating Utah 78-69 before a crowd of 40,000. Sheppard poured in 7 of 14 shots for 16 points in the championship game.

But he was even more remarkable in the national semifinal showdown with Stanford. Sheppard was sensational as he gunned in a career-high 27 points on 9 of 15 field goal shooting, including 4 of 8 three-point field goals. Stanford was tough, but Sheppard's critical baskets sparked UK to rally for an 86-85 win in overtime after a 10-point deficit in the second half.

So, for both Final Four matchups, Sheppard totaled 43 points. Also, in the regional finals victory over Duke, 86-84 at Tropicana Field in St. Petersburg, he was noteworthy, hitting 18 points along with 11 rebounds, both team-highs. (UK's Heshimu Evans also had a double-double with 14 points and 11 rebounds.) As you may recall, the win over Duke was a stunner because the Wildcats had fallen behind by 17 midway in the second half but somehow pulled it off with key downtown jumpers by reserve guard Cameron Mills and Scott Padgett at the end.

Tubby Smith said Sheppard, with his senior leadership, was the main one who held the 1998 team together and [helped them] have success, calling him the "glue." Sheppard, who now lives in London, Ky. with his family, was asked about that Final Four memory in San Antonio with two great performances against No. 10 Stanford and No. 7 Utah in the national spotlight. They were the last games of his collegiate career.

"There's a great life lesson that I learned during my senior year at the University of Kentucky," he said 20 years later during an interview with the author. "When I started the year, I was coming off a redshirt year. Derek Anderson and Ron Mercer were in my position [during the 1996-97 season], and Coach Pitino asked me to redshirt and wait until the 1998 season to have my senior season. So, when the '98 season started, I had a very selfish mentality. I had a mentality that 'this is my team and I'm gonna lead this team.' It was me-centered, and I struggled early in the season. I didn't play well. I believe I didn't play well because my whole mentality was around me.

"After we lost to Ole Miss [73-64] at Rupp Arena, we had a team meeting and completely made a transition as a team and as individuals to be selfless. So, once we started our attitudes being selfless, then we put others first, we put the team first. Then what started happening is we started really making a run as a team, but what happened to me individually is I started having my very best games.

"So, the lesson that I learned is that there's a great irony that exists in life, and when we want great things for ourselves, the best way is to put self on the back burner and put others up front. There's great fulfillment there when you just live for other people. Your attitude is much clearer, but it's a big challenge because we live in a world that is so selfish, and there's a lot of pressure on taking care of self, and it just doesn't work. When your whole focus is about yourself, even if you're successful, you're still miserable because there is no fulfillment there. It's empty. And that's why you see billionaires who are miserable. You see movie stars, musicians, and athletes who just struggle so much with drugs or depression or suicide because there is no fulfillment when you just fill yourself up with self. So, you see the billionaire give money away and become really big in helping charities and being a philanthropist. That's where their fulfillment comes in with helping other people.

"There's just so much pressure that the world system puts on people, and in the United States, we say, 'Take pride in yourself, be successful, make a lot of money, be famous' and that kind of thing. If that's where it stops, then you end up finding out that it's not worth it. So, they're miserable, and I do think it is because of faith. It's the removal of God in our society, in our schools, in our laws, and it causes a major problem.

"But for us, the Final Four's Most Outstanding Player was an individual award, and it came because a group of individuals decided to be completely selfless, and then we played great as individuals. The individuals received by-products of the team being successful and winning. That's a great life lesson for me to try to communicate with my children, my family, and all those I have the opportunity to influence."

Jeff Sheppard (Photo by UK Athletics)

For Sheppard, the 1998 Final Four was not his only trip to the national semi-finals and championship game. He also was a part of UK's other two Final Four teams, including a redshirt season when the Wildcats went to the 1997 Final Four before losing to Arizona. In 1996, the 34-2 Cats won it all, beating coach Jim Boeheim and Syracuse 76-67 in East Rutherford, N.J. behind Tony Delk's 24 points. Sheppard actually went to the NCAA Tournament all five years at Kentucky. How many players can say that? Not many.

Sheppard is grateful for his UK experience. "Well, I feel very privileged and very thankful to be at Kentucky during the era when I was there," he said. "We had wonderful coaches, we had wonderful teammates, and we had an incredible level of chemistry that allowed us to be successful on the court. There was a lot of pressure on Coach Pitino and his staff in the early '90s to win a national championship. At the time he was the best college basketball coach who had never won a championship. He was now at Kentucky, he now was off probation, he was getting the recruits that he wanted, so there was a lot of pressure for him to win a national championship. We felt that there was a lot of pressure, but that was okay. That was good pressure that was put on us to train and to prepare, and the whole season was about preparing for that tournament because that's how you're graded. You're always graded in college basketball based upon the NCAA Tournament.

"For the small school, it's all about just making it to the NCAA Tournament. For the big school, it's about winning the NCAA Tournament, and so, for us, it was always a goal. Not to go to the Final Four but to win the national championship. As the years went on and as we played in the tournament and we experienced the tournament, it really gave us an advantage because players who play in the NCAA Tournament year after year have a distinct advantage – it's a different stage. The lights are brighter, the lights are hotter, the crowds are bigger, and it's a completely different stage than playing at Rupp Arena or on the road in the SEC. Experience becomes a huge factor that helps teams succeed in the NCAA Tournament, and we had a lot of experience. So, we had a distinct advantage, and it showed every single year. When we went into the NCAA Tournament, we were gonna make a run, and we did that."

Despite growing up near Atlanta, Sheppard had dreams of becoming a Kentucky Wildcat. And his sixth-grade class had a writing assignment about who would they like to be.

"On that piece of paper, I wrote that I wanted to trade places with Larry Bird and play for the Boston Celtics in the NBA, but first I wanted to go to the University of Kentucky and play in the Final Four for the University of Kentucky," Sheppard recalled. "So, it was always my dream to play basketball at Kentucky, as it is so many other boys. But I was from Georgia, so it was unusual for me to have a dream to play basketball at Kentucky, but I kept practicing and playing and eventually got the opportunity [to play at UK].

"[In the seventh grade] I came to basketball camp with a friend of mine that his grandparents lived in Richmond, Ky. I came up to basketball camp when Eddie Sutton was the coach [from 1985-89], and I got a taste of Kentucky basketball there. I was a big Rex Chapman fan; I loved watching Rex play. So, there were some influences on me with Kentucky basketball, but as a boy, you always dream about playing for the major programs, and in Georgia, we're such a big football school. I loved Georgia football. I still love Georgia football, but there's just something special about Kentucky basketball."

By the time he was beginning his senior year at McIntosh High, the high-jumping Sheppard, who was an All-Stater during his junior year and had just won the event's Slam Dunk Contest at the AAU Boston Shootout, made a commitment to play basketball at UK, with assistant Billy Donovan doing most of the recruiting. Sheppard's mother wasn't completely happy, fearing that he may have made an uninformed decision. However, for the most part, she was okay. In high school, Sheppard had also worn Chapman's UK jersey No. 3. Sheppard also visited and considered other schools, such as Georgia, Vanderbilt, and Florida.

"Mom always wanted what was best for me," said Sheppard. "She knew I wanted to play at UK. She loves Vanderbilt, and of course, Georgia was just around the corner. But she knew I wanted to play for the Cats."

Added Sheppard, "He [Donovan] came down, and he recruited me. He saw me play at a couple of basketball camps, so it wasn't a hard decision for me to make. It was more of a hard decision for Kentucky to make if they were going to offer me a scholarship or not.

"Once they offered me a scholarship, I pretty much knew where I was wanting to go. It would've been more of a recruitment for other schools if Kentucky had not offered me a scholarship, so not a hard decision for me. Kentucky called, and I answered and said yes."

Sheppard also liked Vanderbilt, especially coach Eddie Fogler, who was leading the Commodores at the time before moving on to South Carolina. "Vanderbilt was one of the favorites for me and for my parents because Vanderbilt University is such a strong educational university, and we really fell in love with Eddie Fogler," he said. "We really liked Coach Fogler. So, they made a really hard push, and it was very compelling, but once again, had Kentucky not offered, I would've continued through the recruitment process. But I didn't even complete all of the recruiting visits because, as soon as Kentucky offered, I said yes because I always wanted to play there. There was somewhat of a recruitment from other schools, but I wanted to go to Kentucky. I had to do some other visits to prepare in case Kentucky didn't offer me a scholarship. I didn't need to go anywhere else to confirm that I wanted to go to Kentucky."

Sheppard was asked about his very first meeting with the charismatic Pitino during the summer of 1992. What was he like? Pitino liked what he saw of Sheppard in the Nike All-American camp in Indianapolis, and he later had Billy Donovan watch Sheppard work out and shoot basketball. After that, Pitino visited Sheppard's home.

"The first time that we met was in our home in Georgia when he came down for a home visit," said Sheppard. "He came down to recruit and offer me a scholarship. I was very nervous because at that time he hadn't offered a scholarship yet, so we didn't really know what to expect; he had such a big name, and the program was doing so well. That was in the early 90s, so he was coming out of probation, shooting all the three-pointers. Jamal Mashburn was at the University of Kentucky. They were starting to really make a run – '92 was the Duke game [in the NCAA regional finals], and '93 was Jamal Mashburn going to the Final Four, and that was my senior year [in high school]. So, that was a really good up-and-coming time at the University of Kentucky with a lot of excitement going on there. It was definitely a dream come true to be sitting there with Coach Pitino in our living room talking to us about playing at Kentucky.

"They showed a lot of videos of three-point shooting and just how the style of play was so much fun and exciting. It was more of a formality of just going through that and him being sold on me as a player. We didn't even eat at home, we went out to eat, but it was a lot of fun for all of our family." Asked what kind of dinner they had, Sheppard smiled. "Steak dinner!"

Sheppard – whose McIntosh team made a special trip to Lexington in January 1993 to play Henry Clay at Memorial Coliseum – finished his prep career on a high note, averaging 28 points, 11 rebounds, and six assists during his senior year and was named Georgia's Mr. Basketball by the *Atlanta Journal and Constitution*. Named as one of Top 40 players in the nation by *Parade* magazine, Sheppard was voted by the faculty at McIntosh High School as the 1993 Academic Athlete of the Year. The Converse All-American also won the state high jump championship with his 7-foot effort in 1993.

For the 1993-94 campaign, the Wildcats only had one other rookie besides Sheppard. And that was 6-foot-2 guard Anthony Epps from Marion County High School. The Jamal Mashburn-less Wildcats, who would finish at 27-7, had four seniors, including standout guard Travis Ford.

And Sheppard almost didn't play that season, as Pitino considered redshirting the freshman from Georgia. But he made his Wildcat debut at Rupp Arena when the Wildcats topped coach Denny Crum's Louisville squad 78-70 in a Top 10 showdown. Kentucky sophomore Tony Delk recorded a double-double, pumping in 19 points, including five three-pointers, along with 10 rebounds. But Sheppard doesn't remember that game much after getting zero points in six minutes of action. Epps just played one minute.

"I really don't remember much," said Sheppard. "My freshman year at Kentucky was somewhat of a blur. It was such a transition year for me; the intensity of practices and the intensity of the games was at such a higher level than at the high school level. AAU basketball and travel basketball existed, but it didn't exist at the level that it exists now. So, it was very difficult for me to make that transition. I don't know how the guys now make the transition and play at such a high level. It was difficult, but it was a whole lot of fun for sure."

It was 5-foot-9 Travis Ford – a *Parade* All-American from Madisonville who is now coaching at St. Louis University – who helped Sheppard adjust during his first year at Kentucky. Ford was there to guide the rookie from the very beginning.

"Travis Ford was probably the best role model, and he was the fifth-year senior that year," Sheppard commented. "As soon as I arrived on campus the summer before my freshman year, they got me a job out at Lane's End horse farm in Versailles. Anthony Epps and I worked at the horse farm every single day, feeding the horses and taking care of the horse stalls, everything like that.

"Then we would work out in the afternoon, and Travis Ford was the guy that really took me under his wing and showed me how Kentucky basketball is. I spent some time with him at Madisonville. He took me back to his hometown. So I got to see Kentucky basketball outside of Lexington, and that's very important for Kentucky basketball players to see just how important Kentucky basketball is for the state. Most of the players that come in today don't because they don't have a Travis Ford that stays around for five years; everybody rotates through so quickly. The dynamic is completely different.

"But my freshman year, Travis really showed me how things are, and I appreciate him doing that. I was able to return that favor when I was a fifth-year senior, and I think that's one of the reasons through the 90s we had such a special chemistry. We spent a lot of time together on the court and off the court. We were together for three, four, five years, and we really have strong relationships still to this day."

Sheppard was asked about Rick Pitino as a coach. Was the young-looking mentor approachable? Was Sheppard comfortable approaching him about a problem?

"He coached with an arm's distance away," said Sheppard of Pitino. "He was very, very strict and very, very demanding, but we didn't know all the things he was doing behind the scenes to help us, to defend us, and we would hear him say things in the media defending us. Yet he would come from a press conference into the locker room and say, 'Don't believe anything I just said. We've got work to do.'

"The way Coach Pitino was is, when you're playing for him, he's very demanding, but when you finish playing for him, he allows you in and embraces you and becomes more of a father figure. So, you just have to make it through. You have to get through all of the difficulties with him, all of the tough practices, and that's just his style of leadership."

But when then-athletics director C.M. Newton hired Tubby Smith to replace Pitino in 1997, Sheppard and his teammates had to adjust to Smith's coaching style, which was the complete opposite, like day and night. Pitino had left Kentucky in early May 1997 to take a head coaching job with the Boston Celtics.

The distraught Wildcats were emotional when Pitino informed the players that he was leaving Lexington after eight memorable years at UK. They weren't happy. "I started crying. We were in the locker room, and it was very difficult," said Sheppard. "Every year when Coach Pitino was at Kentucky, there was always a rumor that he was going to leave and go to an NBA team. So, we heard those rumors all the time, but up until then, he hadn't decided to leave. And we were on a roll. We had just come off several Final Fours, a national championship. We were really rolling, we had a lot of momentum, and he left.

"So, it was very difficult. C.M. Newton did a great job. He came in immediately and addressed the team after Pitino left. He told them that he was thinking about hiring Tubby Smith and working very quickly to get a coach in place. He did a wonderful job with the transition because when Coach Pitino left, all the coaches left. There weren't any other coaches around, so it was a difficult few days there, but we had a lot of confidence in C.M. Newton. I don't remember hearing anybody talking about leaving or transferring. We just stayed together and waited for the next coach."

What about Tubby Smith as a coach? How different was he as compared to Pitino?

"Tubby Smith was quite the opposite," Sheppard said. "Tubby Smith invites you in from day one. It's a completely different style of leadership, both work, but completely different. It was a tough transition for us in 1998 when we transitioned to Tubby Smith, but we were very experienced at that time. We had a lot of players that had played three, four, five years of college basketball. It really helped us.

"Coach Smith, when he first got to Kentucky, the very first thing he did was invite us up to his office. One by one and we were always nervous because anytime we got invited to Coach Pitino's office we were in trouble. But when we got invited to Smith's office, we knew we weren't in trouble; he just wanted to get to know us. He asked us about our family, he asked us about school, he asked us about our relationship with the Lord, he asked us about our girlfriends, he asked us about things socially, and that was foreign to us. He truly led differently, and he wanted us to get to know him so that he could get to know us.

"So, there was an immediate relationship that was starting to build. He had a short window, especially with Cameron Mills, Allen Edwards, and myself as the three seniors. There was a very short window to build a relationship because the season was going to start soon and we had work to do. He did a wonderful job building that relationship, establishing himself as a leader, but also as a fatherly figure as well, so that style of leadership was very successful for him."

As history will show, Smith and his "Comeback Cats" surprised many folks with a national championship in San Antonio.

Sheppard said it was Midnight Madness (now called Big Blue Madness) during a Homecoming weekend in 1992 that pushed him to realize that the UK hoops program was bigger than he had expected. It was that "wow" moment for the high school senior who had already committed to the Wildcats earlier in the summer.

"My parents and I came up to Midnight Madness [during] Jamal Mashburn's last year," he said. "We saw all the people waiting outside. At that time it was at Memorial Coliseum, and there were no tickets. You just had to wait in line outside, and the first people that came got to come in…. It was at midnight also. It was not at 7:00 or 8:00 [p.m.]. It was at midnight, so you had to wait all day. They had the practice at midnight, and it would be full, and that was the moment I realized it was very special.

"A couple of months later during my senior year, I played a game against Henry Clay in Memorial Coliseum, which was full to watch me play in that game. So, there were several moments, but Midnight Madness was the first moment that I realized this is even bigger than I thought."

Kentucky moved its annual preseason celebration to Rupp Arena in 2005, where over 23,000 rabid fans showed up. It seems that Big Blue Madness has gotten bigger every year since then.

During the summer of 2016 in Miami, Fla., Pitino, then coaching at Louisville, held a 20-year reunion for the 1995-96 Kentucky squad, which is often called the "Untouchables." That 34-2 team is considered among the best in UK's storied hoops history. And Sheppard, who was the team's best leaper, attended the event and had a great time.

"One of my favorite stories was at our 20-year reunion," said Sheppard. "We saw a different side of Coach Pitino, a side that was very open and showed appreciation to us as players, and we didn't get that much when we played at Kentucky. He ruled with an iron fist.

"So, when we got to see him 20 years later and he got to let his guard down and share some things, it really completed the process for us. It gave us closure in going through different times, in understanding why he drove us the way that he did but yet kept us an arm's distance away. You never got a pat on the back when you were playing for him. We desired that as young men. We just wanted to please our coach and to hear him open up and just share with us how proud he was to coach us really brought closure in the whole process of being a student-athlete, playing for him.

"We went down to Miami for a couple of days. Stayed down there, played golf, went out to dinner, had several fun events together as a team, and celebrated the 20-year reunion of the championship. [It was] a lot of fun, but I think it was also very important for us to have that moment, and it just gives you closure in several areas of your life. That was a very important and very special moment, and we also got to share that as a team. We were all together with him when he got to share those moments with us."

Unbelievably, that group of Wildcats featured nine future NBA players, including stars Delk, Antoine Walker, and Walter McCarty.

Even though it was Tubby Smith's team that won the 1998 NCAA crown, some UK fans have argued that Smith won it simply because he had players whom Pitino had recruited and coached. That old argument doesn't faze Sheppard.

"Well, it doesn't bother me because Coach Pitino does deserve credit," Sheppard said. "Any time there's a transition, there's nothing Coach Smith could've done. He wasn't going to kick all of the players off the team and bring his own players in. That was something that was out of Coach Smith's control. That statement can be turned, and it's even more impressive for a Coach Smith to be able to say, 'I did win, but I won with somebody else's players.' But I understand the argument. It doesn't bother me because it doesn't bother Coach Smith. Coach Smith isn't bothered with it at all. It's just the situation, so it's fine. I understand what the fans are trying to say, but it doesn't matter—he still won the national championship."

While he was not selected in the 1998 NBA Draft, Sheppard, though, did sign a free agent contract with the Atlanta Hawks and played one season. He also played pro basketball in Italy for three seasons. He gave up his pro career because of the 9/11 terrorist attacks in the U.S.

"I was playing in Rome, Italy, when the terrorist attacks happened," said Sheppard. "My daughter Madison had just been born the summer before, and [wife] Stacey and Madison were here in the United States. They were living in London, and I was living in Rome, Italy. They had plans to come over in November and live with me the rest of the season over there, and then September 11th happened.

"So, things changed. Things were very different at that time. The idea of traveling in an airplane was scary, much less traveling with an infant to another country in Europe was scary. We had some decisions to make, and I didn't really want to stop playing basketball, but I felt like it was what I was supposed to do. A few months later I came home and stopped playing basketball completely and started working, and that was okay. It was fine with me. Basketball was great for me. I got to play a little bit in the NBA, play a little bit over in Italy, and have a wonderful experience in high school and in college and learn some really great life lessons from some great leaders. So, I have no regrets."

Sheppard, who is currently a financial advisor, met his future wife at UK, and they married two months after Kentucky's 1998 national title. She is the former Stacey Reed, a basketball standout who starred for the old Laurel County Lady Cardinals and UK women's team. At Kentucky during the early 1990s, she earned All-SEC honors for three straight years.

How did he meet her?

"We were in study hall, and she gave me a note," remembered Sheppard, whose favorite UK subject was mathematics. "She just said, 'Look, I know you just got to school. I understand that you like to fish, and if you ever want to go fishing, I'd love to go with you. I love to fish.' She was just trying to be my friend. I got her note and threw it in the garbage.

"We knew of each other, but we didn't know each other real well at that time. About a year later, I saw her in the training room, and I asked her out on a date, to a Christian music concert in Wilmore, Ky. We went with Mark Pope and his girlfriend, and we went to the concert together and had a great time. We started dating after that. Then my senior year, we were engaged and then we got married on May 30th."

Sheppard added he often saw Stacey, a 5-foot-7 guard, in UK women's basketball action at Memorial Coliseum. "I watched her play most of her career at Kentucky," he said. "She was [an] incredible player and could've played professional basketball if she wanted to. She had several opportunities to play overseas and decided not to. Actually, when we were in Italy together, our first year in Italy, she was playing basketball. She didn't go over there to play basketball, but some of the teams in Italy saw her play and wanted her to play with them. So, she was working her way up to playing a little bit of professional basketball, but she was pregnant but didn't realize it. She had Madison in her belly, so that ended her basketball career."

At Kentucky, Stacey is among the team's all-time leading scorers with 1,482 points. She led the Wildcats in scoring and rebounding during both her junior and senior seasons, and led in assists and steals during all four years at UK.

In addition to Madison, who plays basketball at Campbellsville University, the couple has a son, Reed, a rising high school star at North Laurel.

For Jeff Sheppard and his family, faith is very important in their everyday lives. They are active in various Christian-related activities, especially youth. Many years ago, his wife established the Backpack Club. The organization, which recently closed due to lack of funding and volunteers, had provided food for hungry children in Laurel County.

Sheppard discusses his faith. "When I was 13 years old, I went forward and gave my heart to the Lord at First Baptist Church in Peachtree City, and it was the single most important decision of my life," he said. "And it's obvious to see how God has opened doors and closed doors, and God has helped me through situations. Introduced me to my wife, blessed us with a family, and given me so many opportunities that I don't deserve.

"When you get a gift that you don't deserve, that's called grace, and you are to be thankful for that. I am so thankful for his grace upon my life individually, upon our family, and faith is the ability to trust, believe. The Bible says faith is the substance of things hoped for and the evidence of things not seen. Just the ability to trust and believe no matter what you're going through is difficult, but it is worth it because God is in control. He's sovereign and knows what He's doing. So, we just have to trust that and apply that to our life, and things will always work out for the best when we do that. When we don't and we try to do it ourselves, that's when we get in trouble. I'm just very thankful for my relationship with the Lord and looking forward to living the rest of my days with Him forever."

Chapter Thirteen
A National Championship Coach

*I*n 2017, on a cloudy and very windy Saturday morning in mid-November, there was a vibrant annual festival for book lovers, called the Kentucky Book Fair, taking place at the Kentucky Horse Park, near Georgetown. Nearly 200 authors, some of them well known, appeared at the popular festival to sign their books. Even then-Kentucky Gov. Steve Beshear attended the affair to promote his hardcover. While I love books, I was there actually to meet someone. That person is a highly successful basketball coach with strong UK ties who has won lots of games, including national championships in 2013 and 2019, with little fanfare outside of the Bluegrass region. He had suggested that we meet at the event, even though his school office was just minutes away. His name is Chris Briggs, the head coach at the National Association of Intercollegiate Athletics (NAIA) Division I powerhouse Georgetown College, who is a former UK graduate assistant and student manager under coach Tubby Smith.

Briggs, who was hired at Georgetown in 2011 after four years as an assistant at the school, is continuing the Tigers' rich hoops tradition with his recent coaching success on the hardwood floor, following in the footsteps of coaching legends Bob Davis (who later coached at Auburn during the 1970s), Jim Reid, and Happy Osborne at the Tiger helm. And all of them, including Briggs, have won national coach of the year honors. Under Briggs' leadership, his Georgetown teams have won at least 24 games every season since he began his head coaching career. Former UK coach Tubby Smith has said Briggs has a high basketball IQ.

Despite his immediate success at Georgetown, Briggs said his first season as the head coach in 2011-12 was difficult as he was trying to uphold the school's winning tradition. "That first year was rough," he added. "It was different. Sliding over a foot in that chair [on the bench where he had been an assistant] made a huge difference."

Briggs said he was very fortunate to learn from different people at UK such as Tubby Smith, David Hobbs (ex-Alabama head coach), and Cameron Hill (director of player development). Hill, who was one of Briggs' best friends at UK, is currently the head coach for the women's team at Trinity University in San Antonio, Texas. "[You] learn from guys like that," he said, adding that he "learned a ton" from Happy Osborne when he was an assistant.

"I could probably write a book about that first year," he said. "You learn a lot, and you try to figure things out. It's stressful at times. There's a time you wonder, 'Am I doing what I'm supposed to be doing?' You just got to keep plugging and keep going. We've had a lot of great players at Georgetown, a lot of great assistant coaches along the way, and feel like I've been able to figure things out and try to do things my own way.

"Because [Osborne] was so successful, I could try to do the same things he did and try to act the same way that he did, but that's not me. You got to be yourself. You got to wade through the waters. Some things are going to work for you that he did, and some things aren't. It's just kind of a process of elimination about what could work and what can't. That's something that I was able to sort of figure out along the way and be able to carry on that success. Hopefully I will still be able to do that in the future going forward."

And Briggs – who recently had ex-UK standout Marquis Estill as assistant coach at Georgetown for a couple of years – is not taking anything for granted while coaching.

Chris Briggs gives instructions during a break at a Georgetown College game. (Photo by Georgetown College's Remington Williams)

"You better cherish every win you get because there's a lot of coaches out there who are struggling to get them," he said. "Everybody's situation is different, so I just try to be relaxed and be myself and coach the guys. [I'll] try to apply the system that I feel is most successful with our personnel and try to be as positive I can with the guys and get them to work hard. I tell them all the time, 'If you'll defend and you'll rebound, you got a chance.' So, I put a lot of emphasis on defense, rebounding, toughness, and just playing hard and unselfish. That's kind of what we go by. Offensive plays will change, defensive styles may change a little bit, but most important is passion, enthusiasm, and hard work. If you can do that, then you got a good shot."

Growing up in western Kentucky, Briggs had lots of fond memories of the Kentucky Wildcats. He often put on his Kentucky gear and played Nerf basketball in the house. Or he would put on a jacket, go outside in the cold, and shoot hoops in the driveway with a little boom box playing music, pretending he's warming up on the Rupp Arena floor.

"[I] remember coming to games when I was little," he said. "Both my parents were graduates of UK, and we had season tickets up in the nosebleeds [at Rupp Arena]. They still have them to this day, and just being a little kid, I was excited to go to Rupp Arena. Watching those games.… That would have been in the mid-80s. When I was a child, obviously like every kid in Kentucky at that time period, it was Rex Chapman and Reggie Hanson. It was pretty cool because I remember chasing down Reggie Hanson on the escalator in the Lexington Center right there by Hyatt [Regency] to get his autograph, and then 15 years later, I'm at UK as a student manager, and Reggie is an assistant coach."

Briggs is also a big fan of Chapman. "I vaguely remember him playing at Kentucky, but when he was playing for the [Charlotte] Hornets, I wore all the Hornets gear in elementary school. [I] was a huge Hornets fan, as was probably most of the state of Kentucky at that time." He also liked UK All-American Jamal Mashburn. They were pretty much his favorite players at Kentucky, Briggs added.

Because of NCAA probation, the inexperienced 1989-90 Wildcats, who only had eight scholarship players, with none of them taller than 6-foot-7, could not play their games on live television. "It was crushing," said Briggs about not able to watch the Cats live.

The games were only seen on local television on delayed basis. "I guess I was like 10 years old [at the time]. If my parents let me stay up [late], I'd watch it. I do actually remember recording some of their games, too. I used VHS tape and then popped it in, maybe the next day [to watch the game]."

Despite the very gloomy preseason prediction when doomsayers forecasted perhaps only eight victories for the undermanned Wildcats, UK coach Rick Pitino and his squad somehow surprised many folks. They finished the year on an incredible note with a respectable 14-14 mark, including an exciting 100-95 win over ninth-ranked LSU and a 10-8 SEC record. That fast-paced, three-point shooting team popularly was called "Pitino's Bombinos." The Wildcats also received postseason individual honors, with 6-foot-8 junior Hanson and 6-foot-5 senior Derrick Miller getting All-SEC recognition as well as Pitino being selected as Coach of the Year by *Basketball Times*.

Before his college days, Briggs played mostly basketball at the old Reidland High School in Paducah. (The school – along with Heath and Lone Oak – later closed in 2013 to become the new McCracken County High School in a consolidation.) The 1999 graduate of Reidland High was a decent hoops player and started during his junior and senior years.

Briggs remembers many tough battles in the 2nd District tournament, which included Paducah Tilghman, Heath, Lone Oak, and Reidland. During his senior year of 1998-99, Tilghman (30-6) advanced all the way to the state tournament at Rupp Arena, reaching the semifinal showdown with defending champion Scott County (which had Kentucky Mr. Basketball Rick Jones) before dropping 78-75 in overtime.

"We had a moral victory with Tilghman my senior year when they only beat us maybe 14 points at home," he said. One month earlier, Reidland had lost in an 88-42 blowout to Tilghman. "They were really good that year. They had that game with Scott County (in the state tourney) where there were some controversial plays called."

After graduating from high school, Briggs didn't have plans to become a part of UK's basketball program. As a freshman, he attended King College (now King University) in Bristol, Tenn., and played basketball. "[I] really like it, had a great group of guys, had fun playing basketball, but I knew I wanted to coach," recalled Briggs. "[It] really wasn't what I was looking for in a college, so I went to UK. Had a friend who was one of the practice players against the women's team [which was then coached by Bernadette Mattox]. Bobby Clifton was his name, and he was from Paducah. He actually played high school baseball with my brother. He said, 'Why don't you go to see Mr. [Bill] Keightley and see if you can be a manager.' He kind of put that bug in me. So, I went and met him a few times. He gave me a chance to work camp and, from there on out, [I] became a student manager."

So, he worked with Keightley, UK's longtime equipment manager who was fondly known as "Mr. Wildcat," in the basketball program for five years (from 2001 to '06), including two as a graduate assistant. "I remember getting Mr. Keightley's autograph when I was a kid," he smiled.

You can add Briggs to a list of successful student managers under Keightley who have moved on to become a high school, college, or pro coach. For instance, Frank Vogel, who was a member of UK's 1996 national championship team as student manager, reached the highest level, coaching the Indiana Pacers, Orlando Magic, and Los Angeles Lakers. Even Jeff Kidder, who was a student manager under coach Eddie Sutton, won the national junior college championship as the head coach at Utah's Dixie State College in 2002. Jeff Morrow, a Louisville native who has been a successful high school coach, including winning a state title with Jeffersontown in 2006, said Keightley was the one who gave him a huge opportunity to be a member of UK's program when he was a freshman at UK. "If it were not for Mr. Wildcat, Bill Keightley, I would not be where I'm at today," said Morrow. "He opened the door to an 'once in a lifetime experience' that prepared me for the success I have had in coaching. I will forever be grateful to him."

On his college days, Briggs added, "We were a tight-knit group year-round."

And UK is where Briggs met his future wife, Elizabeth, who was a student worker for the K Fund, which is the fundraising arm of school's athletics department. They often were in and out of Memorial Coliseum and had the same circle of friends. After two years of friendship, they began dating, said Briggs. His wife is currently the assistant athletics director for premium seating, hospitality, and events at UK.

"[I'm] very fortunate. She's a hard worker, wonderful mother, wonderful wife who understands [his coaching life]," said Briggs. "She makes a lot of sacrifices. She's a great coach's wife."

Briggs' first year at Kentucky was the 2001-02 season, when the 22-10 Wildcats had players like senior All-American Tayshaun Prince as well as junior standouts Keith Bogans and Marquis Estill. And he got to see Prince's stunning display against North Carolina up close from the bench as the slender 6-foot-9 forward gunned in five consecutive three-pointers in the opening minutes helping the Cats to a 79-59 win at Rupp Arena. Prince finished with 31 points.

There are many good stories about Tubby Smith. The Wildcat boss also would often play pickup basketball with the student managers. Briggs particularly remembers a couple of episodes.

Then-Kentucky coach Tubby Smith at a post-game news conference in 2003. (Photo by Jamie H. Vaught)

"He'd [Smith] come pick up with us, and I remember him and Saul [his son] getting into it," said Briggs. "He told Saul one time, 'Come down the lane again, and I'll break your chest' or something like that because I think Saul got on him for trying to take a charge on a pickup game.

"I remember one time there was a loose ball, and D.J. Geddes [one of UK's student managers] was kind of trotting to the backcourt, trying to pick it up, thinking nobody else was going to go after it. Then all of a sudden, here comes Coach Smith sprinting, and [he] dives headfirst like he's diving into home plate, dives on the basketball, kind of takes D.J.'s legs out from under him, grabs the ball, rolls over passing it to somebody, and we're all like, 'Oh, he just took him out.' " Briggs added that Coach Smith was "so good to us managers and played pickup games with us. Everybody talks about how great of a person he is."

Just before Briggs came to UK, Saul Smith played four years under his father at Kentucky and was a backcourt starter in each of his last two seasons. The younger Smith also was a special assistant on the UK coaching staff during the 2003-04 campaign while finishing up his bachelor's degree in economics. Following his dad's footsteps in coaching, he later became assistant coach at Tennessee Tech, Minnesota, Texas Tech and Memphis.

What was his best moment as a student manager? "It's hard to pick one out," said Briggs. "I guess that 2003 season [is the most memorable one]."

Even *Sports Illustrated*, in its online story in 2014, listed that Kentucky squad as one of the 16 best college basketball teams in history that didn't win a national title. It was the year the top-ranked Wildcats, after a slow start, steamrolled throughout the SEC race without losing a single game against the conference foes in finishing at 19-0, including winning the SEC Tournament title. Kentucky, which compiled an overall mark of 32-4, featured All-American and SEC Player of the Year Keith Bogans and All-SEC performer Marquis Estill, both seniors, along with other players like Gerald Fitch, Erik Daniels, Chuck Hayes, Cliff Hawkins, and Jules Camara.

"[We] were on a roll, just winning and playing well. We had lost to Michigan State in December at home. We lost to Louisville. And I remember practicing after that Louisville loss, Coach Smith being intense and really driving them, really pushing them in those practices right there around New Year's, at [the] end of December, early January. [Coach] really drove that team to be as successful as they were and have that wonderful season until we lost to Dwyane Wade and Marquette with Bogans' having the ankle injury [suffered in a previous game against Wisconsin in the Sweet Sixteen]. But Marquette played so well that night. They were going to be tough to beat anyway.

"That winter – January, February, and March of 2003 – these guys were telling us they're excited, they're playing together, they're having fun, we were rolling and just plowing through the SEC. I remember the times just sitting in the hotel, after being out in the court, laughing with Mr. Keightley, Coach Smith and the other managers around the table, just developing the relationships. But obviously, when you're winning, that makes it so much more special."

Against Kentucky in that Elite Eight showdown, Wade, a future NBA star, was phenomenal at Hubert H. Humphrey Metrodome in Minneapolis, as he came up with a rare triple double of 29 points, 11 rebounds, and 11 assists in leading the ninth-ranked Marquette club, then coached by Tom Crean, to an 83-69 victory for a trip to the Final Four.

In 2014, Briggs took his Georgetown Tigers to Rupp Arena for an exhibition game against the powerful Kentucky Wildcats, who were ranked No. 1 in a preseason poll. As expected, the matchup wasn't very pretty, but it was a very good experience for the underdog Tigers, who lost by a whopping score of 121-52.

"That was rough," Briggs told the author three years later. "That was a long night, but a lot of people have a long night with that team. [But] it was an awesome experience for our guys to be able to get in there and play against those guys. You know a lot of teams got blown out by that team, so it is what it is. It's an experience our guys will remember for the rest of their life. A lot of them had played in Rupp Arena in the big tournaments, but it's a little bit different when you're playing Karl-Anthony Towns, Willie Cauley-Stein, Devin Booker, Trey Lyles, and guys like that whom they're watching on *SportsCenter* now."

During the postgame press conference in 2014, Briggs – whose teams like to play up-tempo – told assembled reporters that the Wildcats were that good. "Those (Kentucky) guys are unreal," he added. "I told the guys in the locker room, they could have beaten some NBA teams tonight. There's no question in my mind. Defensively, they're going to be a problem for a whole lot of people because they're so long, so athletic at every position, all the way down to the guard spot. I was really impressed with their intensity, defensively in the press, getting after us, and making it hard for us to do anything."

It was the same UK team that went unbeaten all the way to the national semifinals in Indianapolis, where the 38-1 Wildcats dropped a 71-64 verdict to Wisconsin.

In late October 2019, Briggs' Georgetown club – which was picked as the preseason No. 1 in NAIA by *Street & Smith's* basketball yearbook – met the Wildcats again for another exhibition matchup as it suffered an 80-53 setback at Rupp Arena. For Georgetown, former Western Kentucky University player Jake Ohmer – a junior guard from Taylor Mill, Ky., who starred in the 2017 Sweet Sixteen for Scott High School – took the game scoring honors with 25 points before fouling out.

"It was an amazing experience for our young men," said Briggs told the news media, including the author who covered the contest. "To get the chance to come into Rupp Arena and play the Kentucky Wildcats, it's something a lot of people dream of, and most kids in Kentucky dream of playing for the Kentucky Wildcats, like this young man [Ohmer], and I probably did.

"Proud of this gentleman [Ohmer] right here. He picked up where he left off in the state tournament. We were practicing in here yesterday and I am running up and down and getting a little exercise in here before we start, and I said, 'Jake, how many [points] did you score in here [in the Sweet Sixteen]? About 100?' He looked at me and said, '106, Coach.' He knew, and he got 25 tonight. Proud of him and the way he competes and the way that he battles."

In recent years, Georgetown also faced another Division I school, Eastern Kentucky, in a couple of exhibition matchups, with the host Colonels winning both times. EKU, at the time, had a promising coach by the name of Dan McHale, who had served as a student manager at UK just before Briggs arrived on campus. They met while working at a basketball camp during the summer of 2001 when McHale – who had just graduated with honors with a bachelor's degree in business administration – was a newly hired staff assistant to U of L coach Rick Pitino and Briggs was preparing for his first year at Kentucky.

"I got to know him [McHale] that way because he was already friends with the guys that I was coming in to work with," said Briggs. "He's been great to give us the [exhibition] games. He gives us that opportunity to come down and play. It's good for us. It's not quite Rupp Arena, but it's still a great experience."

While Briggs has said he'd consider a future opportunity to coach in NCAA Division I, he is nevertheless very thankful for the chance to be a coach at a special place called Georgetown College, which is less than 30 minutes away from the UK campus.

Chapter Fourteen

The Gator Boss with Bluegrass Connections

*H*ere's a pop quiz for you:
Who was in charge of UK basketball program's massive publicity machine from 2003 to 2008?

A. John Fitzwater
B. Adrian "Odie" Smith
C. Scott Stricklin
D. Kenny Klein

You say Fitzwater? Incorrect. He is a retired *Gainesville Sun* publisher from Somerset, Ky. You say Smith? Incorrect. He is a former UK and NBA star from the 1950s and 1960s. You say Klein? Incorrect. He runs the publicity machine at U of L.

So, after the process of elimination, the answer obviously is Scott Stricklin, who has strong roots in the state of Kentucky. And he is no stranger to the Southeastern Conference. Before he became the athletics director at Florida in 2016, Stricklin previously had worked at Auburn, Mississippi State, and UK, in no particular order. "I'm an SEC guy," he said after his arrival at the Gainesville school. "I understand the position Florida holds in college athletics."

Before heading to sunny Florida, Stricklin said it was very tough for him to leave Mississippi State, where he had served as the school's athletics director for several years. "It was incredibly difficult to leave Mississippi State for several reasons," said Stricklin. "Obviously, it is my alma mater, but also because nearly all of our family are tied to MSU. Also, I was really proud of all the things we had helped put in place there to build a successful department that could compete consistently in the SEC.

"However, the opportunity to be at Florida was too good to pass up. On a personal level, at my age, I felt like I needed another challenge in my career to see if I could successfully lead another athletic department."

During his early days as a marketing student, Mississippi State was where Stricklin met his future wife, the former Anne Howell, in a class. "We met in a summer school class at Mississippi State before our senior year," said the Jackson, Miss., native. "Anne grew up in Starkville but went to Abilene Christian University, where she played tennis. So, her undergrad [degree] is from ACU, but she has a master's from MSU." Her dad, by the way, is Bailey Howell, a basketball Hall of Famer who was a two-time All-American at Mississippi State and played 12 seasons in the NBA, including six trips to the All-Star Game.

Asked about meeting his future father-in-law for the first time when he was dating Anne, Stricklin added, "Bailey is a quiet gentleman who is a better person than he was a basketball player … and he was a great basketball player. I met him one night after church, and he didn't have much to say. He's opened up quite a bit since then and gives me as much advice as any other fan does these days."

Stricklin also has heard UK basketball stories from Howell. "Any time I've asked him about playing against UK, he talks about how important the games were in the conference standings," he said. "MSU won the SEC for the first time Bailey's senior year (1959), and obviously, they had to beat the Wildcats for that to happen. In his three years with the varsity, the Bulldogs beat Kentucky twice and only lost once. I think he's proud of having a winning record against the Big Blue."

However, Coach Babe McCarthy's 1958-59 Bulldogs (then called the Maroons), who finished 24-1 overall and won an automatic bid to the NCAA Tournament for capturing the conference title, were forced to give up their tourney bid because of an unwritten state policy that forbid Mississippi teams from facing integrated teams. Because of MSU's decision, Kentucky became SEC's representative in the Big Dance. Howell, by the way, led the SEC in scoring for the second straight time with a 27.5-point average that year.

While Stricklin holds a very high-profile post as Florida AD with an operating budget of nearly $141 million for the 2019-20 fiscal year, he has strong ties with the Bluegrass State. His parents are from Johnson County in the Eastern Kentucky mountains and graduated from Paintsville High School, and his uncle still lives there. Two cousins also live in Lexington. As mentioned earlier, Stricklin worked at UK as the associate athletics director in the media relations department.

"My parents moved to Mississippi for a job in the 1960s, so that's where I was born," said the very likeable Stricklin, who was born in 1970. "But we made trips every year back to Johnson County to see family. And we actually lived in Paintsville for about eight months when I was in the third grade."

Florida athletics director Scott Stricklin and Kentucky AD Mitch Barnhart. (Photo courtesy Scott Stricklin)

Growing up in Jackson, Stricklin wasn't all that good in sports, but he loved them and had some favorite teams. "I was a huge sports fan," Stricklin commented. "Football, basketball, baseball … you name it. SEC sports were especially big because we had both Mississippi State and Ole Miss, but as you know, being in the South, every SEC team has a local following, and you end up getting acquainted with all of those schools.

"For the NFL, we grew up as Saints fans because New Orleans was just a couple of hours away, and native Mississippian Archie Manning was their quarterback at the time. And I grew up a [Cincinnati] Reds fan because it was during the Big Red Machine days, and all of my family in Kentucky were Reds fans."

And Stricklin got involved in sports, but he was just mediocre in athletics. "I just knew I wasn't good enough to play beyond high school," said Stricklin, who attended Jackson Prep. "I actually started on the football team in junior high and did the high jump for my track team in high school, but my interest was in the off-the-field stuff such as writing for the school paper." He became the sports editor of *The Sentry*, the school newspaper and did stats and spotted for the radio play-by-play guy who covered the football team.

Eventually, as a student at Mississippi State, Stricklin found a sports-related job. "I began working in the Mississippi State athletic department as a student worker," he recalled, "and my goal upon graduation was to get a full-time job in athletics. You always want to progress and move through the ranks."

After MSU, Stricklin moved on to Auburn, Tulane, and Baylor, working primarily in the field of media relations and communications. Then he arrived in Lexington to work for his new boss, athletics director Mitch Barnhart, in 2003. How did he end up at Kentucky? "Mitch Barnhart and I had never met, but we had a mutual friend who recommended me for the position [as then-assistant AD for Media Relations]."

For the personable Stricklin, he oversaw the day-to-day publicity machine for UK's basketball program. It was a big job with numerous daily responsibilities, including working with high-profile coaches Tubby Smith and Billy Gillispie, among others. He had to deal with one of the nation's largest media contingent that covers Wildcat hoops, but he has fond memories during his Lexington stay.

"There are so many [UK memories] to choose from," commented Stricklin. "Coming back from a big deficit to beat U of L [on Kentucky's Patrick Sparks' three game-ending free throws] at Freedom Hall in December 2004, the double-overtime Elite Eight game against Michigan State in 2005 even though it was a loss, football wins over Georgia in 2006 and U of L in 2007. The baseball team winning the SEC in 2006 was a special accomplishment.

"But two memories really stand out. The first was football beating No. 1 LSU in 2007.... That was just an unbelievable atmosphere and a remarkable win. The other was men's basketball Senior Day in 2008. I ended up standing next to Mr. [Bill] Keightley during the singing of 'My Old Kentucky Home.'

"Even though I didn't grow up in Kentucky, that song has significance to me because every year growing up when the [Kentucky] Derby was run, my mom would make sure all of us kids were in front of the TV for the playing of 'My Old Kentucky Home.' And while we were all sitting there watching it, my mom would be singing along with tears streaming down her face.

"So, here I am in, standing on the court at Rupp Arena next to Mr. Wildcat while 'My Old Kentucky Home' is being sung. I'm thinking about my mom, and I'm also thinking about how many Kentuckians would love to switch places with me at that moment because of what that song meant, what UK basketball means, what Senior Day means, and what Mr. Keightley meant.

"As it turned out, that was Mr. Keightley's last Senior Day because he passed away a few weeks later. So, that's a pretty special memory."

Then his old school came calling in 2008 via former UK high-ranking sports official Greg Byrne, who was MSU's athletics director at that time. The school was searching for a senior associate athletics director for external affairs, overseeing fundraising and football, among other duties. Stricklin said yes and accepted the post, making the jump from media relations to fundraising.

In 2010, his boss left for a similar AD post at Arizona (and later at Alabama), and Stricklin became the top dog at MSU, serving as AD, which fulfilled his lifelong dream at the age of 40. At the time, men's basketball coach was Rick Stansbury, who also had Bluegrass ties. A 1977 graduate of Meade County High School, Stansbury had graduated from Campbellsville University, where he was a four-year starter in basketball.

"That Kentucky connection is something Rick and I have in common, so it comes up from time to time," Stricklin said in November 2010. "He's obviously done a great job as MSU's coach. His program has been the most consistently successful of any SEC West [Division] program over the last decade or so, and he does a great job of evaluating, recruiting and developing players."

In March 2012, Stansbury decided to retire after 22 years at MSU (eight as assistant, 14 as head coach). At this writing, his 293 career wins were the 11th most in SEC history. He also captured two SEC Tournament titles as well as winning five divisional crowns. After spending quality time with his family and two years as an assistant at Texas A&M, he returned to his home state in 2016 and became the head coach at Western Kentucky.

While at MSU in 2015, Stricklin received lots of national attention from media outlets such as *Sports Illustrated* and the *Washington Post*, among others, when he revealed the school was partnering with financial guru Dave Ramsey to help teach athletes in the subject area of personal finance.

In 2016, Stricklin made another career move, going from Starkville to Gainesville, Fla. As mentioned previously, it was perhaps the toughest decision that he has made in his athletics career because of his longtime love affair with MSU.

"I couldn't have left for any other place but Florida," he added. "It's just a special place not only in the world of the SEC but in college athletics because of the success they've had and the way they've had it with the integrity. Florida holds a leadership position in college athletics. And you look at the academic reputation; it is one of the best universities in the country. That's a pretty hard combination to not take the opportunity if it's offered to you."

In coming to Florida, Stricklin certainly understands he has big shoes to fill in replacing highly successful AD Jeremy Foley, who first came to the university in 1976 as an intern in the ticket office. It was Foley who in 1992 replaced then-Florida AD and Kentuckian Bill Arnsparger, the former NFL and LSU head football coach who once served as an assistant under UK coach Blanton Collier for several years.

In an interview with senior writer Chris Harry which appeared on the school's official athletics website, Stricklin was asked about his memories of the Gators when he was younger.

"Well, first off, 'The Swamp.' I came here when I was at Auburn. It was the first time I ever went to a football game there. Just the energy and how close the fans are – right on top of the field – it always felt like it was one of the best atmospheres for that reason alone.

"Next, Coach [Steve] Spurrier. If you're growing up in the '90s in this league, I don't know how you don't think about him. I remember I had a conversation with him on the field before the South Carolina-Mississippi State game in 2011. He reminded me how he interviewed for the Mississippi State job when he was between the Tampa Bay Bandits and Duke in 1986. He said, 'Yeah, they didn't hire me, but I guess it worked out OK, though.' Yeah, it did – for the Gators.

"And then, of course, Billy Donovan and what he did with the program and those back-to-back (NCAA) titles. I was at Kentucky and remember how frustrating it was when they went on that run. At the time, it was like, 'Man, these guys are winning everything. Football, basketball, everything.' "

Stricklin knows there are high and lows in his complex AD job. For example, while at MSU, he was proud to see the stunning rise of the school's football program led by then-coach Dan Mullen, who is now at Florida. But he also has seen the death of a Bulldog football player. In addition, there was an off-the-court fight between two basketball players during the team's Hawaii trip. Added Stricklin, "Sometimes young people make mistakes. That was an embarrassing incident and the type of behavior that we don't tolerate."

One difficult part of his AD job are the times he has to inform a coach that his or her performance wasn't satisfactory and the coach would need to step down from the post. "Managing and leading people in general, whether it's coaches, staff, students, or fans, is the biggest responsibility of a leader and the most challenging part of leadership," said Stricklin, who once received the 2015-16 Athletic Director of the Year award from the National Association of College Directors of Athletics (NACDA). "But making personnel changes are especially difficult because it's hard to tell people that they aren't going to be able to continue doing what they enjoy."

Stricklin realizes the fans and administrators can be impatient when it comes to their favorite team's poor performances and the coaches often get fired fairly quickly, but he also tries to give his coaches an opportunity to get through tough periods.

"I do think we have a lot more impatience than we used to, which is unfortunate, because the commitment that schools are making to coaches is a lot greater than it used to be, too, from a financial standpoint," he said.

"You know, if you have the right people in place, though, I'm going to be really patient. If we have the right person working with a plan, working hard, committed to this place, yeah, you can be patient with that. If you feel like you don't have the right person, you might be a little less patient...."

Throughout the Sunshine state, Stricklin often makes appearances, interacting with the Gator fans at social functions. He is also active on social media, including his official Twitter account that has over 70,000 followers.

"I like social media because I think it's a way you can communicate directly with people," said Stricklin. "And there's a lot of people who care about our athletic programs. That's one of the great things about college athletics is the passion people have for what our young people and our coaches do. And the opportunity to directly communicate to the masses is really cool, something that didn't exist 15 years ago.

"So, I enjoy it. I will try to be judicious.... It's a great tool and a great way to connect. And it's amazing how many people walk up to you – people always like connections, right? They walk up and say, 'Hey, you don't know me, but I know your cousin or I know your uncle or I live next door to your brother.' In this day and age, people walk up and say, 'Hey, I follow you on Twitter.' They feel a connection through social media, which is really pretty unique. I enjoy using that."

On his leadership philosophy, Stricklin, who is a member of the College Football Playoff Selection committee, said, "To be a good leader you have to be a selfless person and look after the needs of those you lead ahead of your own needs and wants. Like many people, I had to grow and mature before I really understood the importance of servant leadership, but to me, it's the only way to genuinely lead others."

His AD job at Florida is practically 24/7, but he makes a special effort to have free time for himself and his immediate family, which includes his wife, Anne, and two daughters, Abby and Sophie. "She's got a great heart, but she's my steel magnolia," said Stricklin of his wife.

In addition to his wife and two kids, some of his extended family members attended the press conference in Gainesville in September 2016 when Stricklin was introduced as Florida's top sports administrator. "We're both really fortunate to have an extended family that's been very supportive and loving throughout our lives, and I'm really blessed to have my parents, David and Eula Stricklin, here with us today," said Stricklin at the news conference. "Thank you, guys, for coming and being here. I want to wish my mom a happy birthday. She told me I couldn't say how old she is, but today is her birthday.

"My brother, David, is here, who's my older brother. He's a pilot for Delta, so it was easy for him to get here. He was born in Jacksonville, and my parents lived there while he was born, and so things seem to come full circle, I guess, sometimes. At least it has for the Stricklins."

In his spare time, he enjoys running several times a week and likes to read. "I usually keep a book in progress, and those tend to be nonfiction, although I just completed a fictional book by Nelson DeMille called *Up Country*," said Stricklin, who often reads on his iPad due to traveling. "This past fall I read *Flash Boys* by Michael Lewis (which is about high-frequency trading on Wall Street) and *Dead Wake* by Erik Larson (which recounts the sinking of the Lusitania)."

And his Christian faith is a very important ingredient in his everyday life. "I've been incredibly blessed, and those blessings have nothing to do with job title or salary or anything that the world might consider a blessing," said Stricklin. "The peace that comes from living in God and his son Jesus is hard to describe. I can't imagine doing a high-profile job in athletics and managing potential stress without that peace. Proverbs 15:33 is a verse I look at often."

Chapter Fifteen

From Coach P to Tubby

For a long time, former UK equipment manager Bill Keightley produced over a generation of outstanding student managers in the school's historic basketball program. And Dan McHale was one of his hard-working and most highly motivated students during the late 1990s and early 2000s. But his path to the program wasn't all that smooth.

McHale, who is from Chatham, N.J., came to Kentucky because he wanted to be a coach someday. Being a part of UK's hoops program is a very good way to start learning about coaching. "I grew up in New Jersey in the '80s and '90s and I knew I wanted to do coaching at a young age," said McHale, now the assistant coach at the University of New Mexico and former head coach at Eastern Kentucky University. "I was a scrappy little basketball player, but I knew my career was going to stop after high school. Rick Pitino was coaching the [New York] Knicks when I was growing up, and that's what I idolized from a coaching standpoint. When he was the coach of the Knicks, I tried to get out to as many games as possible.

"When Coach Pitino took over Kentucky, I was probably in seventh or eighth grade and realized that that's where I want to go. I wanted to learn from him. But I knew it was very difficult [to enter the program]. There were a lot of kids my age without any connections that were going to be able to go and work with the team."

But McHale's father, Dan McHale Sr., had a Kentucky friend in the Navy who had suggested the youngster come down and tour the campus. The friend didn't really know anyone from the UK program but said he would try to introduce the younger McHale to the right people. McHale's dad also was a basketball player at Navy, playing as a 6-foot, 170-pound guard during the 1970-71 season. McHale Jr. said, "I came down and met [future NBA coach] Frank Vogel, to be honest with you. He was from New Jersey as well. He was the manager for Kentucky, and I talked to him. I said, 'Look, this is what I want to do.' He said, 'Well, this is what you've got to come to, you got to get in good with "Mr. Bill." ' So, I met him [but] he brushed me off. He was busy with practice. So, I just wrote him letter after letter after letter.

"And finally I came back down again to the Kentucky-Villanova game [in 1997]. This was Coach Pitino's last year. This was the Tim Thomas vs. Ron Mercer game, and after the game, I finally got to Vogel again and got two minutes in front of 'Mr. Wildcat.' I told him, 'Look, I'm from New Jersey. I want to get into coaching.' He said, 'I've got your stack of letters, son. I've been following you, and I can't promise you anything. Get accepted to school. Be at my office at 6 a.m. first day of class.'

"Again, I came down here not knowing anything. I got something from housing [for a room assignment]. I came down, drove my family. It was the week before Labor Day. I was 17 years old and I pull up to the [Joe B. Hall] Wildcat Lodge [a dormitory that primarily housed the men's basketball team] to walk around, and I see my name on the door. So, I move into the Wildcat Lodge. I had no idea I was officially a part of UK basketball until I drove 12 hours with my family. I [had] said, 'I want to be a part of this team,' and my parents are telling me, 'You got to work for it.' And sure enough, I saw my name on the door of my dorm room at Wildcat Lodge. And that's how I found out I was a part of the team."

With his parents staying over at a Lexington hotel to help their freshman son finish unpacking, McHale decided to work very early on a Friday morning even though classes hadn't begun yet. He knew Keightley would show up early to work, so he set the alarm at 4 a.m.

Said McHale, "I showed up on Friday morning. Practice hasn't started, and back then, he didn't work out with the guys that early, but I knew he got to the office early. I sat outside Memorial Coliseum at about 4:30 a.m. I think he got there right around 5:05, and he looked at me and I said, 'Mr. Bill,' and he goes, 'I know who you are.' I said, 'I'm Dan McHale,' and he said, 'I know who you are,' and I said, 'I just want to thank you again. I just moved into Wildcat Lodge.' He said, 'I don't know nothing about that.' I knew that was his way of welcoming me to the family. You know he was a Marine as well, so he had connections with my father. I think he didn't like Northerners too much, so that's why I got a little tough love, being from New Jersey. I think surely I became one of his favorites. But I remember that was the first impression I made on him. He told me he told other people that story that I was one of the first and only people ever to beat him to the office."

And McHale lived four years at the Wildcat Lodge, which was later razed in 2012. Before coming to Kentucky, the future coach said he "actually grew up a Seton Hall college basketball fan and actually a Duke fan because I was enamored of Bobby Hurley [who played at Duke] and the Jersey guys as well, as crazy as that sounds. He was a scrappy little point guard from New Jersey, and I went to his dad's camps when I was a kid. I remember being torn from the classic Duke-Kentucky game [in 1992]. I'm rooting for Coach Pitino, but I'm also rooting for Bobby Hurley. So, I rooted for Kentucky, but I wanted Hurley to play well."

McHale's parents had some concerns about his early goals to be a basketball coach. "They always told me, 'Follow your dreams, but there are a lot of kids your age that want to do this.' And I said, 'Look, I know what I'm doing. I'm going to kick the door down until I can really establish my marks,'" recalled McHale, who earned high school letters in basketball, track, and cross country.

They advised him to have a backup plan to fall back on in case coaching didn't work out, so he studied business. "I graduated with a degree in marketing with honors," he said. "But I knew as I worked my way up, and my first year was Tubby Smith's first year, I got to know the staff. I knew from early on that I was going to be a part of this program because I just lived and died with it. I was in the gym with the players, in the video room with the assistant coaches as a freshman, taking notes at every practice, so I knew I was going to leave my mark."

As for Frank Vogel, the UK student manager who became the head coach of the Los Angeles Lakers in 2019, McHale said he didn't really know him at Kentucky. "By the time I got here, he left," commented McHale. "We stayed in touch, and it was more of the same connection. Scrappy basketball player from New Jersey who ended up being a manager at Kentucky, and he took off and ended up being a coach for the NBA."

While at Kentucky, Vogel, who had transferred from NCAA Division III Juniata College in Pennsylvania, where he was a point guard, also played on the newly revived junior varsity squad in addition to his student manager duties and served as the video coordinator for UK's 1996-97 Final Four squad. Vogel then joined Rick Pitino at Boston when the coach took charge of the Celtics.

"I think anything can happen," said McHale when asked about Vogel's rise to the NBA. "He's a very smart guy. If you look at the way coaching goes these days, you know, there is a former player route, but there's a lot of coaches either in college or pro who get their start in the film room and work their way up. I'm not surprised at all. He has a very bright mind. I got a chance to really spend time with him [when] the Celtics came to play an exhibition game at Rupp my freshman year. So, they practiced at Memorial Coliseum. I really hit it off with Frank and Kevin Willard [who] was on the staff at that time, both young guys with the Celtics. Obviously, Kevin and I connect a couple years later and go off to our own history together. But Frank was just a great guy. He told me, 'Just live your dreams, live in the film room, [and] listen three times more than you speak.' That is what he kept on telling me."

McHale credits Keightley and Vogel for their guidance. Without them, "I'm not sure I would be where I am today," he added.

After Pitino – who in eight years at Kentucky had rebuilt the Wildcats program after a nasty mess with the NCAA and guided them to three Final Four trips – went to Boston, Tubby Smith was named the head coach at Kentucky in 1997. That meant McHale would be working under a new mentor, not Pitino, his hero. He was upset. "I was really disappointed when he left because he was the reason I was coming to UK, and I was set to enroll in the fall," said McHale. "But I was 17 at the time, so what did I really know about life? I knew my best chance to become a college basketball coach was to take this route, and the University of Kentucky in the late 90s under Rick Pitino was like getting accepted to the Harvard Business School."

McHale remembers a time about the newly hired Kentucky boss when he had his team at his house on Halloween night and they were watching an NBA season opener between Boston and Michael Jordan's Chicago squad. It was Pitino's first game as the Celtics coach, and he had three former Wildcat stars – Antoine Walker, Walter McCarty, and

Dan McHale (Photo by Jamie H. Vaught)

Ron Mercer – playing for his new club. Later, during the season, he also added another ex-UK standout, Reggie Hanson, to the roster.

"He's such a man with class and integrity," McHale said of Smith. "His biggest thing was, 'Never get too high, never get too low.' One of my early memories was Coach Pitino's first game [at Boston]. I remember Coach Smith celebrating like it was yesterday. We all came over to his house, and I remember my parents were in town. He said, 'Bring your parents over.' He was the most welcoming guy in the world, and I just remember him gathering around the TV with his current players.

"Of course, Coach Pitino's players [at UK] had a lot of allegiance to Coach Pitino at that time. And him [Smith] being the biggest cheerleader, the Celtics won that game. They beat the Bulls that night. I can't imagine the range of emotions going through his head because he's trying to develop his own identity, he's trying to win over a team that was loyal to Coach Pitino, but he put the game on TV, and he was the biggest Celtics fan that night.

"And that just showed me about the type of person he was. He wasn't going to run from the fact that he was in Coach Pitino's shadow. He wasn't going to shun his players for supporting him. I didn't realize it at the time, but now that I'm a coach, I look back at certain dynamics of coaching. For him to do that, it just shows the type of guy that he is, not afraid about the past, and he's not afraid to embrace certain things. It just shows how upper class that guy is. But I will never forget that. He invited all of the families over, put the Celtics game on, and he hadn't coached a game as a Kentucky Wildcat coach yet, everyone was still talking about Rick Pitino, and he embraced that."

In Tubby Smith's first year at Kentucky, the fifth-ranked Wildcats continued their winning ways, posting a 35-4 overall mark as well as capturing the SEC Tournament title without superstars. And they, surprisingly, won six straight games in the Big Dance to win the national title. The captains of that "Comeback Cats" squad were Jeff Sheppard, Allen Edwards, and Cameron Mills. As discussed in a previous chapter, the fans unfairly have said Smith didn't actually win the championship since he was coaching Pitino's players. McHale doesn't agree with that argument.

"You don't win games without coaching, and, yes, he had talent, but it wasn't like he inherited that talent from the '96 team," he said. "There were pieces, but he had to blend all those pieces together. I'm not sure if McDonald's All-Americans were on that team, but you look at [6-foot-10 Nazr Mohammed. [He] wasn't a finished product. (6-foot-10) Jamaal Magloire was still a sophomore. [He] wasn't a finished product. Heshimu Evans and Allen Edwards, they're good players, but it wasn't like Walter McCarty and those guys. So, he was able to blend a collection of really good players into a championship team, and you've got to give him all of the credit for that."

McHale also shared some of his UK memories, mostly during his freshman season.

On Kentucky's come-from-behind 86-84 win over Duke in NCAA South Regional finals at Tropicana Field in St. Petersburg, Fla.:

"I remember going into halftime [behind 49-39], and everyone [is] looking around for answers. Coach Smith was really good, but I'll never forget Scott Padgett was the one that stood up and talked to the guys. He said, 'Look, guys, we've been here before. We can't give up 49 points at the half. We got to relax.' That was the thing about Coach Smith. He let the players speak a lot. You could tell Scott was going to be a coach back then because he really got after the guys in a way where they responded to come back and to do it in dramatic fashion. It was awesome." [Padgett is now the head coach at Samford University in Birmingham, Ala.]

Asked if he was surprised about UK's stunning comeback against the Blue Devils:

"Not really. It was a high-level game; I could see the momentum shifting. There were about 12 minutes left in the game, and we got lucky. You know Cameron Mills hit the big shot, Scott hits a big shot, and that's just what happens when you have a good team. At that point, it's the Elite Eight. You can't be surprised about anything. They got tight and we started playing loose, and we got some big-time shots made."

On UK's 86-85 overtime win over Stanford in the national semifinals in San Antonio:

"I remember that one very, very vividly. We didn't come out well, and then we battled back again in the second half, and that's when they started getting the 'Comeback Cats' [nickname]. It was just one of those games you knew the guards were going to win. Jeff Sheppard injured his ankle, and the guys stepped up. Wayne Turner really carrying us in the second half. But it was just a collection of guys that did it together, and they didn't care about who got the credit, and you could just tell there were no egos. There was no one superstar, but we just kept chipping away and it was a huge win."

On the school's 1998 NCAA championship:

"I was a young guy nine months from my senior prom. [I was] at the White House meeting Bill Clinton. [I was an] average player from New Jersey with no connections at Kentucky. We flew to the White House. Coach Smith took us all, even the young guys. If you had told me nine months (earlier), I'd be in the White House getting a ring, shaking the hand of Bill Clinton, it just doesn't happen like that.

"So, there were several great moments. You really bond with these guys, the managers and the coaches. I can remember like it was yesterday with the SEC Tournament [and the NCAA's first/second round games] being in Atlanta, and then we drove down to Tropicana [Field, where] I was at the game against Duke for the regionals. It was special. After coming back [to Lexington] from San Antonio, I'll never forget that – getting off the bus for the welcome ceremony at Rupp Arena and seeing 18,000 people going crazy just for the celebration. That's something you'll never forget."

On his most embarrassing moment as a student manager:

"I think the other guys set me up to this. I was a freshman, and [general manager] Jerry Krause of the Chicago Bulls was in the stands as a scout in Memorial Coliseum. Listen, nobody's been at practice unless we knew about it. I'm pretty sure it was [sophomore guard] Steve Masiello. He was standing on the sidelines with me. He says, 'See that guy right there? He doesn't belong in practice. Go throw him out.' So, I go up to Jerry Krause, who's in watching our guys as a scout for the Bulls back in 1998. Jerry Krause was one of the most powerful men in the NBA, and I told him he has to leave. He was like, 'Awww,' and I was like, 'You have to go.' And I remember [assistant coach] George Felton yelling at me and flagging him down. George was running up in the stands and he said, 'Jerry, he doesn't know, sit down,' and I'm looking around like, 'What did I do?' And George said, 'That's Jerry Krause, general manager for the Chicago Bulls, you idiot! What are you doing?' I knew who he was, but I didn't put a name to a face." [McHale said he then wrote a letter of apology to Krause but isn't sure if the Chicago executive had received it or not.]

Which Wildcat player probably had the most personality during McHale's four years as student manager at UK?

"Well, Scott [Padgett] never stopped talking. He was always the guy that kept going. He talked a lot, I mean, a whole lot. And you've got quiet guys like Jeff Sheppard and Tayshaun Prince. They were very quiet. I would say the most personality had to have been Jamaal Magloire, easily. Jamaal was always joking, always trying to get after the guys. He was definitely a guy that used to clown around a lot. I'm happy for him because he's done very well obviously [in the NBA]."

How did McHale meet his future wife, the former Jackie Hering, at UK?

"When I was a junior, she was a sophomore. One of my closest friends was J.P. Blevins. J.P. and I were very, very close. J.P.'s girlfriend was Jackie's roommate, and they would hang out all the time, and Jackie would come over a lot. J.P. and I lived across the hall from each other. So, then I met her. It took her a good eight months before she would allow me to go out on a date with her. She was a Kentucky girl through and through. She wanted nothing to do with a guy from New Jersey. I remember a late-night shooting in the gym with J.P. I'm rebounding for him and strategizing. I'm like 'Okay, J.P., I got to figure out a way where we could all go out, double date together.' She turned me down three or four times before I could finally win her over." [McHale said his now-wife was really the one who encouraged and pushed him to chase his coaching dream, saying she has been "my rock through the highs and lows."]

On Bill Keightley's attendance at McHale's wedding:

"He came with a blue blazer on. I got married in Lexington and my wife is from Owensboro. We got married at [Cathedral of] Christ the King and [had a reception at] Marriott Griffin Gate. And I'll never forget [when] the power was out in the hotel, and [he was] one of the first guys I saw. [He had] a big red face and a big Kentucky blue jacket, and he just gave me a big hug."

By the time McHale was a junior at UK, he became more involved in the coaching aspects, helping out the assistant coaches.

"Coach Smith was involved with the other stuff going on, but coaches Mike Sutton, George Felton, and Shawn Finney took me under their wing, and I broke down a lot of film with them at night," said McHale. "We'd get back from a road trip and I wouldn't go back to the [Wildcat] Lodge. I'd go to the offices with the coaches and do whatever they wanted me to do, whether it was sharp deflections, break down the offense with them. I give them a lot of credit because they really helped me get into coaching."

Later, in 2001, McHale graduated from UK with honors and earned a bachelor's degree in business administration. However, it was an awkward time for him as Pitino had stunned the sporting world in late March by announcing that he was returning to the state of Kentucky to become the coach at rival U of L. And McHale immediately began working for the new Louisville coach as a staff assistant.

"It was weird," commented McHale. "The last month of the year I was living in the Wildcat Lodge but commuting to Louisville. In March and April, I would go out with a jacket on and get in my car. I'd go out with my Louisville gear on and do my individual instructions in Louisville, and then I'd get back at eight or nine o'clock at night at the Wildcat Lodge. That month was very strange. I'm not sure how the [UK] coaches felt about that. I know the players were looking at me a little funny. But my friends are my friends. They're going to support me either way. A lot of UK fans, including my wife, said we're loyal to people, and that's about it. It took some time [to adjust]."

McHale was asked if Pitino ever knew that the coach himself was the real reason why the youngster came to UK back in 1997. "He knew that early on when he first hired me," said McHale. "He had given me a hard time because he'd just gotten the job at Louisville and he kept on telling me. I was wearing my blue, I had blue underwear on all the time. And I told him, 'Coach, I came here because of you. I had four great years there.' But he knew that early on, and I think that's why he hired me. He heard my story and I got lucky. He knew that the reason I was there was because of him and how much I idolized him growing up."

Like McHale, Jeff Morrow was a student manager at Kentucky. Before becoming a successful high school basketball coach in Louisville, Morrow worked under Pitino and has many memories about the former Wildcat coach, including the pickup games.

"When Coach Pitino came to UK [in 1989], he was known for his early morning pickup games, and he included the managers in these games," said Morrow. "He and Coach [Billy] Donovan were usually the two captains who chose the teams. The assistant coaches – Herb Sendek, Tubby Smith, Ralph Willard, Rock Oliver, Bernadette Locke – all played during their time on staff. In addition, the managers played, and sometimes Coach Pitino's friends would join.

"These games were competitive and fierce. Let's just say Coach didn't like to lose. I played basketball in high school, so I was used to playing. Let's just say that having the head coach at Kentucky scrutinize your game on a daily basis raised the stakes and, for a young college student like myself, added some pressure to the games. I was an average player at best in high school, and I did not want to be the one who caused his team to lose. Often, Coach Pitino would choose me to play on his team, and my roommate Spencer Tatum [who was also a student manager] would be on the other team. It made for long days when you were playing pickup games at 5:30 a.m., usually five days a week, but make no mistake about it, I enjoyed it. What basketball person would not want the opportunity to play with the head coach at UK on a regular basis?"

Then-Louisville coach Rick Pitino smiles at assistant Wayne Turner before the 2013 UK-U of L matchup at Rupp Arena. (Photo by Jamie H. Vaught)

Added Morrow, who was inducted into the Kentucky Association of Basketball Coaches' Court of Honor in 2017, "I recall a specific day that was not too long after he had arrived at UK where Coach gave me a nickname that has stuck to this day for those who know me from my time there. Even if I do not see or talk to someone for years, if I see them, they will refer to me as 'Magic,' the name Coach gave me during an intense pickup game one morning. It was a close game and we were on a fast break, and I was dribbling the ball down the court. Coach was in front of me on a wing, and as I approached the top of the key, I dribbled between my legs and threw a behind the back pass to Coach, who scored, and our team won the game. I had begun to feel more comfortable after getting to know him, so I guess I came out of my shell in that defining moment. He did not expect me to do that. It caught him off guard, and you could tell he was amused by it. He laughed and asked what got into me and began to refer to me as Magic [because of NBA legend Magic Johnson]. From that day forward, he and others who knew me from UK refer to me as Magic. I'm just glad that behind the back pass landed where I intended and not out of bounds ... who knows what my nickname would have been."

In addition to working for Pitino at Louisville, McHale has spent time as an assistant at Manhattan, Iona, Seton Hall, and Minnesota before landing his first head coaching job at Eastern Kentucky in Richmond in 2015. He got to coach against his UK friends, including Manhattan's Steve Masiello and Georgetown College's Chris Briggs. McHale also took his 2015-16 Colonels to Rupp Arena for a date with the mighty Wildcats. As it turned out, the Colonels lost 88-67 to John Calipari's team with UK senior forward Alex Poythress getting a double-double, recording game-highs with 21 points and 13 rebounds. At the time, UK was coming off a road loss at UCLA.

On Poythress, McHale said, "I think he was a difference maker. He is a pro when he wants to be. When that motor clicks and when he starts playing at the speed he did tonight, he's very tough to guard. He's jumping off trampolines and just finishing in traffic. He's a special, special player."

McHale added his first Rupp Arena appearance as the head coach was an emotional one. "It was awesome," he commented. "It was a surreal experience. Now I'd been on the bench before. I've been back before as a Louisville guy, but this was my first time as a head coach. To be honest with you, I did a couple of things. I wanted a tribute, a thank you to Mr. Bill [Keightley who had passed away in 2008], so I left that first chair open as an honor, and that was my tribute to him. I spoke to Hazel, his wife, and Karen, his daughter, about that. I said, 'This is for Mr. Bill. I don't know if he'll sit on the visitors' bench at Rupp Arena, but I'm keeping that chair open just in case he wants to.'

"And then another special friend of mine that I had a connection with was Van Florence [a longtime UK hoops program supporter who later passed away in 2016]. As sick as Van was, I said, 'Van, you need to walk me out at the tunnel. I just need you to be there by my side.' So, Van came in the visitors' locker room, spent the first 10 minutes before the game with me, and asked me how I was doing. You know, [I had] butterflies. For him to walk me out, it was just truly special."

After trailing 50-36 at the halftime, EKU rallied and made the contest much closer in the second half. With 6:06 remaining, the Colonels were only down by eight before the Wildcats finally pulled away for a 21-point victory. Added McHale, "I was proud of our guys. It was a great memory, and I hope I get the chance to do it again."

During his three years at EKU, McHale posted an overall coaching record of 38-55, including a 16-34 record against the Ohio Valley Conference teams, before he was dismissed by the school's athletics director and ex-Wildcat Steve Lochmueller in March 2018. His three teams also failed to earn a trip to the Ohio Valley Conference tournament, which only invites the top eight conference teams. Not long before he left Eastern Kentucky, he was asked if coaching at mid-major schools like EKU was tougher than coaching at big-name places like Kentucky, Louisville, and Alabama.

"I think it's got its pros and cons," he said. "You have to embrace where you are. The pressure obviously isn't as big as it is at those schools, but there is pressure here. But it is tougher because there are limited resources. I have fewer assistant coaches. We have less money to travel. We have to play a lot of guarantee games to bring in money. But I think you can look at two ends of the spectrum. There's less pressure, but you have less resources to win. So, you've just got to embrace where you are, be happy, be excited, I'm just all in. Just thrilled to be the head coach at Eastern Kentucky, and that's it."

A member of the Rick Pitino coaching tree that includes Tubby Smith, Travis Ford, Billy Donovan and Mick Cronin, among others, McHale thanked the EKU followers for their support when he was fired. "On behalf of Jackie and myself, we just want to thank the Colonel fans and the great city of Richmond for a great three years. It was an honor to be your head coach," he tweeted.

After his EKU days, McHale continued to stay involved in basketball during the 2018-19 season, talking hoops on ESPN Sports Radio [Lexington] and on Fox Sports before landing another coaching position. During the summer of 2019, McHale arrived in Albuquerque, where he became assistant coach for the New Mexico Lobos, where their home arena, known as "The Pit," has been characterized as having one of the best atmospheres in the country. On his latest career move, McHale said he was "excited to be part of such a rich basketball tradition" at New Mexico, which has been among the home attendance leaders in college basketball for many years.

As you can tell, McHale is clearly a passionate fellow who loves coaching and basketball.

Chapter Sixteen

Kentucky Mr. Basketball to NBA

On a beautiful summer day in 2018, ex-Wildcat Darius Miller, coming off his fourth NBA season with the New Orleans Pelicans, had just finished the first day of his three-day basketball camp at Tom Browning Boys & Girls Club in his hometown of Maysville. He and another Mason County product, Chris Lofton, had been conducting summer camps together for several years, even though Lofton, a former University of Tennessee star, wasn't around this time as his European team was still competing for a championship. The duo were former Kentucky Mr. Basketball winners who led Mason County High School to separate state tournament titles. In addition to Miller and Lofton, the Ohio River city has had a share of celebrities over the years, including Miss America Heather French Henry, television host Nick Clooney, singer and actress Rosemary Clooney, and even U.S. Supreme Court Associate Justice Stanley Forman Reed.

And Miller, who as a senior helped UK win the national championship in 2012, was glad to be back home and sat down for an interview for this book. He was courteous. The 6-foot-8, 225-pounder was asked about the past season when the Pelicans had five players from UK on their 2017-18 roster. That's like home away home, right?

"It was a whole lot of fun," said Miller, who averaged 7.8 points and 23.7 minutes that winter. "I feel like I had a lot of chemistry. A lot. I knew all the guys, so, me coming back from overseas and being able to join the team with people I was familiar with, it really helped me a lot. I really enjoyed competing night in and night out with those guys because they're all good guys. I'm pretty good friends with all of them."

His New Orleans teammates from UK included Anthony Davis, DeMarcus Cousins, Rajon Rondo, and DeAndre Liggins. Miller and his teammate, E'Twaun Moore, were the only two players for the 2017-18 Pelicans to play in all 82 regular season games. Interestingly, the only other pair of New Orleans teammates who have played in all 82 games were ex-Wildcat standouts Jamal Mashburn and Jamaal Magloire in 2002-03.

Miller's Pelicans went on to finish that regular season with a 48-34 mark and advanced to the playoffs, sweeping the Portland Trail Blazers in four games in the opening round before dropping to eventual NBA champion Golden State Warriors.

During the Pelicans' 2018-19 campaign, Miller also played with three former UK players – Davis, Julius Randle and Andrew Harrison – as they finished at 33-49. He also started 15 games – his NBA career-high. In 69 games, he averaged 8.2 points while shooting 36.5 percent from the three-point line. Miller, who missed the last five games of the season due to an injury, hit a career-high tying 21 points against Oklahoma City.

Nearly four months after the 2018-19 season had ended, Miller signed a two-year pact reportedly worth around $14 million to remain at New Orleans. However, he later suffered a ruptured Achilles tendon during a summer workout and was expected to be sidelined for the 2019-20 campaign.

Darius Miller was born in 1990 and he couldn't get away from basketball. His young father, Brian Miller, was still playing hoops. He was a productive 6-foot-5 guard/forward for Morehead State Eagles. His coach at MSU, Tommy Gaither, told Rick Bailey of the *Lexington Herald-Leader* in 1991 that the elder Miller was "a coach's dream as a player. I've never questioned his intensity. He always plays hard. He's a winner in every sense of the word, and he has asserted senior leadership as he's matured. I'm real proud of him. I've watched him grow up, and I'll be at his graduation in May."

Well, as it turned out, the Millers do love basketball and have battled in pickup basketball ever since. "Yeah, since I was born," smiled the younger Miller. "He's the reason I started playing basketball. I [have] seen my dad playing basketball and I wanted to be like him. I mean, he's been playing since I can remember, and I've been trying to be like him, so definitely a lot of pickup games with him. He never took it easy on me, and I think that helped me to get where I'm at now. So, I definitely looked up to him and tried to emulate him when I was playing the game of basketball."

His athletic father, Brian, was asked about his proudest moment in his son's career so far. "The proudest moment is Darius being a nice young man. [I] raised a good man, a loving father, loving husband," said the elder Miller at the summer camp. "That's the proudest thing that I can take with me. I mean, basketball is just the icing on the cake. But I thank God that he's a great young man.

"He was able to fulfill his dreams. He won a championship. He won one at every level. I'm just glad and thank God every day that he's living out his dreams. It's a proud moment."

On visiting Darius in New Orleans, Brian said, "I visit him while I can. I went down there to the playoff games. I go down there and see what's going on with him and see how the family is doing, and [I] love my grandbabies." Darius and his wife, Brynne, have two daughters, Nadia and Kalani. He even wrote a "Father's Day" note to his toddlers that was published on UK basketball coach John Calipari's CoachCal.com website.

Growing up, Darius also played pickup hoops with other (mostly older) hometown kids, including Chris Lofton, a 2004 Mr. Kentucky Basketball who became a three-time All-American and 2007 SEC Player of the Year while at Tennessee. Even though they are several years apart, they briefly played together at Mason County High School, advancing to the state tournament championship game in 2004 before losing when Miller was in the 8th grade and Lofton was a senior.

Darius Miller and his father Brian at a basketball camp in Maysville. (Photo by Jamie H. Vaught)

"I've been playing against Chris and watching Chris work and watching him play. He really inspired me to work hard and to try to compete at the highest level, and he was like a big brother to me growing up," said Miller. "Even to this day, we still play pick up in the summer when we get together, so it's always fun. It's always competitive."

Miller hasn't forgotten his first state tournament trip in 2004 at Rupp Arena when the defending champion Mason County Royals, coached by Kelly Wells, won three games and advanced all the way to the finals before losing to Warren Central. "That was amazing," he commented. "That was the first time I experienced an atmosphere like that. Growing up watching Chris, he dominated that year, too, like he always did. I really enjoyed it. I was looking up to those guys, going to all their games since I can remember, and I finally got a chance to play with those guys. We made it, and we made it pretty far and to the state championship [game], so it was nice."

By Miller's senior year, his 2007-08 Royals, who had a four-game trip to Hawaii, were so good as coach Chris O'Hearn's squad dominated nearly everyone, finishing with a 34-4 mark and a state tournament title. Named to the *Parade* All-American team, he averaged 19.9 points and 7.9 rebounds.

While Lofton was shooting the lights out with his patented downtown jumpers at Tennessee, Miller said the Vols' star didn't push him hard to come to UT. "Not too hard, really," said Miller of Lofton's recruitment. "I mean, I came to him for advice. I asked him questions, but he never tried to make me go to Tennessee or tell me I should go to Tennessee. [He] kind of let me find my own way, and I appreciate that."

Before selecting Kentucky, Miller considered Cincinnati, Florida, Illinois, Indiana, Kansas State, Louisville, Miami, Xavier, and Tennessee. He became the third basketball player from Maysville to play for the Wildcats since the 1970s. The other two well-known performers from Mason County High School who starred at UK during that period were Deron Feldhaus and Ronnie Lyons.

Miller added it was the friendships that he had developed with several UK players, including Perry Stevenson, Ramon Harris, Jodie Meeks, and Patrick Patterson, which guided him toward Lexington during the recruiting process.

"The relationship I built with the players [is what led me to Kentucky]," said Miller. "Patrick Patterson, who I still call my big brother to this day, really showed me around, kind of took me under his wing. All the guys who were there really showed me a great time. They really looked out for me, kind of took me under their wing, and that made me feel comfortable there and what ultimately made me commit to Kentucky."

Speaking of Patterson, a native of Huntington, West Virginia, who was coming off his co-SEC Freshman of the Year performance in 2007-08, Miller also visited Patterson's hometown on the Ohio River, a little over an hour-and-a-half drive from Maysville, during his UK career. "I've been to his house a couple of times," said Miller. "We always go out to eat or whatever the case may be. Before I had kids, we used to take a trip every summer, go on vacation, but now that I have kids, I don't really have time to do that. We still keep in touch. Every time we're in the same [NBA] city, we go out to eat. We go to do something. I talk to him every week.

"He took me under his wing and showed me the ropes as soon as I got there [at Kentucky], and he's been doing that. Even when I got to the NBA, he helped me. He would talk to me, call me, check on me, still to this day. That's like my big brother. He did a great job of helping me, and we've been close ever since."

By the way, guard DeAndre Liggins, who is from Chicago, and Miller were the only two freshmen on scholarship on coach Billy Gillispie's second Kentucky team that finished at 22-14 with a trip to National Invitational Tournament. (UK's other freshman that season was walk-on Landon Slone, the current coach at Paintsville High School.)

As a typical young kid growing up in Kentucky, Miller had a favorite Kentucky Wildcat player. Who was he? It was sharpshooting All-American guard Tony Delk. And Miller had his picture taken with Delk in Lexington during the mid-1990s, and the future Cat was wearing an oversized Kentucky jersey.

"I think that was at the mall, and I think he was doing a signing or something," said Miller. "I can't really remember. I was really young, but he was one of my favorite players. Growing up I spent a lot of time with my grandmother who was a huge Kentucky fan. [Delk was] one of her favorite players, so he became one of my favorite players, just watching him play and watching how talented he was, one of the best shooters I've seen. So, I got a chance to meet him, and I was really excited that I got to do that." [Delk is currently No. 5 on UK's all-time scoring list with 1,890 points, leading the Wildcats in scoring in three of his four years at Kentucky.]

Along with his teammates, Miller had a new coach at Kentucky after his freshman season. UK athletics director Mitch Barnhart and others weren't very happy with Gillispie's two stormy years, so the school lured then 50-year-old

John Calipari away from Memphis, where he had been coaching for nine years. A year before, he had just led Memphis to the national championship game, and the former NBA head coach had been named the national coach of the year by various organizations in three separate years.

By the summer of 2009, Miller knew things would be different in the UK basketball program under Calipari. In addition, for the coming season, UK would be playing with a talented group led by rookies John Wall and DeMarcus Cousins along with veteran Patrick Patterson.

"Totally different, night and day," said Miller when asked to contrast Calipari's and Gillispie's coaching styles. "The difference between my freshman year and my sophomore year was unbelievable. Billy G. played a more grinded-out type game, played rough, played physical, deny everything, that type of basketball. Coach Cal, as we all know, has a system. He's a player's coach. His teams were like NBA teams, and it was great. I loved it and felt I played really well in it, so it was good for me."

In Calipari's first season at Kentucky, the 35-3 Wildcats advanced all the way to the East Regional finals, where they lost to Coach Cal's friend, Bob Huggins, and his West Virginia club, 73-66 at the Carrier Dome in Syracuse, N.Y. It was a game that Miller would like to forget. Like the cold-shooting Wildcats who hit only 34.3 percent, the sophomore from Mason County missed all six of his field goal attempts. Just a week earlier, Miller was red-hot as he poured in 7 of 9 shots for a then career-high 20 points along with nine rebounds in a 30-point victory over Wake Forest in the Big Dance.

For the 2010-11 campaign, Kentucky made a surprising run to the Final Four in Houston after a mid-season slump that saw the Wildcats drop six SEC road games from early January to mid-February. After a 77-76 overtime setback to the Arkansas Razorbacks and coach John Pelphrey at Bud Walton Arena, the No. 22 Wildcats bounced back and defeated coach Billy Donovan's No. 13 Florida 76-68 in the next game as Miller scored what would be his career-high 24 points at Rupp Arena. UK then finished the regular season on a winning note and took the SEC Tournament title in Atlanta, where Miller was named the tourney MVP. In three SEC Tournament contests, Miller averaged 13.3 points and 5.6 rebounds.

"I had had a rough regular season when we came to the SEC," recalled Miller, who started 37 of 38 games that winter. "That was probably our roughest year as far as the SEC went. We lost some games we shouldn't have, and I was a part of that. I wasn't really performing how I felt like I should. Coming into the SEC Tournament, I was just determined to play the best that I could, and it worked out for me. I had a great SEC Tournament, and my teammates did a great job of trying to motivate me and keep me motivated when I was going through a rough time. Like you said, I happened to play pretty good, and we happened to win, so it was nice."

And the Wildcats – who received a No. 4 seed in the Big Dance – weren't finished. They kept winning in the NCAA Tournament, beating favored teams Ohio State (in the Sweet Sixteen) and North Carolina (in the Elite Eight), and advancing to the Final Four in Houston, where they lost to third-seeded Connecticut 56-55 in the national semifinals. Before a large group of assembled media at the Final Four press conference, Miller was asked about how much the Final Four means to him and the state.

"It means a lot to me," he told the reporters on the day before the UConn game. "I'm from Kentucky. I know what it means to the state. I grew up in an area where they had a lot of Kentucky fans. Kentucky doesn't really have a pro team, so they look to us and Louisville like their pro teams. They take a lot of pride in basketball in Kentucky, in my opinion. For us to make it, like I said, me being a part of it, it is amazing for me. It's something I've dreamed about since I was little. I'm glad to be here."

Brad Stevens-coached Butler, which had junior guard Shelvin Mack of Lexington Bryan Station High School, was also in that Final Four. Miller also visited and talked with Mack, who would be a future NBA guard.

"I went over to his room a couple of nights ago, spent a little time with him," said Miller. "We have a really close relationship. I grew up playing basketball with him. I talk to him pretty much every day."

Kentucky, whose leading scorers were freshman guard Brandon Knight and freshman forward Terrence Jones, finished the year at 29-9.

UK had one of its best teams ever in school history in 2011-12 when the Wildcats practically played with a six-man rotation made up of Anthony Davis (national player of the year), Doron Lamb, Terrence Jones, Michael Kidd-Gilchrist, Marquis Teague, and Miller. All six eventually were picked in the 2012 NBA Draft, including four in the first round. One of preseason favorites to win the whole thing, the Wildcats dominated college basketball with a stunning 38-2 mark. To win the school's eighth national title, Kentucky rolled over Western Kentucky, Iowa State, Indiana, Baylor, Louisville and Kansas in the Big

Dance. And Miller – one of the team's only two seniors (the other was 6-foot-11 Eloy Vargas) – was the "glue" that helped the Wildcats – who were unbeaten at 16-0 in SEC action – win the whole thing. For his efforts, he was named the coaches' SEC Sixth Man of the Year.

Moments after Kentucky stopped archrival Rick Pitino's U of L Cardinals 69-61 in the national semifinals, Miller became very emotional when asked how far he had come after his ups and downs throughout his collegiate career, beginning with his freshman year. "I was in the NIT. I was terrible," he told the reporters, including the author. "We've worked extremely hard to get to this point. I feel like we've all done a great job throughout the whole year. This is what we've been reaching for. At the end of this game, we have a chance to win a national championship. It's an opportunity that not most people get. Can't explain it in words. You have to experience it. For me to be able to experience it with these guys who I've grown to be brothers with, it means a lot to me."

Miller only started 11 games during that memorable campaign while averaging 26.1 minutes and 9.9 points, but Calipari said he was good enough to start the entire year.

"Darius basically has started for me for two years," Calipari added. "But he's accepted coming off the bench. There are times I started him this year, times he started in the second half because he was playing so well…. People love him. All the calls I'm getting about him, people want him on their team for the simple fact he's got to be a great kid. We have six starters. Someone had to come off the bench. He said I'm good.

"He's the most unselfish player I've ever coached. Sometimes it drives me crazy because I don't think he understands how good he really is, but he's done great things for us."

Recalled Miller several years later, "I didn't really care about starting. I didn't think it was very important. I still played major minutes. I still felt like I was a part of the team, a big part. We had such a talented team. It really didn't matter who started, honestly. Anybody could've started, and it really didn't faze me at all. It [sitting on the bench] actually helped. I really enjoyed it. A lot of time I would get to come in, and I had already seen how the game was being called. I had already seen the pace and flow of the game, so it's actually an advantage in a lot of the cases."

What did the team do between games on Sunday during the 2012 Final Four? "Nothing really, rest," said Miller who couldn't recall if the team visited some of the popular sites in New Orleans. "I think most of the time we just hung together as a team and just rested."

What about watching game videos? "We didn't really watch a lot of film at all when I was there with Coach Cal," Miller commented. "He made it more about us. We took care of what we could control, which was our attitude and our effort. We came out and tried to play as hard as we could and tried to play as a team, and it worked out for us pretty much every time. We watched a little bit of film, personnel clips to know what players like to do and stuff like that but not a ton. It was more about rest and recovery."

Even though the fans and the media had high expectations for the Wildcats, Miller said there wasn't that much internal pressure on the team. "We never really put pressure on ourselves," he said. "We took every day, day by day, trying to get better that day. We were just worried about what we could control. That's playing as good as we can. We're not thinking about any pressure or anything like that. Of course, people outside of us try to put pressure on us, but we don't listen to people outside of what we call 'the family' anyway. It's been basketball for us the whole tournament. I think that's probably the reason why we're so successful."

In the NCAA championship showdown, history will show top-ranked Kentucky was victorious over coach Bill Self and the Jayhawks by a score of 67-59 before a crowd of 70,913 fans at the Mercedes-Benz Superdome. It meant Calipari had joined Adolph Rupp, Joe B. Hall, Rick Pitino, and Tubby Smith as the Wildcat coaches who have won at least one national title.

"I can't really explain it in or put it into words," said a jubilant Miller when asked about becoming a national champion several minutes earlier. "All the hard work that we put in this year, the sacrifices that people have made on this team means a lot, especially with these guys. We've grown as brothers. We've had a lot of fun with this. I can't really put into words how it feels."

Earlier in that championship season, there was a marquee showdown between No. 1 Kentucky and No. 5 North Carolina on a Saturday afternoon in early December in Lexington. The CBS broadcasters Jim Nantz and Clark Kellogg were there to cover the event, which at the time was possibly the best game in Rupp Arena history in terms of national rankings.

It was an extremely exciting game, and the fans definitely got their money's worth as Anthony Davis blocked North Carolina's John Henson's shot in the waning seconds to preserve UK's dramatic 73-72 win. Miller had 12 points on 4-of-8 shooting in 23 minutes of action in a backup role. Asked about the last play of the game, Miller said, "I was nervous. Anthony came up with a crucial block and saved the game for us. I just knew if he got that shot off it was going to go in, so I was just nervous."

Since the beginning of the season, Miller said there had been lots of talk and hype about the Kentucky-North Carolina matchup, and he was glad the Cats came out on top. "It is a very big win," he said. "We felt like this was a test to see where we are at, playing against one of the best teams in the country, and we come out with a W. I think we are pretty happy and proud about it, but we know we aren't exactly where we want to be. It's still early on in the season."

North Carolina coach Roy Williams said, "I think that, for us, it was a very disappointing last couple of seconds to say the least. It was a big-time college basketball game. There were some very talented and gifted youngsters out there really playing hard.... At the end you just have to congratulate [Anthony] Davis who blocked that shot. It was a big-time play on their part."

During his freshman season, Miller got to witness a historical game when Kentucky visited Tennessee at Thompson-Boling Arena. Junior guard Jodie Meeks, the team's leading scorer, set a single-game school record for most points scored when he poured in 54 points, including 10 three-pointers, to spark the Wildcats to a 90-72 win over Coach Bruce Pearl's squad. Meeks passed the previous record of 53 points by All-American Dan Issel in 1970.

"I definitely will remember that forever. That was amazing," said Miller. "One of the best scoring performances I've seen in person, and it was amazing. He was on fire, he couldn't miss, and the team was really happy for him. Our chemistry was great, so everybody was feeding him. He dominated the game. It was an amazing performance."

Ellen Calipari, the wife of Coach Cal, often bakes brownies or cookies for the players' birthdays. She plays an important role as the team's so-called mom away from home. The players often call her Mrs. Cal. Miller says her brownies are delicious.

"The brownies are amazing, definitely," smiled Miller. "And when you had a birthday, she would make you some. She's really a huge part of the team, Mrs. Cal. She does a great job of making everybody feel at home when they're away from their home, on campus and driving on their own during the college years. When we watched the Selection Sunday [after the SEC Tournament in March] at Cal's house, she was always there, she was making stuff, she was making everybody feel at home, and she was like a mother away from home.

"When we had our little camp where we were doing two a day, we would go there [their house] after the first practice and stay. Mrs. Cal was always inviting, she always made us feel at home."

A No. 46 overall selection by the New Orleans Hornets [now Pelicans] in the NBA Draft, Miller had to adjust to his new professional life, especially off the hardwood floor. It was not easy. During his NBA rookie season, Miller saw limited action, averaging 2.3 points and 1.5 rebounds in 52 games. Against Denver, Miller hit 16 points.

"Being on my own, taking care of my body [was tough]," said Miller of his rookie year. "There were no UK food programs where we could go eat. There was nothing. Nobody calling me, telling me to come to the gym. You're completely on your own, you're a man at this point. At UK, I had [assistant coach] Kenny Payne, I had [assistant John] Robic, Cal, they come looking [for you]. You come to get some extra work in at that time.

"So, at that point I had to grow up really fast, and then on the court just the speed of the game, the talent. When you're playing in the NCAA every now and then, you might run into a star or something like that. In the NBA it's every single night. Everybody has talent and speed, and the discipline it takes to play 82 games in a season with the traveling on top of that. That was probably the biggest adjustment."

It helped that his UK teammate Anthony Davis, the NBA's No. 1 draft pick, also played for New Orleans.

"Coming in with AD helped a lot," said Miller.

Darius Miller greets Washington's John Wall after an NBA exhibition game in 2013 at Rupp Arena. (Photo by Jamie H. Vaught)

"Like I said, we're pretty close friends, so just coming in with him and seeing how he took to it, how he was going about it helped a lot, but still it was rough for me. He handled it way better than I did, I think. It [having AD] definitely helped a little bit. I think it would have been a lot rougher if I didn't have someone to experience it with."

A couple of days before Miller held his 2018 hoops camp in Maysville, he visited Davis at his summer camp in Lexington. "I went to his camp the last day," he said. "I didn't really help him out too much, but I came to show my face and say 'hi' to some of the kids and to see how he was doing."

Miller said Davis, Patrick Patterson, Shelvin Mack, and DeMarcus Cousins "are probably the people that I'm closest to as far as people in the NBA."

Miller's last collegiate appearance, which came against Kansas in the national championship game, marked his 152nd game at Kentucky, breaking Wayne Turner's school record of 151 games during the late 1990s. That meant Miller has played more games as a Wildcat than any other player in UK history.

On the day before the Kansas game, Calipari was asked what Miller's legacy would be at Kentucky with many teammates over a four-year period. Miller "has won a ton of games now," said Calipari. "[He] is Kentucky's own. They love him. If he wants to get into politics, he could run for governor and win. He's beloved. He's going to be one of those guys 50 years from now they're going to be talking about."

Miller added, "I am very proud of it ... in playing that many games for a program that I consider one of the top programs ever in the history of NCAA basketball. So, just to do something like that on a team of that caliber is amazing to me. And I really appreciate it, especially coming from where I come from. It's just something I take pride in, and I'm happy about."

Chapter Seventeen

A Classroom Star

*L*ike most youngsters growing up in the foothills of Kentucky, Dillon Pulliam had dreams of playing college basketball, especially the Kentucky Wildcats. He even pretended he was UK All-American Tayshaun Prince when playing pickup basketball in his backyard in Harrison County, the home county of UK legend Joe B. Hall. And he and his younger brother, Zack, often had friendly but fierce battles against each other for many years and had fun.

"I always dreamed of playing basketball in college," said the 6-foot-3, 195-pound Pulliam, a former Wildcat guard who graduated after the 2017-18 campaign. "I'd say Tayshaun probably was my favorite [UK] player. I especially remember the time he hit the five straight threes against UNC. I also enjoyed watching Gerald Fitch, Keith Bogans, and a lot of those guys in the early 2000s under Tubby Smith when the program was really rolling.

"Later, as I got to middle and high school and Coach Cal came to UK, I really enjoyed watching that first team with [John] Wall, [DeMarcus] Cousins, [Eric] Bledsoe, and that squad. I felt like the success they had that year was crucial in terms of getting the program back on the right track and chasing championships on a yearly basis.

"Zack and I played countless one-on-one games. The number I'm sure is in the thousands. Those games are some of my best memories, and they really helped us to grow closer to one another. Early on I won pretty much every time, but eventually Zack caught me in height, and our games started to become ultra-competitive, sometimes too competitive [where his parents got a little concerned].

"Whenever it was NCAA Tournament time, we would print off the bracket, choose teams, and play out the entire tournament one-on-one until we had a champion. Our court back home has seen its fair share of buzzer-beater moments, and to this day, we still play one-on-one when we get a chance."

Pulliam has fond memories of his first Wildcat matchup at Rupp Arena even though he sat in nosebleed section in the upper deck. "The very first UK game I attended, I literally sat at the top of the arena, my back was actually against the wall," remembered Pulliam. "I can't remember exactly who we played since I was in elementary school at the time, but I know I had a blast, and we won. Looking back on it, it's crazy that years later I had the opportunity and was actually out on the court playing in front of 20,000-plus screaming fans." Pulliam added that his other favorite players during his childhood were NBA stars Kobe Bryant and Tim Duncan.

Pulliam became a hoops standout for Harrison County High School, where he earned All-Region team honors three times during his five-year prep career. He once established a school record for most three-point field goals made in a contest with nine. As a high school player, the ex-Wildcat said he doesn't really have one favorite moment and the former district tournament MVP finished No. 5 on the school's career scoring list.

"In terms of a favorite moment from high school basketball, there really isn't one that specifically stands out," said Pulliam, a member of Harrison County's 1,000-point club. "I could say winning district back-to-back my last two years or hitting nine threes in a game my freshman year, but, looking back on it, these really aren't my favorite memories.

"What really stands out for me is just all the little moments; the games, the bus rides, and the practices with my teammates. We all grew up together playing elementary, middle and high school ball, and just being around those guys for so long and growing up together was really cool. I also had the chance to play with my brother and one of my best friends in Trenton Thompson [who was a two-time All-American at Asbury University], so that was awesome."

Pulliam also excelled in the classroom as an honor roll student. A member of the prestigious Beta Club, he was the valedictorian at his high school. Unfortunately, while in high school, UK wasn't interested in him as a college basketball player. But there were several small schools which actively recruited the shooting guard. He ended up going to Transylvania University in Lexington.

"The schools that were most interested in me coming out of high school were Transylvania University, Rose-Hulman University [in Terre Haute, Ind.], and Washington University in St. Louis," added Pulliam. "These schools all recruited me very heavily. All had very good basketball programs and coaching staffs with extremely strong academic programs. Choosing which university to attend was a tough choice for me, as all universities would have been a considered an excellent decision."

Pulliam said he already had developed contacts with Transylvania, and that pretty much sealed his collegiate decision. "I had a strong connection with head coach Brian Lane and assistant coach Barrett Meyer. Growing up every summer, I went to Coach Lane's basketball camp and slowly fell in love with the university, the team, and the way the program was run," he said. "Not only is Coach Lane a tremendous coach, but he's an even better Christian person. I knew Coach Lane would help me to grow both on and off the court.

"I also chose Transy because it was close to home and made it easy for my family to attend games and for me to see them on a somewhat regular basis. The university has a strong academic reputation and is known for developing talented professionals in all aspects of life. Overall, choosing Transy was an excellent choice and helped me to grow as a person, as a player, and as a student during my first year of college."

His brother, Zack, later played at Transy, also. They were teammates at Harrison County High for a while. "My senior year Zack was our team's sixth man [as a sophomore] and even started some games," said Pulliam of his high school days. "That year was fun because we got a whole lot of time on the court together, which was something we had always talked about growing up. Zack is a tremendous player and essentially a 6-5 shooting guard, which is a very rare thing in high school basketball. To this day, when he gets hot, he can pull up and hit threes from 25 feet plus. He was also a very good athlete with hops and lateral quickness. I'm sure my parents enjoyed only having to follow one team, which made their travel schedule a whole lot easier."

But, for one year, his parents often had to alternate between UK and Transy basketball games in Lexington on some Saturdays when their sons' teams played basketball on the same day. "Zack and I definitely kept them busy that year, but I'm sure they loved every minute of it," said Pulliam.

At Transylvania, during his freshman year, Pulliam averaged 4.8 points and 3.4 rebounds in 25 games. However, he didn't stay very long at the private university, which has about 1,000 students. He found another school which is actually less than a 10-minute walk. That school was University of Kentucky, and he also would get to play hoops for the Big Blue.

"Transferring to the University of Kentucky was a no-brainer," he said. "Growing up, I always dreamed of playing basketball at the highest level, and

UK gave me the chance to do that. Every single game is in front of 20,000-plus screaming Big Blue Nation fans. At UK, I also had the chance to play for a Hall of Fame coach in Coach Cal and the rest of his tremendous staff. I knew at UK I would be challenged to become the best version of myself and that I would have to bring it every single day in practice while going against some of the best players in the country.

"Transferring to UK also made sense for reasons other than basketball. At Transy, I was involved in the pre-engineering program, where I took an engineering course at UK through Transy each semester. Transferring to UK allowed me to directly pursue the computer engineering and computer science degrees I wanted and take courses that were both interesting and would help prepare me for the future. Overall, it was a great fit both athletically and academically, and I'm glad I had the opportunity to make it happen."

But how did Pulliam end up on the UK basketball team? "[During] my first year at Transy, UK had three senior walk-ons in Tod Lanter, Brian Long, and Sam Malone," he said. "I knew that, after the season, these spots would open and that I might have an opportunity to join the team. After discussions with the staff, it all ended up working out, and I was able to make the transfer. Having the chance to play ball at UK under Coach Cal was a dream come true, and I thank God every single day for this blessing and the numerous others He has given me throughout my life."

During the 2015-16 campaign, Pulliam had to sit out because of NCAA transfer rules. After that, he made his Wildcat debut in November 2016 during UK's 93-69 win over Canisius. As for his Kentucky career, he didn't play much, seeing action for a total of 11 games. But that's okay. No problem. Pulliam understood that Kentucky was loaded with future NBA standouts. Was it hard for him to practice and stay motivated as a member of the program, knowing that he wouldn't get to play much, if any?

"It wasn't difficult at all," he said. "I knew I played a vital role on the team, regardless of playing time, and I knew my efforts on the practice court helped tremendously regarding our guys improving and being ready to take on the competition. Basketball has always been something I've loved, and simply having the opportunity to play at the highest level against the best competition was a blessing.

"Now, obviously as a competitor you want to be out on the court playing as many minutes as possible, but the only way to do so is to prove yourself in practice. Therefore, staying motivated to give my best every single day was a no-brainer and something I always did."

At Kentucky, Pulliam, however, got to see lots of big games up close from the bench, including the NCAA Tournament. He was a part of UK's three SEC Tournament and two SEC regular-season titles. What was his favorite memory or game at UK?

"It's difficult to choose one specific game or moment," said Pulliam, a three-time SEC Academic Honor Roll member. "While at UK, I was a part of three SEC championship teams, and those tournaments were always a blast. Another good memory was the Bahamas trip [in the Atlantis Showcase] during the 2016-17 season. We went down there two days early, and Coach Cal let us run around the resort, go to the

Dillon Pulliam at UK pre-game practice. (Photo by Jamie H. Vaught)

water park, and even go to the beach and get in the ocean. That trip was also great for me because on the last day we beat Arizona State by over 40 points, which allowed me to see more playing time than I typically did.

"However, I'd have to say my favorite memory in my three years was beating UCLA in the Sweet 16 during the 2016-17 season. UCLA had beaten us earlier in the year at Rupp [by a score of 97-92], and all season long we were hoping to get another shot at them. The funny thing is, Coach Cal even said after the game at Rupp that we would see them again and that next time we would be ready for them.

"Even though the UCLA game was a Sweet 16 game [in Memphis], it had a Final Four feel to it. It featured two of the most historic teams in college basketball history, and numerous lottery picks and pros. We were under-seeded as a No. 2 seed, and UCLA was vastly under-seeded as a No. 3 seed. The game was ultra-hyped up as it featured the two best point guards in the country in [De'Aaron] Fox and Lonzo Ball, and we couldn't wait to play them.

"Overall, the game was close throughout, and we pulled away and won by 11 at the end. Fox absolutely went off with 39 points and couldn't be guarded all game long. That was a game I'll remember forever and definitely one of my favorite moments as a player, as it was a big-time game in the NCAA Tournament, and we were able to get a great win and advance."

But the next game – an Elite Eight showdown – was a disappointment as Kentucky dropped to North Carolina in a 65-62 thriller. "The most heartbreaking moment in my time at UK was our Elite Eight game against UNC," said Pulliam. "We had beaten them [103-100] earlier in the season in Las Vegas in a close one. That's the game everyone remembers for Malik [Monk] dropping 47 on them. We knew going into the Elite Eight game it was going to be a challenge and would come down to the wire. The game went back and forth throughout, and, in the end, Malik ended up hitting a contested three-pointer to tie it up with about eight seconds left or so. The rest was history as Luke Maye hit that shot [with 0.3 seconds left].

"That game was heartbreaking, as we were playing so well as a team, and we really thought we were on the right path to cut down the nets for championship No. 9. Our team was ultra-talented and peaking at the right time, but it simply wasn't meant to be for us that year."

UK completed that remarkable season with a 32-6 mark, including the SEC Tournament title in Nashville, with a final No. 6 ranking in the Associated Press poll. Three Wildcats – Fox, Monk, and Bam Adebayo – were selected as lottery picks in the first round of the 2017 NBA Draft.

❖ ❖ ❖

Pulliam has seen a handful of prep All-Americans at Kentucky who became NBA standouts and has practiced against them nearly every day during the season. He usually was matched up against a first-rate guard. Who was the toughest one to practice against?

"This isn't an easy question to answer as in my three years we had numerous pros," said Pulliam. "The toughest guy I've had to try to score against in my time would either be Tyler Ulis or Shai Gilgeous-Alexander. Although T was only 5-9, he truly has the heart of a lion and has one of the best basketball minds I've ever seen. T was so hard to score against as it's just impossible to get around him since he's so low to the ground and has quickness off the charts. Shai, on the other hand, was hard to score against because of his length. He's a legit 6-6 with a 7-foot wingspan. Even when you get a little air space – which is not an easy task to do with his quickness – he's able to recover ultra-fast with his length and have a solid contest on any shot attempt.

"In terms of the hardest person to guard, I'm again going to have to give you a variety of answers. De'Aaron [Fox] was hard to guard due to his speed and quickness, particularly on the fast break, where he's downright impossible to stop. Jamal Murray was another tough cover with his ability to score at all three levels and his ball-handling ability. His skill level was simply off the charts. And then finally you can't have this discussion without talking about Malik [Monk]. When Malik gets hot, he can't – I repeat cannot – be guarded. Malik could simply one or two dribble pull-up going left or right jump over you to get a shot off. He also could rock his way into a three-pointer off the dribble, and like I said, when he gets hot, the game is over."

On Murray, Pulliam pointed out the 6-foot-4 guard from Canada often "would warm up before practice by shooting with his left hand. I'm not just talking layups and floaters – he would shoot threes with his left hand. And what's even crazier is he would hit them at nearly a 50 percent mark uncontested, and his form was so fluid that, if you had never seen him play before, you would think he was left-handed with the way he could shoot."

Pulliam was asked about UK coach John Calipari. What is his favorite Coach Cal memory?

"My favorite Cal story would have to be the time we visited the National World War II Museum when we played in New Orleans [where UK lost to UCLA 83-75 in the 2017 CBS Sports Classic]," said Pulliam. "What most people probably don't know about Cal is he's really into history, and I mean really into history. He said at the time we were visiting the museum so we could see firsthand the stuff our textbooks taught us growing up about the war. However, looking back on it, I think we actually visited the museum because he really wanted to and because he couldn't leave the city without doing so.

"Overall it was an effective team-building experience, and it was neat having Coach teach us facts about the war and about some of the tactics and strategies used in it. You can tell right away that he has done his research and knows his stuff. He was as, if not more, excited about the history than the tour guides themselves. For me, it was interesting getting to experience this other side of Cal outside of basketball. Once you get to know him, he's down-to-earth, relatable, and has hobbies and interests just like the rest of us. He also just happens to be an incredible coach that always puts his players first and that's in the Hall of Fame."

Calipari wasn't really sure if his players enjoyed the experience at the World War II museum in the Big Easy. "I don't know what it was for them, but I did it because I wanted to go and I said 'You're coming with me,' " commented Calipari. "So, I tried to explain some things to them about Normandy, the D-Day landing. I tried to explain the Battle of The Bulge. I said you probably would hear this at some point. I tried to explain [the Siege of] Bastogne and how that was, and there were things that I asked them. They knew about the airmen.

"So, you just want them to acknowledge that we had a chance of losing that war and all of our lives changing and these men, what they did. That museum [had] very vivid videos where you could see. Some of it where they're in snow, and they're trying to fight. I wish I [had] had five hours. I would have enjoyed five hours. We were there about an hour. But I think it was good for them."

Calipari also enjoys reading nonfiction books and his favorite topics include history, biographies, self-help and motivation. While on the road, he often carries a book with him.

During his UK tenure, Calipari has brought people from all walks of life to Lexington to speak to his team. For Pulliam, his favorite speaker was the superstar rapper from Canada.

"Hands down my favorite person that spoke to the team in my three years was Drake," said the Harrison County native. "Over the course of my lifetime, he's really blown up and is now considered one of the greatest rappers of our generation, if not all time. I've grown up listening to his music, watching him host the ESPYs, perform at All-Star Weekend, etc., so to have the opportunity to meet him in person was really cool. At Big Blue Madness [in 2017], he made an appearance and talked to our team afterwards about hard work, dedication to your craft, and belief in yourself. To hear someone who is at the top of their game and considered the best at what they do speak with that same passion and that same energy that helped get them to the top was inspirational. Right away I could tell Drake has a genius for his craft, and his work ethic and self-belief is something we can all strive to emulate."

Another highlight of Pulliam's UK career was capturing the school's Male Scholar-Athlete of the Year at the annual CATSPY awards in 2018, sharing the same honor with two other athletes.

"Winning Male Scholar-Athlete of the Year this past season along with Chris Meuth [men's golf] and Gus Benson [men's tennis] was an incredible honor and one of my proudest moments in my time at UK," said Pulliam. "Having the chance to be recognized and speak to all the other amazing athletes, coaches, and athletics staff members was awesome. I never imagined that I would win a CATSPY so being chosen for the award was incredibly humbling. The CATSPYs were always one of my favorite parts of the year as they are one of the few times that all the UK Athletics community come together and connect as a group.

"The event has always been, in my mind, a fantastic way to close out the year one last time before everyone goes their separate ways. To go along with that, I feel as if winning Male Scholar-Athlete of the Year was also a terrific way to close out my career at UK. It was an honor receiving recognition for the dedication I had put into the game of basketball and into my studies throughout my career."

While at UK during the summer of 2016, Pulliam also had a very memorable trip. He took a mission trip to Belize, a small country located below Mexico in Central America.

"The mission trip I went on with the Sports Reach Organization and Robbie Speer was truly life-changing," said Pulliam. "It was the first time I had been out of the country for an extended time without my family, so it was really a time for me to grow. The purpose of the trip was to spread God's message through basketball.

"Essentially our schedule most days was to play a game against a local team and afterward [spread the] message to the them and to the fans. During this time, we would read the Word, pray with them, and just hang out and connect. In between games, we also took time to visit children's homes as well as some local families that the Sports Reach Organization had connected with over the years.

"Traveling to Belize was the first chance I'd really had to see how people live outside of the U.S. The trip made me extremely thankful for everything I've been blessed with. It allowed me to connect and make friends with other Christian college basketball players, guys I still, to this day, communicate with on a regular basis. Belize helped to inspire me and show me that life is bigger than basketball. It reminded me that basketball is one of the abilities and platforms I have been blessed with and to use it to honor God and spread his message to others."

A classroom star, Pulliam is serious about academics. He also tried to help other students, including his teammates, if they had a question, including mathematics.

"If they ever have a math question, they always know they can come to me," he said in 2017. "Or sometimes when we're traveling, I may have to pull out my laptop and do homework on the plane. So I guess I try to set a good example."

He certainly finished his UK career on a high note. Not athletically but academically. He maintained a 4.0 grade-point average and graduated with honors in May 2018, earning undergraduate degrees in computer engineering and computer science. He also minored in mathematics. In addition, he was admitted to Carnegie Mellon University's master program in Pittsburgh for the fall of 2018, where he studies electrical and computer engineering.

In addition, Pulliam served as a research assistant for NASA Kentucky at UK. He built an electronic pitch detection device capable of recognizing which string had been played on a guitar and developed a mobile application for both iOS and Android devices.

Calipari said he is proud of Pulliam's work. "Dillon was a great teammate and an important part of what we do in practice every day," said the UK coach. "He earned a partial scholarship at different points because of his contributions. Suffice it to say, he was a great student. I've been stopped by professors who ask me, 'Do you know how smart he is?' Being from Pittsburgh, I know what it means to be accepted into Carnegie Mellon. I also know my application wouldn't have even made it to anyone's desk. I'm just as happy for Dillon as I am for our other guys who go on to pursue their genius in other areas, whether it be in the NBA or in the business world. My guess is Dillon will be in the middle of a program to put people on Mars before it's all said and done. Proud of him."

Said Pulliam, "Before I say anything, I'd first like to thank God for all he's done for me over the past three years. When you put your faith in him, it really is amazing the doors he will open for you."

Pulliam also commented that his parents had the most influence on his academic success. His mother, Debbie Pulliam, teaches art, while father, Bill Pulliam, is a longtime employee as an engineer at Toyota manufacturing plant in Georgetown, Ky.

"They taught me from an early age that education could take you far in life and could lead you to incredible places," said Pulliam. "Growing up they encouraged me to do the best I possibly could in everything I pursued and to always give 100 percent effort. They encouraged me to pursue my dreams both on the court and in the classroom. I truly believe my parents' faith in me helped to build my own confidence and has been a major factor of the success I have had. To them I'm thankful for everything they have done and for the way I have been brought up."

Less than two months after graduation from UK, Pulliam received a 2018 Phi Kappa Phi (PKP) national fellowship worth $5,000. Nationally, he was one of the 50 award winners for the fellowship entering the first year of graduate or professional study. PKP is the nation's oldest and most selective all-discipline academic honor society, having over 300 chapters across the nation and more overseas.

Pulliam said the fellowship "will be a tremendous benefit in helping me grow as an engineer and prepare for a future in the field. I have always been fascinated with technology and how it works. From a young age, I have dreamed of having a hand in one day developing the innovations that will shape tomorrow."

Before he started classes at Carnegie Mellon in the fall of 2018, he and his former Wildcat teammate Jonny David, who is from Pittsburgh, spent some time together in the Steel City during the summer, and David helped his friend look for a place to live. "While I was up here, we were able to meet up and go downtown and hang out a little bit," said Pulliam. "We went to eat at the world famous Primanti Brothers restaurant downtown."

Asked about living in Pittsburgh during his first year there, Pulliam said, "The most interesting thing about the city has definitely been the people. The variety of different cultures, particularly at Carnegie Mellon University, is very cool. Just having the chance to develop relationships and interact with other people from literally all corners of the globe has taught me a ton, helped me to grow, and it's also exciting."

He said he hasn't become a Pittsburgh Steelers or Pirates fan. "And that isn't going to happen any time soon," smiled Pulliam. "Go Bengals and Go Reds!"

By the way, after receiving his degree in kinesiology from UK in May 2019, David, a former 6-foot-2 guard who played all four years at Kentucky, has returned to his hometown. He was planning to attend graduate school at the University of Pittsburgh to pursue a master's degree in physical therapy.

While at Kentucky, besides academics and basketball, Pulliam managed to find time for hobbies, including winning the ping-pong championship among the UK basketball team members. He loves to hang out with his friends and family, and to play video games.

"One of my favorite sports to play other than basketball is ping-pong," he said. "One little-known fact is I'm the reigning UK basketball ping-pong champion. I'm going to brag a little and say that, in my three years, I was the best ping-pong player on the team. We had a few other guys who were pretty good

– [De'Aaron] Fox, Jemarl [Baker], Shai [Gilgeous-Alexander], Vando [Jarred Vanderbilt], Mike Mulder, to name a few – but none of them could beat me consistently, although I'm sure some of them would say otherwise. I also enjoy playing the video game *Fortnite*, and in my spare time, I also like to read sci-fi books and tech articles."

Pulliam also enjoyed reading the best-selling *Harry Potter* book series by author J.K. Rowling. "Definitely some of the best books ever, no doubt," he said with a smile.

Chapter Eighteen

Coach Cal and His Early Days

*L*ess than a year after John Calipari and his Wildcats celebrated their 2012 national championship crown in New Orleans, he found himself coaching in a postseason tournament in front of his hometown crowd in the Pittsburgh suburb of Moon Township, where he grew up near the Ohio River.

Since the struggling Wildcats, playing without 6-foot-10 freshman star Nerlens Noel, who had suffered a knee injury during his team's setback at Florida in Gainesville in mid-February, didn't finish the 2012-13 campaign on a strong note, they ended up going to the 32-team National Invitational Tournament instead of the NCAA Tournament. UK had dropped three of the last four games, including a one-game appearance in the SEC Tournament (a loss to Vanderbilt), and its record of 21-11 wasn't good enough for a ticket to the Big Dance.

The Wildcats were disappointed, but they received a No. 1 seed in the NIT. They were set to host a first-round game, but Rupp Arena wasn't available since the first weekend of the NCAA Tournament was taking place there. UK also didn't have enough staff to handle the game at Memorial Coliseum. So, No. 8-seed Robert Morris University, UK's NIT opponent, hosted the game at its 3,000-seat Charles L. Sewall Center, which was later demolished in 2017 to make room for a new campus arena.

For Calipari, it was a homecoming of sorts as he grew up next door to the campus of Robert Morris. The private university was also the site of the famed Five-Star Basketball Camp, where many high school standouts, including Michael Jordan, caught the attention of scouts and coaches.

In a pregame interview with the assembled media, Calipari was asked about going back to his hometown of Moon Township. "Well, it's funny. I've coached about 24 games in that gym," said Calipari, who had worked at the camp during his much younger days.

But it was going to be a very short trip for the Kentucky coach and the team. "I told my wife [Ellen], don't even come. [It's] too quick. I mean, we get in there late tonight and leave late tomorrow night. It's not worth that. There will be some guys at our practice tonight that I'll see."

As it turned out, this NIT game wasn't a very memorable one for the Big Blue Nation as Kentucky was upset by Robert Morris 59-57 in a stunner before 3,444 emotional fans, then the largest basketball crowd in RMU's history. And Calipari obviously wasn't too happy.

As Calipari later said, "They deserved to beat us. We deserved to end our season right there."

Looking back, Calipari agreed that he even felt weird about the entire situation. "What had happened was our building wasn't available for us to play in the NIT at home. We probably would have gotten a home game, and it would have been different," he told the author during a 2017 interview at his Joe Craft Center office. "The options were that we were going to have to go on the road, and I recommended, 'Let's go to Robert Morris. I can go home.' There was a Catholic church with a lot of grass and a little neighborhood between our house and Robert Morris. You could see Robert Morris College [as it was called back then] from our front porch, like you could see the buildings.

"My grandmother worked in the cafeteria there. Gus Krop was one of the original basketball coaches and athletic directors that brought sports to Robert Morris. I had all kinds of family, mostly cousins, aunts, and uncles, that were there who came to the game. To be back home and to see friends, it was kind of neat. We lost the game. That wasn't fun. But it was a big game for Robert Morris College, and I think it put them on a little different path [to respectability and recognition]."

Calipari added Robert Morris today is practically nothing like during his younger days. "When you look at Robert Morris now, with its football stadium, and they're building a new basketball arena [now completed], the student population and what it stands for, and the buildings, it's not even the same place," he commented. "They've done great work there."

❖❖ ❖❖ ❖❖

When he was a young kid growing up in Pittsburgh during the 1960s and '70s, Calipari followed local professional teams like the Pittsburgh Steelers and the Pittsburgh Pirates "back in the day when they [the Pirates] had Willie Stargell, Roberto Clemente, Dick Groat, Bill Mazeroski, Richie Hebner, and Manny Sanguillen.

"But I also liked the Yankees when they were good, the Red Sox when they were good, and everybody says you couldn't have liked all those teams. And [manager] Billy Martin was one of my favorites. The Steelers [during the Super Bowl championships in the 1970s] – when they were good and when they brought great pride to our city – they were fun to watch.

"I'm talking baseball and football because, where I grew up, it was mostly baseball and football. And basketball was like the other sport. We (high schools) started late because they wanted all of the football players to play their season before you started basketball. A lot of what we did was based on football. But I've grown up with sports teams, watching leadership, watching coaching, watching excellence, watching committed players, and, obviously, it was a pleasure."

During his elementary school days, he was even a ball boy – all dressed up – for a local basketball team, Moon Area High School. He did similar chores for Moon's baseball squad as a bat boy. And when he got older, he became more of a gym rat who had help getting into the school gym during the offseason. It was easy for Calipari to get involved with his high school activities as his home, located near a major airport, was within a very short walking distance.

"When I grew up, my home, our property, was butted against the high school property," said Calipari. "So, the school was right there. I could throw a rock from my house and hit the school. During the off times where, if you wanted to go in, it was locked up. They had the doors chained, but I was so skinny I could slip through.

"We also had combs, which we knew how to [use to] open doors. We'd go in there, and we weren't vandalizing anything. We were just getting in the gym. So, people knew we were doing it but never said anything because we never damaged anything. We were in there playing basketball. The only thing they [school officials] were afraid of is if someone got hurt. All right, who are you going to sue? But my parents – that's not how we did that."

In high school, Calipari, who was also senior class president, was a pretty good player and became a three-year starter at point guard, guiding his teammates. During his senior year of 1977-78 when he averaged 20 points along with seven assists per game, he – as a team captain – helped his Moon Area High School team to the postseason playoffs for the first time in nearly three decades. It was a really good memory for Calipari. His basketball coach was Bill Sacco. "We're still close friends," Calipari said of Sacco, who has attended many UK games. "I just saw him three weeks ago at a clinic I did up in Pittsburgh."

On his high school team, Coach Cal added, "The thing – my high school team, for like 25 years, had never been to the playoffs. My senior year that summer, our players were together just about every day. We went and played pickup all over the state. We went to Center [Township], we went [to] Monaca, we went to Aliquippa. Wherever there were courts in the summer, we went and played pickup as a group. So, the five of us would go and play. We got to know each other, we got to be about each other, we got to grow together, and each kind of take on roles.

"And that year we ended up being in the playoffs for the first time in 25 years. If we had been to the playoffs the year before, I think we would have advanced. We lost to New Castle, if I remember, but it was a big game. I can remember walking out, saying, 'Oh, my gosh, this is a team that we didn't know, with officials we didn't know, and an arena we didn't know.'

"At that period of time, it's a proud accomplishment that a team did it. It wasn't me. It was the WPIAL [Western Pennsylvania Interscholastic Athletic League] tournament, which would lead into state tournament. So, you had to advance to a certain level. But it was a fun time."

Coach Sacco was "an absolute grinder, worked year-round, had great relationships with all of us as players, knew when to have fun, and knew when to get tough," said Calipari. "There was time in practice that he would break it up by doing something goofy, tackle somebody, we'd all be jumping and piling on, where we knew we could have fun. [He] took a team that had lost for 30 straight years, took them to the playoffs, and created pride in all of us that we could. Just because we went to this school doesn't mean we can't play in state championships, the state playoffs. We were able to do it."

Calipari graduated from Moon in 1978.

One of Calipari's teammates at Moon Area High was Joe Fryz, an All-Stater who later signed with West Virginia, where he became a teammate of future WVU coach Bob Huggins. He was two years ahead of Calipari. Fryz, who remained close friends with Calipari and Huggins, eventually developed Lou Gehrig's disease (better known as ALS) and died during the summer of 2017.

When Coach Cal visited ailing Fryz about a month before his death, the Kentucky coach said Mrs. Fryz had asked him to carry her husband, just like a family member would do, according to an obituary piece by Mike White of the *Pittsburgh Post-Gazette*.

"When I was a sophomore at Moon and he was a senior, I ended up starting with him," said Calipari in *Pittsburgh Post-Gazette*. "He took me under his wing. He was like a big brother to me, and I never forgot that."

Another high school teammate, Tommy Hill, also dealt with ALS. Calipari, who visited him in New Jersey in mid-February 2019, tweeted, "… A kind soul and a great person who was my protector!! Praying for you daily, my brother." Sadly, Hill passed away several weeks later.

At UK's annual Media Day festivities in October 2015, Calipari talked about that crippling disease that has taken thousands of lives. He had been asked by a reporter what keeps him grounded after being inducted into the Naismith Memorial Basketball Hall of Fame in the previous month of September as well as winning an NCAA title.

"You know, it's funny, my high school coach called me today because a teammate of mine, we found out, has Lou Gehrig's [disease], and I've lived with two people that have had that disease, and it's the most dreaded disease you could get," said Calipari. They chatted about life in general and discussed ways to alleviate the suffering. Coach Cal said he loves to help folks in any way he can and motivates his players to overcome obstacles and find success.

Besides his parents – Vince and Donna Calipari – along with two sisters in a blue-collar community, Calipari was fortunate to have had several role models during his school years. Calipari, known for his bubbly and charming personality, was asked if he was a model student back then.

"Yeah, look, all my role models were the teachers and coaches," recalled Calipari. "We grew up in a neighborhood where other than people that worked at the airport [like his father], people were laborers. And I say the professionals were the teachers and the coaches, not the lawyers, the doctors. They didn't live where we lived. So, those were the role models. When I grew up, I just wanted to be a teacher and a coach. That's what I thought I'd be. Didn't know if I wanted to teach, and then I thought maybe business so that if I didn't want to be a teacher, I could do something else if I felt like doing it. But I never had any thoughts of being anything more than a high school coach and teacher.

"Then I went to college [at University of North Carolina Wilmington before transferring to Clarion State in Pennsylvania], and my eyes opened up, and you start saying, 'Well, maybe I can do this. Maybe being a college coach would be something more rewarding and something I'd enjoy more.' I'm still in touch with some of the teachers now that were there from Skip Tatala [the high school coach at the time when Calipari served as a ball boy], Ray Bosetti [baseball coach when Calipari was a bat boy], and obviously Bill Sacco. There are other teachers that you look back on and you say, 'Boy, they had a big impact on me.' Really, I can think back to whether it was English or any other speech class and different things I had to do, and it was all good stuff for me."

And his mother has always encouraged him to dream big, and his father showed the younger Calipari what hard work is. Calipari discussed his parents' influence in his 2015 speech when he was inducted into the Naismith Memorial Basketball Hall of Fame.

"She was the dreamer," he said of his mother, who wanted her children to live in a $100,000 home. "She would always say 'dream big dreams.' The other thing she taught all of us was to dream beyond our surroundings. 'You can be whoever you want to be.' I miss her uplifting spirit, but I know she is here tonight.

"And then my dad, Vince Calipari, the hardest-working man I've ever met. He taught me what the grind was. He would work double shifts, then come home and work in the yard and drag me out there with him on my hands and knees, pulling weeds. He also would create relationships with everybody. He was the pied piper. He learned to be a gatherer, and he taught me what a gatherer was."

On the day before his Hall of Fame speech, Calipari had a press conference and admitted he was somewhat nervous about the induction ceremony. He also talked about his upbringing and his parents, among other things. It was an emotional time for Coach Cal and his family.

"When I was growing up, her goal was for us all to be college educated – my two sisters and I are – and she wanted us to live in a $100,000 house," Calipari told Darrell Bird of *The Cats' Pause* and other reporters. "Now, I grew up in Pittsburgh. The house we grew up in was $16,000. The mortgage was $63 a month."

Like the folks from eastern Kentucky in the Appalachian Mountains which basically runs through Pittsburgh in the northeast, Calipari grew up in a mountain city which, in the old days, was famous for having steel mills all over. Listed as the second-most livable city in the U.S. in 2018 according to an annual report by a well-respected research group (The Economist Intelligence Unit), Pittsburgh was once the thriving center of U.S. steel industry. It was a blue-collar city, just like the eastern part of Kentucky which was loaded with laborers who worked in the coal mines.

So, it isn't really a big surprise that Calipari and the Kentuckians, many of whom are Kentucky Wildcat faithful, have similar upbringings. But the Kentucky coach didn't really recognize it until after he arrived in Lexington to become UK's new basketball coach in 2009.

"It's all the same, really, the same kind of people," said Calipari, pointing out several regions like eastern Kentucky, western Pennsylvania, West Virginia, and the Appalachian region. "I didn't realize until I got here. I didn't know that's what it would be like. I see family and friends in the faces of the people I meet here, especially when I go to east Kentucky. My grandfather was in the mines. His brother was in the mines."

Calipari also discussed his family history when he was introduced as the new Wildcat boss at a televised press conference after agreeing to an eight-year, $31.65 million contract with UK.

"My grandparents came through Ellis Island on my father's side. They were uneducated," Calipari told a large crowd at Joe Craft Center, including former Kentucky coach Joe B. Hall and ex-Wildcat Herky Rupp (son of legendary coach Adolph Rupp) as well as representatives from the news media, including the author. "My grandfather worked in the coal mines in West Virginia, died of black lung at age 58. My mother's family were from Webster Springs, West Virginia. Dandelion soup. I heard all the stories. So, I want you to know that my wife and I are not the grand pooh-bah, I'm not the emperor. That's not what I want to be. We're regular people."

John Calipari and then-UK President Dr. Lee Todd in 2009. (Photo by Jamie H. Vaught)

After Moon Area High School, Calipari received a scholarship to play basketball at the University of North Carolina Wilmington, which was an independent at the time. Then-UNC Wilmington coach Mel Gibson really liked Calipari's deep understanding of basketball. And Calipari went to Wilmington partially because he had a close family friend who was coaching football in the area.

"He mastered the fundamentals," Gibson told Eric Detweiler of the *Wilmington Star News* in 2015. "That's what really allowed him to get a scholarship in college. He wasn't going to outrun you or outjump you or outshoot you, but he was just a savvy player."

But he didn't stay very long at the university because of limited playing time. During his freshman year of 1978-79, he was a 6-foot, 158-pound backup guard averaging 1.2 points in 25 games as the Seahawks finished with a 19-8 mark. In his second year at Wilmington, he was listed on the team's roster at the beginning of the campaign, but he didn't play with them as he had decided to transfer early.

Next stop was his home state of Pennsylvania, where he played hoops at Clarion State College (now Clarion University). The school is located northeast of Pittsburgh and is less than two hours away from his home. And that's where his high school coach, Bill Sacco, graduated from.

While his future friend, Joe B. Hall, was coaching the Wildcats with star players like Sam Bowie, Melvin Turpin, Dirk Minniefield, Derrick Hord and Jim Master, Calipari was playing as a canny point guard for the Golden Eagles for two years, including the school's first NCAA Division II tournament appearance in 1981. That nationally rated team, coached by Joe DeGregorio, compiled a 23-6 mark and lost in the national regional finals. A quick look at the statistical records on Clarion's official athletics website reveals that Calipari played 19 games and averaged 3.1 points as a junior. As for free throws, he struggled from the line, hitting only 16 of 26 tries for 61.5 percent during that 1980-81 season. Calipari, who had fractured his cheekbone during the campaign, had to wear a wrestling mask while playing.

As a senior on a 16-11 team which was once ranked No. 3 in the nation after a quick 7-0 start, Calipari had a team-high 143 assists, which were the ninth best in school history at the time, and 34 steals, third best on the squad. He also averaged 5.3 points and hit 38 of 53 free throws for 71.7 percent before graduating with a bachelor's degree in marketing in 1982.

"I've never seen a more positive, upbeat, passionate person every day in my life," said Calipari of DeGregorio at Clarion. "You'd walk in tired, and he would be absolutely whistling and skipping every day until you're almost like, 'I don't even want to see him because he's making me feel bad because I'm a little tired, this guy is whistling and skipping.' "

Nearly 30 years later, Calipari invited his alma mater to play an exhibition game at Rupp Arena, not long after he had taken the Kentucky job. Not surprisingly, it was huge mismatch as No. 4 Kentucky dominated Clarion 117-52 before a crowd of 23,802, but Clarion had a nice paycheck of $20,000 to help with its athletics budget. Freshman superstar John Wall poured in 27 points in his unofficial collegiate debut.

In a pregame ceremony, Coach Cal was given two framed Clarion jerseys bearing his name and No. 21. His high school and college coaches, Bill Sacco and Joe DeGregorio, attended the game. Calipari was also the guest speaker at a reception hosted by Clarion the night before the exhibition contest.

John and Ellen Calipari also have honored coaches Sacco (who is a graduate of Clarion) and DeGregorio by establishing two endowment scholarships for basketball at Clarion. Over the years, he has stayed in touch with them and often invites them to games, including the Final Fours, even when he was the head coach at Memphis and UMass. And both of them saw Calipari capture his first national title in 2012 in New Orleans.

In 2016, both schools met again in an exhibition matchup at Rupp Arena, with UK winning 108-51.

In a *Pittsburgh Post-Gazette* story in 2008, Sacco quipped, Calipari "might be a Gucci kind of guy, but he still likes to go to Kmart once in a while."

While the retired coaches occasionally come to Lexington watch the Wildcats, they still get visits from Coach Cal when he returns to his hometown. "There's not a time that I don't go to Pittsburgh that I don't see both of them," added Calipari.

With his marketing degree in hand, Calipari was now anxious to enter the real world. He wanted a coaching job. And he ended up at Kansas, the storied institution where basketball legends came from – the game inventor Dr. James Naismith, Dr. Forrest Clare "Phog" Allen, and Adolph Rupp. "It was the best time of my life," said Calipari of his early days at Kansas. "I had no worries. I had no money. I had a car. We had different places we ate on different days 'cause it was the cheapest place to go. I mean, it was a fun time."

Calipari has said he was very excited for the opportunity at Kansas, even though his was a part-time position with no pay in his first season there. Ted

Owens was the head coach, with future NBA coach Bob Hill serving as an aide. "Bob Hill was an assistant coach there, and I was working at the Five-Star Camp," said Calipari. "[He] saw me working the camp and said, 'Why don't you come out and work our camp [at Kansas]?' I said okay. I went out and worked his camp. Ted Owens watched me do a station. He said, 'Why don't you stay here? I can't pay you. If you want to help out and be in the office and stuff envelopes and learn about college basketball, I'd love to have you here.' I went, 'Are you kidding me?' So, I went out there with two pair of shoes, three pairs of slacks, a blue blazer, three shirts and two ties. Happy as hell."

Added Calipari, "I was a volunteer. To eat, I worked at the training meal.... I would serve peas or corn. That's what I did. I lived with Dolph Carroll, who was the part-time coach. We didn't have furniture because we had a choice between ESPN or furniture, and we chose ESPN. We sat on pillows.

"But you know what, it was the greatest time of my life. I remember the first time in Allen Fieldhouse, the old locker room. I went in, and it was old. I'm thinking, Phog Allen showered in this shower. And I said, 'This has been here since the building, right?' They said yeah. The storied history of Kansas. The environment to live, to raise a family. It was tough for a 25-year-old because you're not going to hang around the students. You didn't have any money to go to the country club. But what it made me do, I just got into basketball. I was in the office all the time doing stuff. It was a great time."

Calipari recalls a crazy story involving a television movie, *The Day After*, which first aired in late 1983, featuring a nuclear war that was filmed around Kansas City and the college town of Lawrence. And the attack had forced many wounded victims to Allen Fieldhouse, which became a makeshift hospital.

"I tell you the bed thing because I couldn't afford a bed. That's one of my sins," smiled Calipari. "[In the movie] the triage was Allen Fieldhouse. I had no bed and they had all these cots in Allen Fieldhouse. So, Dolph and I were leaving one day, and I saw a double-wide cot. It was that wide. We went back that night, and I scooped up that cot, and that was my bed. Think about that. I slept on a cot for a year. Two years."

The 1982-83 Jayhawks didn't have a winning season, posting a disappointing 13-16 mark, and Ted Owens was fired after 19 seasons with an overall 348-182 record. And Calipari took a job at Vermont University as recruiting coordinator. But when new head coach Larry Brown was hired at Kansas, he asked the young Calipari to come back as an assistant with more responsibilities. Calipari stayed there for two more years as the improved Jayhawks posted 22-10 and 26-8 marks. Danny Manning, a 6-foot-11 freshman, was on Calipari's last Kansas team. He was a future All-American who later helped Brown and Kansas to the 1988 NCAA championship as a senior.

Calipari pointed out that he was thankful for the extended coaching opportunity at Kansas after Owens was dismissed. "I was blessed to be able to stay with him [Brown] for two years, and I look back fondly," said Calipari in 2016. "I had nothing except basketball. I think I had a Plymouth Arrow at that time. Do they still make Plymouth Arrows? I don't think they do. But no worries. I stayed with Randolph Carroll. He let me stay with him. It was a great time for me because can you imagine being 23, 22 and your first opportunity to be around the game is in a program like Kansas? I just felt every day I woke up, I was like, 'I can't believe this.'

"And I had the same feeling when I got this [Kentucky] job. And [assistant] John Robic looked out and saw Kentucky across that wall out there, and it was glitter, and I'm like, 'Can you imagine that we're here at Kentucky?' It's the same thing. Kansas is exactly the same kind of program."

For Calipari, Brown has been a mentor and a friend for years. "He threw me a life raft when I was fired [by the Nets] in New Jersey [in 1999]. Hired me at the University of Kansas [in 1983] when I had no business being hired. He's just somebody that I take great faith in. When he says something to me, I listen."

Coach Cal, who became an assistant to Brown for the Philadelphia 76ers for one year, recalled that getting fired from a head coaching position is "like falling down a flight of steps. A lot of times there were people on the sideline kicking you to fall faster. And that's part of life. Anybody that's been in a position that you find out who your friends are. I had a hundred calls when I got the job. I have to say, three calls when I got fired. Larry Brown, my father, and Howard Garfinkel [who co-founded the famous Five-Star Basketball Camp]. Those were my three calls.

"You know, for me, it was a great experience to learn and try to stay positive instead of being vindictive or mean or mad. I tried to stay above it all, didn't blame anybody, and learned from it."

While at Kansas, Calipari also served as head coach of the junior varsity team in addition to scouting and recruiting. He was also in charge of the "Little Jayhawks," a ball-handling squad which often performed during halftimes at Allen Fieldhouse. And the school was where he met his future wife, the former Ellen Higgins, who worked in Kansas' athletics department. The UK coach added that Mrs. Calipari "grew up two-and-a-half hours from there" on a farm in Missouri.

Then Calipari left Lawrence and returned to his hometown of Pittsburgh in 1985, taking the job as the assistant coach for the University of Pittsburgh Panthers. He couldn't say no for the chance to coach at home. And after his first year at Pittsburgh, he married his sweetheart from Kansas during the summer of 1986.

Guess who came to Kansas as a graduate assistant after Calipari left? None other than Bill Self, the current head coach at Kansas. Self had just finished his playing career at Oklahoma State, where he averaged nearly eight points and four assists per game as a senior guard.

"I've known Cal for quite some time," said Self in 2008. "I was actually a player when he was starting out coaching at Kansas. He had got the job at Pitt right before I got there as a graduate assistant. So, our paths never crossed as far as working. But, you know, everybody knew Cal and liked Cal.

"I'm sure he did have a lot of those jobs. I think my jobs were much more meaningful than serving the peas and the corn. I was in charge of making sure we rented out the correct bowling alley on game days and numerous things like that because if you know Coach Brown, he's very, very, very superstitious. If you bowl and you play well, you probably played well because you bowled on that lane, had nothing to do with Danny [Manning].

"So, you know, I had many responsibilities like that. Cal is right in this regard. Making $4,500 a year, being a grad student, all that stuff. I don't know if I could have had more fun than what I had that grad assistant year in Lawrence."

Self later worked as an assistant to former UK boss Eddie Sutton at Oklahoma State during the 1990s before moving on to the head coaching ranks. Interestingly, Self and Calipari have met twice in the national championship game, with Self's Jayhawks beating Coach Cal's Memphis club in 2008 and Calipari defeating Self's team in 2012.

When the 26-year-old Calipari came back to the Steel City in 1985, Coach Dr. Roy Chipman's Pittsburgh Panthers were coming off a 17-12 campaign, including an NCAA tourney loss to Louisiana Tech in the first round. The Panthers' future was bright in then-tough Big East Conference as they featured two former *Parade* and McDonald's All-Americans in sophomore Charles Smith and freshman Jerome Lane on their 1985-86 roster. Also on the team was senior guard Joey David, who would be the father of future UK player Jonny David.

And the young assistant also joined his former college coach at Clarion, Joe DeGregorio, who was starting his third year as assistant coach at Pittsburgh. In addition, Drakesboro, Ky., native and ex-Cat Reggie Warford was beginning his sixth year as an assistant there.

But the 1985-86 season ended on a disappointing note as Pittsburgh finished at 15-14, and the school was looking for a new head coach since Chipman earlier had resigned from his position in December but stayed with the team. For the next two years, Calipari remained on the Panthers' staff under new coach Paul Evans, and Pittsburgh posted 25-8 and 24-7 seasons, winning Big East regular-season titles both years.

At the University of Pittsburgh, Jim O'Brien – a well-known sportswriter – was the assistant athletics director for public relations working in the sports information office, and he knew Calipari.

"John is a good man," wrote O'Brien in an email in 2017. "He is like Joe Namath [of Beaver Falls, Penn.] when he comes home. He has time for everyone and touches everyone in the room. He remembers where he came from and who helped him in his early years."

O'Brien, a Pittsburgh native who was the founding editor for *Street & Smith's* basketball yearbooks, has written numerous books about Pittsburgh sports, covering the Pirates, the Steelers, and Roberto Clemente, to name a few. One of his latest books is a basketball memoir, *Looking Up: From the ABA to the NBA, the WNBA to the NCAA*, and Calipari is featured in that volume. O'Brien and the author have been friends for 10 years. We often catch up via many emails and meet in Pittsburgh during the summers while covering the Pirates at beautiful PNC Park.

O'Brien gave me permission to share some of his Calipari stories from the 480-page paperback.

John Calipari called me on the telephone in the summer of 2014, as he promised he would. The celebrated coach of the University of Kentucky men's basketball team was traveling on the highway to Louisville to conduct a basketball clinic in rival territory.

'This is my fifth clinic in as many days, and I have to get up so early and I haven't gotten much sleep lately,' complained Calipari, 'and I'm not going to do this anymore.'

To which I said, 'Yes, you will, John. You wouldn't be John Calipari if you didn't work as hard to promote your program and yourself.'

'We'll see,' came back Calipari, conceding that I could be right, something coaches are loathe to do at times with sportswriters.

Calipari has always called back when I called the UK sports information office and requested an interview. Calipari comes from Coraopolis, out of Moon Township High School and Clarion University, and he was an assistant to Paul Evans at Pitt in the mid-80s when I was the assistant athletic director for public relations at Pitt. He gets back as often as possible to visit family and friends. He's never forgotten where he came from, or who helped him along the way. Many people do forget. He may arrive in a University of Kentucky jet airplane and that has to impress the citizens of Coraopolis who knew him as a kid.

His coach at Clarion, Joe DeGregorio, had helped him connect at Pitt when DeGregorio served as a volunteer assistant coach for Roy Chipman, who preceded Evans as the coach at Pitt. Calipari has never forgotten DeGregorio and has invited him to join him at the NCAA men's basketball tournament and even got DeGregorio a championship ring when he won at Kentucky.

Another Calipari story as written by O'Brien:

I like Calipari. I like the way he carries himself and the way he handles interviews and the coolness and charm he wears so well. He doesn't shrug off interviews and he is never rude in the manner of Gregg Popovich of the San Antonio Spurs. I don't know why media types bother to talk to him. Why set yourself up for a putdown?

Calipari was a kid in Moon Township who was a gym rat and hung around the Robert Morris University campus there when the Five Star Basketball Camp was conducted on its campus over the years. He would do anything to make himself useful, just to spend time with some of the greatest high school basketball players in the country and, more so, to spend time with some of the greatest college coaches in the country.

While Calipari was coaching in Pittsburgh, his parents were no longer around, as they had moved to another state. "They weren't living there at the time," Calipari told the author. "My parents were in Charlotte, North Carolina. My sisters were going. It was mostly aunts, uncles, and cousins. I was able to be around people that I cared about.

"The first full-time job that I had in my life was to be the assistant at Pittsburgh. I was paid $30,000 and thought I'd just became a millionaire because I'd never really been paid as a job. Six months before I realized I had insurance benefits that I needed to sign up with, they called me and said, 'Are you ever going to sign up for your insurance?' I was just happy to have a job.

"And then to be back, to be around friends, to be around the people there that I thought were just salt of the earth kind of people, people that I grew up with."

But his hometown folks still liked to treat him as if he was a teenager, and young Calipari had to face some awkward moments. "It's hard going home, to be honest with you, because they still look at you like the 15-year-old kid or 19-year-old you were. All of a sudden you're 24, 25, 26, now trying to get established as a coach. It wasn't easy, but I enjoyed my time there," he said.

In 1988, Calipari found his first head coaching job at the University of Massachusetts in Amherst at the age of 29. Even though UMass's basketball program was in a horrible mess, he had to start somewhere. The ambitious Calipari wanted to be the boss. A former player and a graduate of UMass, Rick Pitino, then coaching the New York Knicks, served on the coaching search committee and endorsed Calipari for the job.

According to an article by David Nathan of *Worcester Telegram & Gazette*, the newly hired Calipari appeared on a radio talk show and had to answer a touchy question from a skeptical fan. A caller asked Calipari, "What makes you think you're any different than the last three guys that were fired?"

"We'll be different," Calipari assured the caller.

As it turned out, Coach Cal – called Pitino Jr. at the time by some folks – did a miraculous job during his eight years at UMass and led the rising program to NCAA appearances in the Sweet Sixteen, Elite Eight and Final Four during the 1990s. And Pittsburgh, his hometown university, was very interested in him after the school fired Paul Evans in 1994, but things didn't work out. Calipari had become a rising star in college basketball.

In November 1995, his 35-2 Minutemen, along with 6-foot-11 junior star Marcus Camby, even defeated mighty Pitino's Kentucky club 92-82 in a non-conference matchup. (Yes, that's the same UK team which captured the 1996 national title after senior guard Tony Delk and his seven three-pointers helped the Wildcats beat Syracuse in the finals in East Rutherford, N.J.)

With his team's stunning success during that 1995-96 campaign, Calipari received several national Coach of the Year honors.

Calipari's UMass also faced UK four other times, all during the 1990s, but Pitino's Cats had the upper hand, including a 1996 Final Four showdown.

Asked in 1996 about his relationship with Pitino at a Final Four news conference prior to the UK-UMass matchup, Calipari said, "I would rather not play Rick Pitino unless it was the very last game for both of us. The reason is, I owe him a lot. I'm very grateful for the opportunity he's given me and my family. You don't want to play great friends unless it's the last game for both teams. We have to do this, so we're going to play. Between now and game time, before it ends, he's the other coach. When the game ends, I'll hug him, win or lose, and tell him how much I appreciate what he's done for me and my family. But until then we're both going after the jugular."

The next day after that press conference, Pitino and the No. 2 Wildcats avenged their earlier loss to UMass by beating the top-ranked Minutemen 81-74 in the national semifinals, advancing to the championship game. "I was proud of our guys," Calipari told the reporters. "We played hard. It's just that they played with a little more emotion than we played. We gave ourselves a chance to win against a great basketball club. We refused to lose. We never stopped playing. We played right down to the end. I told the team after this game in the locker room that I learned more about myself as a coach and a person this year than I have in all my other years of coaching. I thanked them because you're talking about unbelievable human beings that I coached this year.… It's about the kind of people and character they had.… You don't win close games like we do without kids with strong character and smart kids like we have."

By the way, the UMass game with Kentucky was Calipari's last one at the school in Amherst, Mass., before he took a lucrative job in the NBA, becoming the head coach and executive vice president of basketball operations for the New Jersey Nets. His five-year pact with the Nets reportedly was worth $15 million. At UMass, he reportedly was making $800,000 a year. Certainly, it was a dramatic jump in pay for the 37-year-old Calipari, who wanted the challenge of running an NBA club. Not long before that, Pitino, ironically, had turned down the same job from the Nets and stayed with the Wildcats.

Looking back, Calipari said that 1996 Final Four – his first one – was a great experience, but it was definitely a challenge to deal with the circus-like atmosphere. He has since learned and become a better coach in handling the postseason tournament distractions.

"I was in my 30s, was overwhelmed with everything, from the phone calls to preparation to tickets, everything," he recalled 12 years later when he took Memphis to the 2008 Final Four. "I walked out on this floor, and my whole thought was, 'This is the next game. I did not look at this like it was anything other than the next game.' And I told those guys. I didn't know, but that's how I felt. I did not feel that way when I was 34 or 35, whatever I was, at that age. So, I was a little bit overwhelmed with the whole environment. But I've mellowed out [smiling]."

Unfortunately, the NCAA later vacated a couple of Final Four appearances in 1996 and 2008 by Calipari's teams at UMass and Memphis due to NCAA violations, but the coach was not blamed or charged in either case.

After four years in the NBA, including two-plus mediocre years with the rebuilding Nets, and a successful nine-year tenure at Memphis, he landed a prestigious job – head coach of the Kentucky Wildcats – in 2009. And he got an eight-year, $31.65 million contract, according to UK. Calipari also brought three assistant coaches from Memphis, including longtime aide and Pittsburgh native John Robic, to Lexington. Robic also worked with Calipari at UMass.

In my syndicated column in Kentucky outlets, I wrote that "UK has hit a grand slam home run heard around the world in the hiring of its new basketball coach." He was easily my top choice if the Wildcats couldn't lure either Billy Donovan or even Rick Pitino – very hot commodities at the time – to the Bluegrass.

After two fruitless seasons of Billy Gillispie's coaching regime, Kentucky was fortunate to have Coach Cal on board. He was a glamorous, charismatic 50-year-old mentor with a proven record as a successful college coach with NBA experience.

Calipari had a lot to say about nearly everything in his introductory news conference on the UK campus. The new Wildcat boss said he had called former UK coaches Joe B. Hall, Eddie Sutton, Rick Pitino, and Tubby Smith. "All I can tell you is, none of those coaches would trade their time here for anything in the world," he commented.

Calipari said taking the coveted position at Kentucky "is pretty heady stuff for me. But this was a dream I had since I brought our team here [UMass in December 1991]. We had won the Alaska Shootout, came out to here to play [before dropping to the Cats 90-69], and I could not believe the environment. At that point, I said I'd love to coach there someday." Current UK assistant Tony Barbee, by the way, was on that 30-5 team which later faced Kentucky's "The Unforgettables" again for the second time in NCAA Sweet Sixteen. It was the matchup before the famous Kentucky-Duke showdown.

UK was the dream job, Calipari added. He had heard a lot about Joe B. Hall and the Wildcats since the early days. Like the big-time programs, Kentucky was on national TV a lot. As a young player, he even got to spend some time with Wildcat star Kyle Macy at the Five-Star Basketball Camp, and he didn't really know what to think. "He [Macy] came up to do a shooting station, and I was his assistant. What a gentleman and what a good guy," recalled Calipari. "I couldn't believe it, a guy that had that much notoriety and passion, that he was that good of a guy." And Calipari once pretended he was Macy. "I used to try to emulate Kyle Macy," he said. "As a matter of fact, one college game someone yelled at me 'Kyle Macy,' and I was so excited I couldn't play the rest of the game."

Former UK standout and current broadcaster Mike Pratt was one of the very few individuals who helped bring Calipari to Kentucky. "He was the No. 1 choice and the only one we talked to about the job. Lawyers got involved after that to work out financial details," Pratt said in 2017. "His predecessor, Billy Gillispie, had become such a pain to all around the program that the powers to be decided to make a change."

Pratt said it was very helpful to know Calipari, who was the nation's third winningest active coach at the time, really wanted to come to Kentucky during the coaching search. "I think Cal is a terrific communicator, with excellent people skills," added Pratt in a separate interview in 2009. "He will push his teams to reach their potential but still not do it in a demeaning way. [There are] exciting times ahead for UK basketball. What sealed the deal was that John communicated his desire to be at UK from the start."

Former All-SEC standout Derrick Hord, a McDonald's All-American who played for the Wildcats during the early 1980s, was impressed with Calipari's performance at the introductory press conference. Hord liked Calipari's approach of including or recognizing the former Wildcat players or mentors in the Kentucky program. "There was an obvious display of respect for the program, and the way he reached out to former coaches and players was very admirable," Hord said. "I particularly appreciate how he has prioritized thus far. Heck, and the guy can recruit and coach, too. I'm looking forward to this era and hope I have a ringside seat."

Added Calipari, "We're here carrying on their tradition, and they're always welcome in here."

When he was a young head coach, Calipari had a good share of major college coaches with experience who became good buddies. They helped and advised him in many different ways. That group included older folks like Jack Leaman and Gene Bartow. Of course, Joe B. Hall became a very early supporter of Calipari when the latter arrived at UK. "I listen to their opinions," said Calipari.

Nationally, Leaman was probably best known as Julius Erving's coach at UMass during the early 1970s. Erving, nicknamed "Dr. J," later became one of the hottest stars in the ABA and NBA. Leaman also coached Rick Pitino there and later became a broadcaster for the UMass games. Also, UMass' hardwood floor at its basketball arena is named the "Jack Leaman Court," honoring his contributions to the university.

"If he wanted me to do something, he'd say, 'Let's go get a cup of coffee.' That meant I want to talk to you about your team," Calipari said of Leaman. "And he wouldn't say anything until I said, 'Tell me what you think.' Then he'd talk for 30 minutes."

Calipari said Hall is kind of the same way. He is grateful that Coach Hall has been a great fan of him and the Cats, and they enjoy a special relationship. Coach Cal loves "seeing him in the gym. Love hearing what his thoughts [are]. I've been blessed that I've had guys that have never tried to overwhelm me or be over-opinionated. If I ask him, he's going to tell me. He called, and we talked the other day. We were talking about guard play, and he said, 'This is what you're trying to do, isn't it?' And I said, 'Yeah.' He said, 'That's what I thought.' Who else would have followed Adolph Rupp up here? Dude had to follow Adolph Rupp. What he's done for this university, for this state, Cynthiana [his hometown], he deserves our adulation. I love it when he does the 'Y' [cheer] and people go crazy on his birthday. They're singing 'Happy Birthday.' He deserves all of that. He earned it."

Another well-known personality who was nice to Calipari during his early coaching days was Gene Bartow. Remember Bartow? He was the one who replaced legendary John Wooden at UCLA and coached the Bruins for a couple of years. During the early 1970s, he was the head coach at Memphis State (now called Memphis), leading the Tigers to the 1973 Final Four, where they dropped to UCLA in the championship game. When Calipari was at Memphis, beginning in 2000, Bartow was around and supported him. At the time, Bartow was working for the firm which owned the Memphis Grizzlies of the NBA and FedEx Forum, later serving as its president.

Bartow, said Calipari, was one of the great gentlemen. Coach Cal added, "He was good to me when he was at UAB [University of Alabama at Birmingham]. He always was kind to me even before I got to Memphis, but I've been blessed in that way."

During the early 1980s, it was Bartow's unranked UAB club which upset Hall's eighth-ranked Wildcats and 7-foot-1 sophomore center Sam Bowie 69-62 in the 1981 NCAA Tournament, shocking the college basketball world. Earlier that season, Kentucky had defeated UAB for the University of Kentucky Invitation Tournament championship.

Calipari mostly has enjoyed a respectable relationship with the media over the years. It also helps that he has a marketing background. One veteran journalist who knows Coach Cal well is Pittsburgh native Mike DeCourcy, the college basketball columnist for the *Sporting News*. They first met when Calipari was an assistant coach at Pitt but became much better acquainted during his UMass coaching days.

"I had covered high school basketball in Pittsburgh prior to becoming the beat writer for the Duquesne Dukes, who were in the same league as UMass," recalled DeCourcy. "So, I knew the players John was recruiting [for UMass]: Jim McCoy and Will Herndon. Jim became the school's leading scorer, and Herndon was a 6-3 power forward who could jump over a car. But he couldn't shoot. That's why he was a power forward.

"In his first year at UMass, the Minutemen played at Duquesne. My seat on press row was adjacent to the visiting bench. He spent a lot of that game carrying on a running conversation with me, frequently the subject being the not-stellar quality of his team.

"I think that's the only time that ever happened in three decades of covering college hoops. But John always has been one of a kind."

John Calipari at a preseason practice held at Joe Craft Center before the 2019-20 season. (Photo by Jamie H. Vaught)

Both DeCourcy and Calipari grew up in the same area, and both have crossed paths numerous times during their careers. "John and I grew up in Pittsburgh at almost exactly the same time," said the writer. "He's a year older than me, and we grew up on opposite sides of the region. He was from Moon Township, out by the airport, and I was from Elizabeth Township, in the Mon Valley in the southeast part of Allegheny County, where a lot of the steel mills were. But once he went to UMass, we were in touch a lot."

DeCourcy has some Coach Cal stories to share. "One of my favorite stories is when he got UMass to the Sweet 16 in 1992, just four years into taking over one of the worst programs in Division I," recalled DeCourcy, who covered his 30th Final Four in Minneapolis in 2019. "I still laugh at the people who say he can't coach and just gets five-star recruits and wins on talent. Were they around in '92, when he made the Sweet 16 with Jim McCoy and Will Herndon? Please. Duquesne and Pitt right there in Pittsburgh wanted nothing to do with them. And here they were starting in the Sweet 16.

"I covered the tournament for the *Pittsburgh Press* and saw John at the news conference on the day before UMass would play Kentucky. Bumped into him in the hallway, I think. He said, 'What are you doing tonight?' I had no plans. He said, 'Why don't you come to dinner with the team?'

"It was a tremendous night. We went to a great Italian restaurant in South Philly, and I got to observe him around his players and staff. It was a great opportunity to see how he connected with both. He has been generous many times with his time and access.

"The next night, this team built from largely unwanted recruits – I'd guess Tony Barbee would want me to note that he was an exception and had been pursued by big-time programs – nearly beat the No. 2 seed Kentucky. The biggest blow to UMass was a technical foul called against Cal by official Lenny Wirtz, who was on the opposite sideline and at the opposite end of the floor. Wirtz was actually right in front of me, and I couldn't have heard anything Cal said if I'd had the hearing of a superhero. But Wirtz tagged him for stepping out of the coaches' box. It was one of the most ridiculous calls I've seen made in three decades of covering the NCAA Tournament."

While working for a daily newspaper in Memphis, DeCourcy covered the Memphis Tigers during the pre-Calipari days and could see the enormous potential for the school's basketball program. He certainly helped Coach Cal land at Memphis in March 2000.

"I don't know how much I had to do with John taking the job at Memphis, but it wasn't nothing," said DeCourcy. "I believe I was the first person to publicly say he was the ideal candidate for the job after Tic Price was pressured to resign before the 1999-2000 season. I appeared weekly on the Memphis radio show of my friend George Lapides, one of the most influential media figures in the city during the past half century, and I said almost immediately that Cal and Tigers basketball would be an ideal marriage.

"I worked for four years in Memphis for *The Commercial Appeal* newspaper, and Tigers basketball was my beat during that time. I knew what the potential of the program was. And I was still covering the league, so I knew he could make it happen there. It was my final season on the [Cincinnati] Bearcats beat at the *Cincinnati Enquirer* [where he worked from 1997-2000] before I moved on to work full-time for *Sporting News*. So, I spoke with John a few times about why it would work for him there, how much I believed he and Memphis basketball could be successful together.

"Memphis is one of America's best basketball cities. They love the game there. They live the game there. I didn't know that before I moved there, but I felt it every day I was there. I knew Cal would be perfect in that environment. That's what I told him. I remember he called me once when I was in Boise for a game the Bearcats had to play on the day before New Year's Eve and us having a long conversation about it.

"But the funniest talk we had came a month before that one, just a few days after Price vacated the Memphis position. I had gone to lunch with several Memphis media friends at a downtown Cincinnati restaurant on a Friday afternoon. They were in town to cover a football game between the Tigers and Bearcats the following day. The basketball [job] opening was huge news at that point, so of course we talked throughout the lunch about the job, and I talked mostly about why I knew Calipari was the perfect candidate.

"We were still on that same subject when we'd left the restaurant and were just getting ready to say goodbye, outside on Cincinnati's Fountain Square. My cell phone rang. I answered.

"Hold on a minute, John," I said.

And the other guys there howled in laughter.

"John's timing always has been impeccable, and we talked some more about why he needed to get that job," said DeCourcy. At the time, Coach Cal was serving as assistant coach for the NBA's 76ers.

DeCourcy added that Calipari is "as sharp and insightful as anyone I've met."

Coach Cal, who has posted five 30-win campaigns at Kentucky going into the 2019-20 season, has coached some of the greatest UK teams in school's tradition-rich history. Some of his best ones include:

♦ Second-ranked 2009-10 Wildcats, which featured freshman stars – National Player of the Year John Wall and 6-foot-11 DeMarcus Cousins, along with junior standout Patrick Patterson. Kentucky nearly made the Final Four in Calipari's first season in Lexington as the 35-3 Cats lost to Bob Huggins and his West Virginia team in the regional finals.

♦ Top-ranked 2011-12 Wildcats, who had 6-foot-10 rookie and National Player of the Year Anthony Davis. Kentucky, 38-2, won the school's eighth national title in beating Kansas in New Orleans. Davis and teammate Michael Kidd-Gilchrist later became the No. 1 and No. 2 NBA Draft picks overall.

♦ Top-ranked 2014-15 Wildcats, who had All-Americans in 6-foot-11 Karl-Anthony Towns and 7-foot Willie Cauley-Stein. Kentucky was on its way in becoming college basketball's first 40-0 team in history, but it got derailed in the national semifinals, dropping to Wisconsin 71-64 in Indianapolis. Instead, the Cats finished at 38-1, which is still a stunning achievement.

Calipari said he doesn't compare his teams, adding, "I've had good teams here. I've had good teams at UMass. I've had good teams at Memphis. Like really, really good teams. This [2014-15] team's a good team. This may be one of the deeper teams I've had. I'm doing stuff, platooning and doing stuff I've never done before. This is a good group."

During the 2015 NBA All-Star festivities, Anthony Davis said his 2012 Kentucky Wildcats were better than the 2015 Cats. When Coach Cal heard that, he just smiled. "Did he say that? But if you ask DeMarcus [Cousins], what would he say? The same thing. Then if you asked Brandon Knight, Terrence Jones and that group [from UK's Final Four team in 2010-11], what would they say? We would kill them. So, that's fine. I would tell you this – they will all root for each other."

When UK loses in the NCAA Tournament in the first or second weekend before the Final Four, it isn't a surprise to see some folks – the so-called "Monday Morning" coaches – in the Big Blue Nation go bonkers. For some, the BBN is the only hobby they have in their lives, and they have no other interests to keep them occupied. It's sure fascinating to see that some fans really go crazy on social media and even want Calipari gone. A handful of opinionated media folks also have complained and howled about Coach Cal, who has successfully rebuilt his team every year after losing top freshmen to the NBA on annual basis.

I wrote a syndicated column about this shortly after the favored Wildcats failed to make a coveted trip to the 2019 NCAA Final Four when they suffered a heartbreaking overtime loss to SEC foe Auburn. Here's what I wrote (beginning with the second paragraph):

Sure, we are saddened with the painful outcome in Elite Eight, but we certainly don't need to blame Calipari and the student-athletes for the setback. It's okay to be very disappointed but we don't need to whine and carry on. Yes, we have high expectations at tradition-rich Kentucky. That is wonderful, but we need to understand it's not going to work out every time for the Wildcats during March Madness even with McDonald's prep All-Americans.

If you want to advance, especially in the latter stages of the Big Dance, you also need to have a little luck and hope the ball will bounce your way. We didn't have it this time against a more experienced Auburn club. Even Duke, with three freshman stars expected to be selected among the top 5 in the 2019 NBA Draft, didn't make it to the Final Four, either.

And ESPN's Jay Williams tweeted that UK fans should not complain under Calipari and listed some of his accomplishments at Kentucky.

I wholeheartedly agree. Why complain? My goodness! Since Calipari arrived in Lexington in 2009, he has taken the Cats to Elite Eight seven out of 10 times, which is more than any other school during that period. That's a record of 70 percent! Amazing! And the 60-year-old hall of famer has sent UK to the Final Four four times, including a national championship in 2012.

In addition, the Wildcats have posted five 30-win campaigns under his watch. During his overall coaching career, which include stops at UMass and Memphis, Calipari now has 11 30-win seasons, third most among all active coaches.

Yes, I know Coach Cal has won only one national title at Kentucky. Sure, the BBN would like to see more championships, but we have to be realistic during the one-and-done era. Calipari doesn't like the one-and-done, which isn't healthy for college basketball and most folks don't like it, either. But he and Coach K from Duke are going to take advantage of the rule and snatch the nation's top high school players until it is changed.

And remember legendary Adolph Rupp won four national titles in 41 years. Coach Cal has captured one in 10 years. Calipari also has 31 NCAA Tournament wins as compared to Rupp's 30.

A big reason Coach Cal loves Kentucky is BBN's passionate fans who care about the program and follow the Cats 24/7. I remember that he discussed the fans during his postgame press conference following his team's 71-58 win over Louisville back in late December. He acknowledged there are fans who will complain.

'I don't pay attention to any of the chirping,' said Calipari. 'I don't watch it, I don't read it. If it gets crazy, I will say to [publicist] Eric [Lindsey], "Is there anything I need to deal with?" I don't watch it, I don't read it.

'[But] let me say this though, we have the greatest fans. Kentucky is what you want. You never have to sell a ticket, you never have to worry about people being excited about games. You could play in a storm and there's 20,000 people in that building. You know the hardcore people adopt these players and they become their sons and grandsons.

'There's also a small percentage out there that are just crazy. I don't pay any attention to them. Now here is the good thing. They will never steal my joy. They never will. I don't listen. You just make yourself angry and go crazy.... And I will be smiling.'

As for this [2018–19] season, it sure was fun to follow the 30-7 Wildcats, who had victories over North Carolina, Louisville, Kansas and Tennessee, among others. UK finished No. 7 in the final Associated Press Top 25 poll.

The Wildcats had a fun-loving group. PJ Washington, Reid Travis, Tyler Herro and others were a joy to watch.

Now, keep in mind that I don't agree with everything Coach Cal has done, but you have to agree his accomplishments are stunning and they certainly speak for themselves. Enjoy while you can. We may never see another coach like him. In the future, the school could end up with someone not as good or a good coach who melts under intense pressure. Just remember several 10-, 12-, 13- or 14-loss seasons that we experienced under previous coaches at UK.

A majority of the faithful Big Blue Nation will approve that Calipari, who earlier agreed to a so-called 'lifetime' contract by UK, is a pretty darn good CEO of UK Basketball, and we can look forward to more notable campaigns with hopes of capturing the school's ninth national crown down the road.

Indeed, the future is still bright in Lexington.

Speaking at a packed news conference during the annual Media Day festivities held on the UK campus in October 2019, Calipari added his wife, Ellen, wasn't too happy about the Wildcats not making the Final Four, either. "My wife was mad," said Calipari. "I had to explain it to her that you don't get to the Final Four every year. And there's times buzzer-beaters knock you out in overtime games, and you move on to the next group. But she didn't understand. I'm like, 'Are you crazy?' That's how it is.

"Look, our fans are crazy, and I love them, but please don't take this wrong, I don't listen to them. I don't read it. Can I go [on] Twitter, Facebook? I give you stuff and never look at anything that comes – not one thing, never since I've been here. If you write me a letter, and it's not addressed, it doesn't even make my desk. It's thrown away. If you have a letter, I'll respond, and usually I handwrite it.

"But here's what I do know about this position when you're coaching here. If you're worried about all that stuff, the clutter that's out there, you can't do this job, and you can't be about the kids. You can't. You'll be under the desk in a fetal position. Your secretary will come in, 'Where did he go? Coach, what are you doing under there? Come out of there.' [Smiling] So, this is not one for the faint of heart, whether you're playing here or coaching here. And that's the first I heard anybody was mad that we haven't done enough."

Despite UK's 10-year unparalleled success under Calipari's watch, a reporter said he had thought the fans were all happy. "I did, too," said Calipari. "So, I'm saying the next 10 [years] got to be better. And they're saying it wasn't enough? Whew."

After three previous trips to the Final Four in 1996, 2008, and 2011 when his different schools failed to win the national title, Calipari finally won his first NCAA title in 2012. The Wildcats, despite Anthony Davis' cold-shooting performance, beat Kansas with their outstanding defense and rebounding. It was Davis – named the Final Four's Most Outstanding Player – who grabbed a team-best 16 rebounds and blocked a game-high six shots. Sophomore guard Doron Lamb had the hot hand, hitting 7 of 12 shots for a game-high 22 points, including 3 of 6 three-pointers.

Moments after the horn sounded at the lively Mercedes-Benz Superdome, Calipari turned and motioned for his wife, who went through security, to come to the hardwood floor from her first-row seat behind two press rows and the Kentucky bench. Surrounded by his family, including his then 15-year-old son and future Wildcat Brad, they hugged and kissed as the confetti fell to the floor from the ceiling. Even actress Ashley Judd sat on the same front row with the Calipari family. A jubilant Kentucky athletics director Mitch Barnhart, who sat directly behind the UK bench, celebrated, raising his arms with clenched fists. It was a joyful time in the Big Blue Nation, tons of whom flocked to the Big Easy. Kentucky had just captured its first NCAA championship in 14 years.

A relieved Coach Cal – who also has two daughters, Erin (who played basketball at UMass for two years while her dad was at Memphis) and Megan – was asked if this NCAA title meant something to him. "You know what it is, I told my wife, I'm glad it's done," he said. "Now I can get about my business of coaching basketball and getting these players to be the best that they can be, helping young people, you know, create better lives for themselves and their families, and also helping them prepare for life after basketball. I can get on with that. I don't have to hear the drama. I can just coach now. I don't have to worry. If you want to know the truth, it's almost like, 'Done, let me move on.'

"I don't feel any different. I'm not going to feel any different in the morning. I'm going to go to Mass in the morning. I'm going to be the same guy I am. I'm telling you. It's over now. I can get about my business of coaching young people and not have the drama of all the other stuff."

But there has to be some happiness in winning a national crown, right? Added Calipari, "Oh, yeah. Listen, this team deserves all the accolades that they've been getting. And what I wanted them to show today is that we were not just a talented team, we were a defensive team, and we were a team that shared the ball. I wanted everybody to see it. We were the best team this season. The most efficient team. We shared the ball. I've wanted that. I told them I wanted this to be one for the ages. Go out there and show everyone what kind of team you

John Calipari and the Wildcats celebrate the 2012 NCAA championship in New Orleans. (Photo by Jamie H. Vaught)

are, even though we were young. It doesn't matter how young you are – it's how you play together."

Before advancing to the national finals, UK had to face Rick Pitino's tough Louisville club for the second time that season (Kentucky won 69-62 in a Top 4 regular-season showdown at Rupp Arena on New Year's Eve). Shortly after Pitino – obviously unpopular in the Big Blue Nation after taking the job at rival U of L – saw his Cardinals drop a 69-61 verdict with Anthony Davis sparking Kentucky to victory with a double-double of 18 points and 14 rebounds, both game-highs, the U of L coach, to his credit, praised the 2012 Wildcats.

"To tell you the truth, I haven't always liked some of the Kentucky teams. I'm not going to lie to you," Pitino commented. "But I really like this team a lot because of their attitude and the way they play.

"I'll certainly be rooting for them hard to bring the trophy back to Kentucky because I'm really impressed with them, not only as basketball players, the way they carry themselves, their attitude. They're a great group of guys, doing a tremendous job. Louisville will be rooting for Kentucky, which doesn't happen very often, to bring home that trophy to the state."

In college basketball, Calipari is one of the more animated coaches you will find on the sidelines. He said there isn't any coach that he tried to emulate about not getting too emotional.

"You are who you are when you're coaching," said Coach Cal. "And I never tried to be anybody else. But whether it's the guys I played for, Bill Sacco [at Moon High] and Joe DeGregorio [Clarion State], I thought everyone that went into coaching was Italian for a while. I didn't learn until I left high school that there were other people who coached basketball. And then I worked for Larry Brown [at Kansas]. I've worked for great people. Paul Evans [at Pittsburgh]. They were all different. I learned from each of them.

"But I don't think any of us in this profession can try to be anybody else. I wish I was less animated. I wish I was less emotional. But I was born this way."

It is a well-known fact that Calipari has helped the other UK sports teams, including football, in recruiting. Many pigskin recruits on an official recruiting trip at Kentucky often get wide-eyed at seeing the basketball coach as well as his star players, saying "Wow!" Calipari enjoys watching coach Mark Stoops' football Wildcats, who have found success with bowl trips during the late 2010s along with record-breaking performances by Josh Allen, Benny Snell Jr. and Lynn Bowden Jr. Said Coach Cal of Allen, who later became college football's top defensive player, "The guy is ridiculous."

Said associate head football coach and recruiting coordinator Vince Marrow, "I remember we took a lot of guys on 'Junior Days' [when] we have basketball games. And when they get down there, they look at Cal like he's a god or something, but then you see how down-to-earth he is.

"So, basketball has been very huge [in football recruiting]. Cal really supports us. Those guys do a good job helping us. I can't thank those guys enough."

In 1967, Vanderbilt's Perry Wallace broke the color barrier by becoming the first African-American to play varsity basketball in SEC. Other standouts like UK's Tom Payne, Alabama's Wendell Hudson, and Tennessee's Larry Robinson, to name a few, followed a similar path in the next several years, becoming the first African-Americans with a basketball scholarship at those schools.

It was former UK player and Naismith Memorial Hall of Fame member C.M. Newton who became a pioneer in SEC racial integration, encouraging Hudson to attend Alabama while he was the head coach at the Tuscaloosa school. Later, as UK's athletics director, Newton hired Tubby Smith and Bernadette Locke-Mattox, the first African-Americans to coach the men's and women's team, respectively, at Kentucky. A former All-SEC standout at Georgia, Locke-Mattox had previously served as an assistant on Rick Pitino's staff at UK, becoming the nation's first *bona fide* female assistant on a prestigious men's squad.

While at Alabama, Newton wasn't very popular after signing Hudson. It didn't help that Newton had just completed his first season at the Crimson Tide helm with a horrible 4-20 mark, including 1-17 in the SEC. "It was controversial," Newton once told the author. "He [Hudson] and I developed a very close relationship during that time because I got a lot of heat, too. We weren't winning, and we'd signed the first black in any sport, so that doesn't endear you to the populace.

"It was hard on him. It was not just hard on the road. It was hard on him right in Alabama. It was hard on him in Bryant Hall [dormitory]. There were some guys who didn't want us to bring black guys to Alabama. It was a very difficult situation for Wendell.

"The reason I say we were lucky was because he was the perfect person for that [in handling racial tension]. He had a way about him of not being, you know, some namby-pamby guy. He had maturity and a wiseness about that whole business of relationships. It was unbelievable to see him [to deal with the circumstances well]."

Coach Cal believes he could've done the same thing as Newton's, but he isn't really sure, though. After learning Perry Wallace had passed away in 2017, Calipari said, "I always say, whether it's C.M. Newton or others, the courage that they had, and I always wonder, if I were put in that situation, would I have the courage to do the right thing? And a lot of times the right thing is not popular. I would hope that I would. That I would go against the grain, which I've tried to do most of my career, but I don't know.

"I mean, would I have the courage enough to say I'm doing right even though it's going to hurt my career? Or I'm doing right even though this is going to be the most uncomfortable thing that I could do, but I know it's right? And I'm going to do right? I don't know if I were put in that situation.

"I know this. When C.M. Newton was put in that situation, you know what he did. When they had players come in the SEC or Kentucky or other places, they had to have courage now. And they had to know – I don't know at the time if they thought what they were doing was groundbreaking, but it was."

For years, Calipari has joked with the media about his possible retirement down the road. He doesn't really know. He has said earlier that he wouldn't coach over the age of 60. At this writing, he is already 60 years old. As long as he is happy, he'll keep coaching for a while. He isn't burned out yet. He has more energy than most of the men in his age group. Having hobbies helps, too. As he began his second decade at Kentucky, just before the 2019-20 campaign, Calipari added, "I'm looking forward to it. I'm excited. I feel refreshed."

On preventing burnouts, Calipari had earlier commented, "I don't live and die with this stuff. The people that know me know I have other interests. I'm focused on helping these kids reach their dreams. Their dreams are my dreams. I sit on the same side of the table as them and their families. [I] want to win for the university I work for, want to win for the program.

"But the reality of it is, our season ends [in late] June here. That makes this different for me anyway. Whether I'm with my family, I like to travel. I like to go to baseball games. I like to go to football camps. I like to go to different events and hang out. I love being with my friends, big dinners. That's who I am, what I do."

In recent years, after the Wildcats finished playing in the SEC Tournament, coach John Calipari and his wife, Ellen, often invite the Kentucky-based media to attend the Selection Sunday party at their spacious home near downtown Lexington to watch the announcement of the NCAA Tournament pairings. After the announcement, Coach Cal and selected players would speak with the media about the Big Dance. Afterwards, the party attendees would enjoy their delicious meals.

If you were a visitor at the 2019 Selection Sunday party at Coach Cal's home, which is located near the famed Ashland plantation, the home of U.S. statesman Henry Clay, in the TV room, you would notice a coffee table book. And it was a pictorial hardcover about the country of Italy, where Calipari's ancestors, including his grandfather, came from.

Calipari has talked about his Italian heritage over the years, and he is proud of it. When his Tyler Ulis-led Wildcats – who were coming off an SEC Tournament title after an overtime victory over Texas A&M in Nashville – faced Stony

Brook and Indiana during the first weekend of the 2016 NCAA Tournament in Des Moines, Iowa, Coach Cal attended a Catholic church while meeting a priest who also shared similar Italian heritage.

"Coach Calipari came to visit our parish [St. Anthony] in March of 2016 while traveling here for the NCAA Tournament," recalled Monsignor Frank Chiodo in an email. "He introduced himself to me. We had a great conversation. He commented about the beauty and sacredness of our church building, and the loveliness of our Masses.

"He was very warm, a typical southern Italian. I learned that our families hail from the southern region of Calabria in Italy. We both share dual Italian citizenship. Our grandfathers both worked as coal miners after coming to the states.

"The coach was pleasantly surprised to find an Italian parish in Des Moines, especially one with so rich in history. Southern Italians like Calipari and I bring a lot of passion into their lives. As a coach, I expect John is very passionate about sports. We didn't discuss sports much – just St. Anthony parish, and our common backgrounds.

"We found commonality between our faith and our roots. Where you are from shapes your outlook on life. It was a pleasure and a privilege to meet John. After leaving Mass at St. Anthony on March 17, he tweeted snapshots of the mural outside the Italian American Cultural Center of Iowa on Indianola Avenue near our church. He commented that he knew there was something about Iowa he loved. He said he was sent to the right region."

Calipari obviously was very impressed with Des Moines. "We're excited about being here," he said. "Me, personally, I got the three things I need. I have the Catholic church. I have the Dunkin' Donuts, and I have the Italian American Cultural Center of Iowa. What else do I need?"

Coach Cal also tweeted, "Monsignor Chiodo at St. Anthony's gave me the history of the Italian heritage in Des Moines. Similar to my own family. Pretty cool."

Calipari said his Catholic faith is the centerpiece of how he tries to treat people. He also points out he's not perfect, either.

"To be Catholic for me and to have that faith, it alleviates a lot of the stuff you go through life with," Calipari told the author. "The one thing with the Catholic faith is, there's confession, absolution for your sins. It's just kind of neat.

"My wife doesn't agree with it. She says your sins are your sins. But in the Catholic faith, confession is a part of it. And then [taking a] communion – being able to every day listen to the Word and be able to tie yourself through the communion – is, for me, a great way to start the day. I'm not out touting myself as anything special. I'm a sinner. I'm a flawed human being, I know that.

"But for me, every day is trying to be better and trying to be better at what I do. It doesn't mean that I'm better than anybody else. It means that I'm Catholic, and I try to follow the faith." On his family's faith, Calipari added, "My dad was Catholic, my mother was not, kind of like Ellen. I'm Catholic; my wife is not."

While he doesn't openly talk about his faith to his basketball players, Calipari, who teaches servant leadership, tries to set a good example for them through his "down-to-earth" everyday actions and his players-first coaching philosophy. Coach and his staff also have taken the players to several community service or charity activities such as Samaritan's Feet, the Salvation Army and fundraising telethons to aid earthquake and hurricane victims, to name a few.

"We don't talk about it, and I'm not in the position I'm in [to discuss his faith]," he said. "I try to influence them through what they see, not what I'm saying, how I treat my wife, how I am as a father. Hopefully, they can learn from that. And they know I go to Mass, and they know that I'm here for them in that way.

"I wasn't the Catholic I am today even 20 years ago. So, it, for me, came a little bit later. I've always been Catholic, but I haven't been this Catholic like where I'm really leaning on the faith and being a part of it."

About the Author

Veteran sportswriter Jamie H. Vaught has covered the University of Kentucky's basketball program since his early college days, including the team's NCAA Final Four appearances in 2012 and 2015. He is a longtime credentialed sports columnist in Kentucky, whose articles over several decades have appeared in many outlets, including the *Middlesboro Daily News*, *Harlan Enterprise*, *KyForward.com*, *NKyTribune.com*, Somerset's *Commonwealth Journal*, and *The Cats' Pause* magazine. Vaught, who is also a photographer, has written five books about UK basketball, including *Crazy About the Cats: From Rupp to Pitino*. He is the founder and editor of the growing *KySportsStyle.com Magazine*.

While a college student at UK during the late 1970s, Vaught served as a sportswriter and sports editor of *Kentucky Kernel*, the campus daily newspaper, before graduating with two degrees – a bachelor's in accounting and an MBA. During the 1980s and early '90s, he worked for *The Cats' Pause* as a sports columnist for 13 years. His articles also have appeared in *The Cats' Pause Kentucky Basketball Yearbook*.

Vaught, who grew up in Science Hill, Ky., is a graduate of Somerset High School where he began his future career in sportswriting. Vaught is also a full-time professor at Southeast Kentucky Community and Technical College in Middlesboro, a position he has held since 1991. He and his wife, Deanna, live in Middlesboro with their two children, Janna and Warren.

INDEX

V

W

Y